Acclaim for Pico Iyer's

The Global Soul

"Pico Iyer is the poet laureate of wanderlust. His perennial subject is the strange confluences and poignant idiosyncrasies born of our world's dissolving borders, and he explores it with a rich mix of astonishing erudition and wide-eyed wonder." —*Literary Quarterly*

"The formidable and elegant travel writer has come up with a philosophical look at the effects of globalization on humanity. . . . The book is rife with unusual insight and unique detail." —*The Boston Book Review*

"This brilliant and restless celebration of cultural plurality is a godsend." —Caryl Phillips

"Iyer is a good writer with a sharp eye, a well furnished mind, and a keen moral sense."
—*The New York Times Book Review*

"Engaging and thoughtful." —*The Philadelphia Inquirer*

Pico Iyer

The Global Soul

Pico Iyer is the author of five previous books, including *Video Night in Kathmandu* and *The Lady and the Monk*. He lives in suburban Japan.

The Global Soul

THE GLOBAL SOUL

Jet Lag, Shopping Malls, and the Search for Home

PICO IYER

Vintage Departures
Vintage Books
A Division of Random House, Inc.
New York

FIRST VINTAGE DEPARTURES EDITION, MARCH 2001

The Library of Congress has cataloged the Knopf edition as follows:
Iyer, Pico.
The global soul : jet lag, shopping malls, and the search for home / Pico Iyer. — 1st ed.
p.   cm.
ISBN 0-679-45433-0
1. Iyer, Pico—Journeys.   2. Voyages and travel.
3. Popular culture.   4. Internationalism.
5. Technological innovations—Social aspects.   I. Title.
G530.I97I97   2000
910.4—dc21   99-35758   CIP

Vintage ISBN: 0-679-77611-7

Author photograph © Mark Richards
Book design by Anthea Lingeman

www.vintagebooks.com

Manufactured in the United States of America
10   9

In memory of my father,
who tirelessly explored the notion of
a Twenty-first-Century City of Man—
a Novus Ordo Seclorum—even as he
was making one available to me.

What is man but a congress of nations?

—RALPH WALDO EMERSON

It is necessary not to be "myself," still less to be "ourselves."
The city gives one the feeling of being at home.
We must take the feeling of being at home into exile.
We must be rooted in the absence of a place.

—SIMONE WEIL

Contents

THE BURNING HOUSE

Philosophy is really homesickness: the
wish to be everywhere at home.

—FRIEDRICH NIETZSCHE

Suddenly, the flames were curling seventy feet above my living room, whipped on by seventy-mile-per-hour winds that sent them ripping across the dry brush like maddened horses. I tried to call the fire department, but the phone was dead. I tried to turn the lights on, but the electricity was gone. I went upstairs again, to see that the flames, which minutes before had been a distant knife of orange cutting through a hillside, were now all around me, the view through the picture windows a wall of flames.

I picked up my mother's cat and ran out of the house, with two friends who had just arrived to try to be of help (my mother and father were out of town). But there was nowhere for us to go. At our feet, a precipitous slope that fell towards the road. On every other side, fires that were rising to a crest. We jumped into a car and drove down the orange-licked driveway to the narrow mountain road, and saw that we couldn't go up, we couldn't go down. Bushes were bundles of orange, and flames were looping over the slope beside us like dogs jumping at a fence. The way down led to a blaze of burning; the way up led into the conflagration.

Beside us on the road was one other vehicle—a water truck driven up by a Good Samaritan who found himself now as trapped as we were, and stood alone in the road, in his shorts, extending a forlorn hose towards the fire. Already the smoke was so thick, we could not even see the helicopters above as we sat in an angry orange haze listening to their blades. One friend, and our new companion, stood in the road and pointed the water at every new roar of fire that flamed over the ridge.

I had never known that fire moves so fast, so purposefully. We could see it cutting through the slope across from us as if with a letter opener, and scrambling up my driveway as if summoned to an execution. We sat in the car, the cat coughing in my lap, and for two hours saw and felt nothing but flames and more flames.

After night fell, at last a fire truck came up, and led us back to a safer spot a little down the mountain, from which, as an opera played on the radio, I saw the fire up above lick at my room, reduce the second floor to a skeleton, charge down towards the city below.

Along the road, a horse was running madly. A man caked in soot appeared, not knowing where he was going. Below, we could see cars burning placidly along the side of the road.

At last, after another hour, the fire having already shot into the suburbs below and leaping the eight lanes of the freeway, which leads all the way to Canada, we were free to drive down, through a wasted world of steaming cars and ravaged houses, the black hills all around wearing necklaces of orange.

I got taken to a friend's house, went across to an all-night supermarket to buy a toothbrush, and started my life anew.

The next day, in the early morning, I returned to the road along which I'd been driving for all my adult life and found it blocked off, exhausted firemen sitting on the pavement at the foot of the mountain, bowing their heads or gulping from bottles of water. I was allowed to climb it, as a resident—the fire having retreated back into the hills—and so, for the first time in twenty-five years, I walked all the way up the road, past houses reduced to chimneys or just outlines of themselves, past occasional houses, just as randomly, entirely intact. Here and there wisps of smoke still trickled up through the asphalt, and beside the hulks of cars along the road, the aluminum from their hubcaps had made little pools of silver.

When I arrived at my house, high up on a ridge, two-thirds of the way up the mountain, it was to find a smoking ash gray sea. Bronze statues had been reduced to nothing; filing cabinets were husks. All the props of my parents' sixty years, all the notes and prospects I'd been collecting for fifteen years, all the photographs, memories—all the past—gone.

I'd often referred to myself as homeless—an Indian born in England and moving to California as a boy, with no real base of operations or property even in my thirties. I'd spent much of the previous year among the wooden houses of Japan, reading the "burning house" poems of Buddhist monks and musing on the value of living without possessions and a home. But now all the handy metaphors were actual, and the lines of the poems, included in the manuscript that was the only thing in my shoulder bag when I fled, were my only real foundations for a new fin de siècle life.

A little later, California being what it is (a society built on quicksand, where everyone is getting new lives every day), just as the final touches were being applied to a new house on the lonely ridge, an earthquake shook its foundations, and all our neighborhood trembled. Then, a few months later, as finally we moved back into our old address (and days after an earthquake shook my other adopted home, in western Japan), huge rains came down and sent whole parts of the slope underneath the house sliding towards the city below.

I, alone and lost in writing at my desk—and used, besides, to mud slides that regularly washed away parts of our road—got ready early, and, for almost the only time that year, put on my only semi-respectable set of clothes (blue jacket, gray trousers, white shirt, and tie): I had to speak to a women's club a hundred miles away in Los Angeles.

As I began driving down the road, I found huge branches—large parts of trees—blocking the way. Boulders stood in the middle of

driveways, and overhead, ominously, I could hear the whir of helicopters. But such disruptions are not uncommon in the California
winter, and so I drove on, swerving past rocks and edging past the
debris, until, within a hundred yards of leaving my house, I accelerated past a piece of the road that was just dirt and scrabble, tried to
speed through a long puddle, and found myself buried, three feet
deep, in a muddy river.

I had no choice but to get out, of course, and as soon as I did, I was
heart-high in mud. My clothes were waterlogged, my shoes were
thick with gunk, and my broken umbrella seemed only to protect the
elements from me. Thus encumbered, I began slipping and falling
and rappeling my way towards the nearest house on the desolate
mountain. Below me I could see the red roof and Spanish-style white
walls of the only house that had survived the fire (thanks to a swimming pool and capacious water tank), and so, my umbrella bouncing
against me in the wind, my trousers soggy and thick with mud, half-
sliding down a brown liquid slope, I made my way through groves of
avocado trees across to the distant place of calm.

When I got to the landscaped driveway, it was to find it empty in
the rain, with all its gates closed, and no answer to my bell. A security
system winked above the door to remind me that I was an intruder (a
postmodern neighbor, that is, who'd never even been to this house
maybe five minutes from my own), and I realized that my only hope
lay farther down, through another ravaged orchard, where I could
see some figures moving.

I began slipping, shoes all brown and legs stiff with mud, my
umbrella extended like some contraption ready to take off in the
wrong direction, down the squishy slope, over fallen branches, and
tangled up in trees, reckless now, and hardly caring what got
torn, until I came to a small white trailer sitting precariously in the
shadow of a slope that looked ready to collapse. The owners of
the house were far away, I heard—in Puerto Vallarta, for all I knew:
their full-time laborers, now, were trying to carry their few posses-

sions out of the two-room trailer before the hillside crashed down upon them.

My neighbors, unmet for more than twenty years—I hadn't even known of their existence here, or of this temporary house—welcomed me into their room and handed me a cell phone with which to call the women's club. The lines were all cut, though—fourteen inches of rain had fallen in less than a day in this arid, subtropical town—and so there was nothing to do but sit there and catch my breath for a moment as the men, in sturdy galoshes and thick sweaters, went uncomplainingly about their evacuation.

There were a couple of mattresses on the floor, an empty can of Yuban coffee, and a couple of tapes of John Sebastian singing Spanish songs. A crucifix hung on a wall; a Mexican movie star smiled back from a frame; a comic book told the story of *Estephania, Defensor de los Indios.*

"We were five," an older man explained, the traditional civilities in place as he took it upon himself to make me feel at home. "But now only four. My sister and two brothers—in Jalisco. The other died when I was young. An *epidemia*—is that what you say?"

He had nine children of his own, he went on, but six of them were girls. "My daughters are too old now," he said, though he looked to me as if himself only in his forties. "Thirty and thirty-one. My youngest—he is the boy you saw on the hill."

We looked out to where the younger ones were putting their lives into a pickup; they moved as efficiently as if mishaps were a fact of life.

"Always my daughters tell me, 'Come back to Mexico,'" the man said. "'Live here. Take it easy. We'll take care of you.'" He looked up at me almost helplessly. "But I cannot do it. It is my duty, my obligation, to take care of them." Sometimes a hundred dollars saved up to send back; sometimes two.

The rain was still coming down in torrents, and the small dirt road was a tangle of fallen trees. The stables, my host explained, would be safer: down a slope from the trailer, they were a set of gated, white-walled buildings—Spanish-style—that looked fit to withstand all the calamities in the Bible.

"I want to improve my English," the father said as we retreated into the warmth and shelter of the stalls. "Is terrible."

"No," I said, thinking of my Spanish.

"I try," he said. "I want to try."

He'd lived here, my unknown neighbor, for twenty-eight years now, more than half his life, I figured, "here" being Texas and Arizona and all kinds of other places from which he was able to visit Mexico for two weeks every year. His eyes lit up when he spoke of "our Mexico," of the village rituals of his place, of the beauty of Guadalajara, of the international airport not far from where he owned eighty acres in Aguascalientes. Here, of course, he had next to nothing except neighbors he'd never met and a trailer that looked perilous.

"You must miss your country, your family?"

"Is sad." We heard shouts, excited cries, as the boys finished loading up the truck and began making plans for walking into town to party. "I am buried here." It sounded ominous until, reflecting, I realized he'd said "bored."

"At night, I've got this"—he pulled out a brand-new copy of the 1995 *World Almanac* in Spanish, though this was only the tenth day of January 1995.

"You don't have a television?"

"We do. But is broken. Two months already. I don't like to watch the television."

The man wanted to be an American, though. "I had an interview, last September," he said, the two of us shivering a little in the chill, dark stables, "September fourteenth. But I missed it."

Outside, the sky had begun to clear a little, and I'd grown almost used to looking like some member of an Amazon tribe whose notion of dressing up was putting on coat and tie and smearing himself in mud. The young workers, bearing spades, suddenly began walking off into the rain, tramping up the tree-crushed slopes, and the man smiled out at them.

"Every night they go to town. Even walk. Is three miles to the supermarket."

Below us, though we couldn't know it yet, waters fourteen feet high were actually burying underpasses, and kids were surfing on the transcontinental highway; the heaviest rains in five hundred years, people were saying (assuming the Chumash and early Spaniards kept records of these things). But my host was still anxious to make me feel welcome, and he asked me about India, about whether it was in Europe, about whether there were many poor people there.

He shook his head when I said it took twenty-four hours to fly there, and told me that his nephew-in-law—the boy on his way to town now—was on his way to Baltimore.

"America must be hard."

He shrugged. They didn't get much money, but they could eat a big meal for $1.50, and they had security. After you'd been working five years in this place, you could take a three-week vacation. Life wasn't so bad; they just needed papers. "They studied in California," he said of the boys; "they speak English."

We looked out through the sludge and drizzle to a nearby house, rebuilt since the fire. "Is a Spanish word," he said, a little proudly, holding it gently on his tongue. "*A-do-be.*"

When I decided the storm had broken enough for me to clomp back up to my house (my clothes so caked in filth that I ended up stripping naked at my front door, and leaving all the sodden clothes outside), I turned to my new friend and said, "*¡Qué lástima!*"

He waved and smiled. "Is a nice word."

. . .

It is a classic story in a way, of fire and flood and migration; the two moments I've just described could almost come from some Old Testament parable. The words themselves, of exile and homelessness and travel, are old ones that speak to something intrinsic to the state of being human. But it is a modern story, too, of a person with an American alien card and an Indian face and an English accent, on his way to Japan, meeting a neighbor who lives down the street in a universe that has never touched his own; and a man coming to a country where he can scarcely speak the language and passing twenty-eight years as an "illegal" to support a family scarcely seen. Two kinds of cross-border experiences meet, one postmodern and fueled by technology, the other tribal almost; over the Atlantic and under the border fence.

The other truth is that they are crossing all the time these days— the new and the old—and producing encounters seldom seen before. Two different worlds are coming together now, and both of us, aliens and unofficials for twenty-eight years in the great immigrants' Land of Promise, were being tossed about in the fast, driving winds that were blowing the world all around.

The century just ended, most of us agree, was the century of movement, with planes and phones and even newer toys precipitating what the secretary-general of the UN's Habitat II conference in 1996 called the "largest migration in history"; suddenly, among individuals and among groups, more bodies were being thrown more widely across the planet than ever before. Therein lay many of the new excitements of our time, and therein lay the pathos: in Cambodia recently, I heard that the second city of the Khmer people had been a refugee camp; even in relatively settled Central Europe, the number of refugees is greater than the populations of Vienna and Berlin combined.

For more and more people, then, the world is coming to resemble a diaspora, filled with new kinds of beings—Gastarbeiters and boat people and *marielitos*—as well as new kinds of realities: Rwandans in Auckland and Moroccans in Iceland. One reason why Melbourne looks ever more like Houston is that both of them are filling up with Vietnamese *pho* cafés; and computer technology further encourages us to believe that the remotest point is just a click away. Everywhere is so made up of everywhere else—a polycentric anagram—that I hardly notice I'm sitting in a Parisian café just outside Chinatown (in San Francisco), talking to a Mexican-American friend about bicultur-alism while a Haitian woman stops off to congratulate him on a piece he's just delivered on TV on St. Patrick's Day. "I know all about those Irish nuns," she says, in a thick patois, as we sip our Earl Grey tea near signs that say CITY OF HONG KONG, EMPRESS OF CHINA.

Up the hill, in my hotel, a woman named Madame Nhu is waiting in a corner of the lobby to talk to me.

"Are you from Vietnam?" I ask as we introduce ourselves, follow-ing the implication of her name.

"No. America."

"You never lived in Vietnam?" I press on, not very diplomatically (and mostly because I want to share with her my enthusiasm for her country).

"I'm from Hue."

"But"—I don't want to make it hard for her—"you left when you were young?"

"Yes. I never lived there; I am American."

I feel a little uneasy about this line of questioning, knowing that I would squirm just as restlessly if someone asked the same of me: those of us who live between categories just tend to pick the nearest (or handiest) answer so we can move the conversation along. In any case, "Where do you come from?" is coming to seem as antiquated an inquiry as "What regiment do you belong to?"

"I remember once, in Vietnam," this highly cultured woman goes on, understanding, perhaps, that I'm only looking for a point of con-tact and, in fact, that I probably have more in common with her than someone from Hue or from the Berkeley Hills might, "the chambermaid at my hotel finally picked up the courage to ask, 'Are you one of us?'"

"In English?"

"No, in Vietnamese."

"And you must have found it difficult to answer?"

"No. I said, 'Yes. Definitely. Yes, I *am* one of you!'"

"Even though, when I asked just now, you didn't sound so sure. Maybe it depends on whom you're talking to?"

Unfair again, though doubtless true: after all, nearly all the cultures of which she'd been a member had been at war with one another during her lifetime, and wherever she was, whether it was Paris or English boarding school, New York or San Francisco, she must have felt that many of her lives were far away. The previous night, I'd met a man at dinner who'd told me that he dreamed in Swedish, English, and Italian (though only his Italian dreams were in black and white).

The surprising thing about such encounters, really, is that they don't seem surprising any more. Already we're taking yesterday's astonishments for granted.

Though none of these mixtures are new, as I say—Homer and Dante tell us everything we need to know about exile and abandoned homes—what is changing, surely, is the speed at which the world is turning, and sometimes I feel as if I'm going through the existential equivalent of that game I used to play as a child, in which I'd spin myself around and around where I stood, till I collapsed in a dizzy heap on the floor. The two great engines of our age—technology and travel (now the largest industry in the world)—give fuel to each other, our machines prompting us to prize speed as an end in itself, and the longing for speed quickening a hunger for new technologies.

The external effects of this are everywhere—1 million transactions every minute on the New York Stock Exchange, and the speed of silicon chips doubling (as their price diminishes) every eighteen months. Yet the internal effects may be even more disquieting, as memory itself seems accelerated, and yesterday's dramas become as remote as ancient history. At times, it can feel as if the whole planet is joyriding in somebody else's Porsche, at ninety miles per hour, around blind curves. As even Marshall McLuhan, the hopeful (if somewhat absentminded) godfather of the "electronic cottage," confessed, "You get going very quickly and you end up in the wrong place."

In the final winter of the old millennium, to see what the official caretakers of our global order make of all this, I accepted an invitation to go as a Fellow to the annual meeting of the World Economic Forum in Davos, Switzerland. The Forum gathers hundreds of "leaders of global security" in Davos each year—captains of industry, heads of state, computer billionaires, and a few token mortals such as me—to map out the future of the planet. For six days in the tightly sealed mountain village, surrounded by teams of armed Swiss guards (the same village, skeptics always note, where Thomas Mann placed his sanatorium in *The Magic Mountain*), we walked through heavy snowfall, met for panels amidst the buzzing screens of the Congress Centre, gathered for lunch and dinner in elegant hotels.

If globalism has a formal, corporate face, it was surely here, amongst the pinstriped CEOs and faces familiar from our TV screens gathered to discuss the theme of "Responsible Globality." Fellows were given "global calendars" on which they could compute the time in Karachi, Rio, and Sydney, and a World Electronic Community was set up to allow us to network on-line as well as off. The first session on the opening day was devoted to the perils of jet lag, a scientist telling his groggy audience that attention skills fall 500 percent after a long-distance flight. Beside the narrow, slushy road, along which Bill Gates and Warren Beatty and Yasir Arafat could be seen trudging, one Institutional Partner had erected an enormous snow sculpture in the shape of a Coca-Cola bottle cap.

Of all the bodies on the planet, multinationals have the greatest stake—quite literally an investment—in telling us that the world is one (and Everyman, therefore, a potential consumer). CNN, part of the new media conglomerate for which I work—the largest such in the world—forbids the use of the word *foreign* on its broadcasts, and IBM, aiming, like most large companies, to be local everywhere, tells us in reassuring tones, "Somehow the word *foreign* seems foreign these days." Globalism has become the convenient way of saying that all the world's a single market.

Yet what the members of the Forum were contemplating in 1999 was the fact that a small world is a precarious one; and in our closely linked planet, a fire in one place soon becomes a blaze in another. Day after day, flanked by large-screen images of themselves, leaders came out onto the main stage of the Congress Hall to assure us of what Al Gore had called the "wisdom of connectedness," and to say that the conflagration was under control. We were all joined now, they said, for richer and for poorer, in sickness and in health; all we could do was make the most of it.

Yet as the days went on, another strain began to rise up from the corners of the gathering as spokesmen for the world's poorer nations began to address us, somewhat in the manner of children with their hands extended outside a private party in some Fashion Café. "Our global village has caught fire," Hosni Mubarak said in the fluent English that almost everyone seemed to use, "from where we do not know. We have put out some of the flames . . . but we do not know where to begin rebuilding." Kofi Annan told us that a quarter of the human race seemed condemned to starvation, and one of his colleagues reminded us that more than a quarter of the human race was actually poorer now than before the end of the Cold War. "Is globalism only going to benefit the powerful?" asked Nelson Mandela, in his farewell address to the gatekeepers of the new world order. "Does it offer nothing to men, women and children ravaged by the violence of poverty?"

The other sound I heard, unmistakably rising up in the shadows of the Congress Centre, under the collective breath almost, was an undercurrent of anxiety about what the global order was doing to those parts of us that do not show up on screens. Even Global Man cannot live on bread alone, the Ecumenical Patriarch of Constantinople reminded us; values do not figure on the currency charts, and all the globalism in the world could not add up to universalism.

Such whispers, to my surprise, were coming even from those most in tune with the planet's synergies. A young scientist credited with the invention of massive parallel computers held a dinner at which he outlined his dream of creating a "Millennium Clock," an instrument that would toll every thousand years, to remind us, in our accelerating world, of the virtue of slowness, and of the need to think of generations we could not see. A futurist spoke of "High Touch" as the necessary complement to "High Tech": consumer technology was the largest industry in America, he said, but the flight from consumer technology was the second. A film producer led a dinner at which he asked, straight out, "What happened to home?" The only home he knew, he said, had come in two unexpected moments of stillness— spiritual epiphanies, really—while traveling through rural Ireland.

At least along its fringes, the unspoken message of the conference, for me, was that it was not just goods and data (or even "gypsy capital") that were being sent around the world in ever greater quantities, but souls, and souls not always used to living without a sense of orientation; and that the "global" we so readily attach to every product we wish to make seem desirable struck a less happy note when it came to "global hearts" or "global loyalties." All the new joint ventures we celebrated so happily in the public sphere had private correspondences, and sometimes, I suspected, they were the more significant precisely because they were the less considered. Borders, after all, were collapsing in lives as much as on the map (borders between now and then, or here and there; borders between public and private). The way in which nearly all the world's conflicts now were internal ones—

twenty out of thirty in 1995, according to a Swedish agency—had a
counterpart, surely, in the way in which more and more of us had to
negotiate a peace within, in our own private Sarajevos or Cape
Towns, made up in many cases (as in Madame Nhu's) of several
clashing worlds. And the fact that the world was moving in two directions at once (countries breaking down into smaller units, while companies straddle more and more continents) had a parallel in our lives,
where we may find that we have more and more "connections" in the
telephone, or airplane, senses, and fewer and fewer in the classic
human sense.

It made me wonder, not for the first time, whether humans were
really meant to cross five continents in an afternoon, and what effect
it must have on us to be (in Mr. Toad's immortal phrase), "here today—in next week to-morrow!" And I couldn't help but notice that in
the midst of all the talk of a world without borders, the most recent
Nobel laureate in economics was detained for ninety minutes at
Zurich's airport—prevented from joining the global discussion—
because his (Indian) passport lacked a (Swiss) visa.

One day, as I was listening to all the talk of open markets and the
Euro, a pioneer in artificial intelligence leaned over to me and said,
quietly, that he'd never forgotten a trip he'd taken to a monastery.
What had moved him most, he said, was just the way the stone on the
monastery steps had been worn down, by centuries of monastic feet,
all anonymous, but all walking on the same path to the chapel, to sing
the same hymns every morning.

My own steadying point, ever since I could remember, had been the
essays of Emerson, with their translation of Asian and ancient Greek
wisdom into a code of New World optimism that turned into a private declaration of independence. Experience, but also something
deeper and more innate, led me to believe that there was a higher
component to the collective unconscious—that we converge as we

rise, as Teilhard says—and that, in fact, almost everyone, in his better moments, longed to subscribe to the creed of universal loyalty
voiced by Thomas Paine ("My country is the world, and my religion
is to do good"). There is a "universal soul" behind us, Emerson
writes in *Nature*, and shining through us, that is "not mine, or thine,
or his, but we are its; we are its property and men." We are "children
of the fire, made of it," he declares in "The Poet," and "only the
same divinity transmuted and at two or three removes, when we
know least about it."

The key to this global soul, for Emerson, lay entirely in perception:
it was not so much that man had been exiled from the Garden as that
he had ceased to notice that it was all around him. In that sense,
our shrinking world gave more and more of us a chance to see, in
palpable, unanswerable ways, how much we had in common, and
how much we could live, in the grand Emersonian way, beyond petty
allegiances and labels, outside the reach of nation-states. When
Edward Bellamy, inspired by the same impulse, envisaged the year
2000 in his novel of 1888, *Looking Backward*, he saw us all united
by a system he called "Nationalism" (in which, ironically, there was
"neither selling nor buying," neither money nor trade).

Yet the chance to rise to this higher sense of kinship was shadowed
by the fact that more and more of what we seemed to share was on
the merest surface, and global unity was most often defined in terms
of common markets and linked networks; sometimes it could seem
that the main force carrying the "Novus Ordo Seclorum" around the
world—our new order of man   was the dollar bill (on which that
noble motto is inscribed above the Masonic seal). And though the
world was available to many of us in ways inconceivable to our grandparents, that also meant that all the age-old human problems played
out now on a planetary stage, with "centers everywhere and margins
nowhere" (in McLuhan's digital upgrade of Augustine's God).

When my parents were growing up, in the heart of an old-style
empire (their hometown of Bombay the largest "British" city outside

London), they were part, willy-nilly, of a worldwide web of such schoolchildren, learning the same poems and reciting the same catechisms, thousands of miles away from London; the British Empire exported Shakespeare and the hymns of Wesley around the globe just as determinedly as the Disney Company distributes *Aladdin* or *Mulan*. By the nineteenth century, in fact (not least because its origins lay in the commercial undertakings of the East India Company), the Raj had set up a global transportation and staffing system—linking Wellington to the Falkland Islands, and Kingston to Nairobi—that was not so different from a multinational's today.

What was different, though, was that in the British Empire every child was born to the immigrant's bifurcation—torn between the home he carried in his blood and the one he had on paper; colonials were all condemned to living with two faces. Yet in the modern world, which I take to be an International Empire, the sense of home is not just divided, but scattered across the planet, and in the absence of any center at all, people find themselves at sea. Our ads sing of Planet Reebok and Planet Hollywood—even my monthly telephone bill in Japan speaks of "One World One Company"—yet none of us necessarily feels united on a deeper level.

Reflecting on all this, I began to wonder whether a new kind of being might not be coming to light—a citizen of this International Empire—made up of fusions (and confusions) we had not seen before: a "Global Soul" in a less exalted (and more intimate, more vexed) sense than the Emersonian one. This creature could be a person who had grown up in many cultures all at once—and so lived in the cracks between them—or might be one who, though rooted in background, lived and worked on a globe that propelled him from tropic to snowstorm in three hours. She might have a name that gave away nothing about her nationality (a name like Kim, say, or Maya, or Tara), and she might have a porous sense of self that changed with her location. Even the most ageless human rites—scattering his father's ashes, or meeting the woman who might be his wife—he might find himself performing six thousand miles from the place he now called home.

This Global Soul, to use the convenient tag, lived in the metaphorical equivalent of international airspace (the human version of cyberspace, in a sense): his currency might be "air miles" (40 percent of which are now earned on the ground), and the main catechism he knew by heart might involve "fastening your seat-belt low and tight across your lap." His memories might be set in airports that looked more and more like transnational cities, in cities that looked like transnational airports. Lacking a binding sense of "we," he might nonetheless remain fiercely loyal to a single airline.

High above the clouds, in an alternative plane of existence—a duty-free zone, in a way, in which everyone around him was a stranger—the Global Soul would be facing not just new answers to the old questions but a whole new set of questions, as he lived through shifts that the traditional passenger on ocean liner or long-distance train could never have imagined. His sense of obligation would be different, if he felt himself part of no fixed community, and his sense of home, if it existed at all, would lie in the ties and talismans he carried round with him. Insofar as he felt a kinship with anyone, it would, most likely, be with other members of the Deracination-state.

"One country's not enough," said a sweet, unplaceable soul who approached me one night at a gathering in rural Japan, introducing himself as half-English and half-Japanese, though he thought of himself as Malaysian (he'd spotted me, clearly, as a fellow in-betweener). "When I'm in England, there's a part of me that's not fulfilled; that's why I come here—to find the other part."

One spring day in London, I went to see Kazuo Ishiguro in his home along the Northern line, near "J.J. Town," as he wryly calls it (for its large population of Jewish and Japanese émigrés), a house he shares with the Glaswegian wife he met while both of them were working with the homeless, and a young daughter. "Ish," as he is generally known (like many a Graham Greene character, he goes usually by his last name), seems in many ways a quintessential Global Soul, not quite a part of the Japan he left when he was five and not really a part of an England where his name and face (though not his manner) brand him instantly as a "foreigner." One reason his fiction speaks to readers across the world is that Ish is a seasoned translator of sorts, used to converting the values of Japan into terms the West can understand, while bringing to both his not-quite homes a nostalgia and an amused detachment that few natives could quite muster.

Ish in conversation, I soon notice, uses "they" for both his apparent homelands, calling the English the "natives" even as he pronounces Nagasaki with the short *a*'s no Japanese would ever use; he speaks only a child's Japanese, he keeps assuring me, yet in English he uses the word *aeroplane* with the careful articulation of one who's learned it as a foreign term, while a boy (and at a time when the things themselves were not so common). In recent months, he says, he's been spending much of his time trying to find the perfect name for a half-Japanese, half-Scottish daughter who will be growing up in an England very likely full of Muslim fundamentalists (and their enemies). His prose, of course, is of the classic, antique sort you seldom find in England anymore, and bespeaks the keen attentiveness of a lifelong mimic.

"I can actually remember this process," he says, "of listening to words I didn't know the meaning of and literally copying the sounds." The only "un-English" boy at all the schools where he found himself, he realized that his survival depended on impersonating an English boy, while also putting his exoticism to occasional good use. "Whenever it was convenient for me to become very Japanese, I could become very Japanese," he says disarmingly. "And then, when I wanted to drop it, I would just become this ordinary Englishman."

And suddenly, in a flash, I am taken back to myself at the age of nine, going back and forth (three times a year) between my parents' home in California and my boarding school in England and realizing that, as a member of neither culture, I could choose between selves at will, wowing my Californian friends with the passages of Greek and Latin I'd already learned in England, and telling my breathless housemates in Oxford how close I lived to the Grateful Dead. The tradition denoted by my face was something I could erase (mostly) with my voice, or pick up whenever the conversation turned to the Maharishi or patchouli oil. With any of my potential homes, in fact, I could claim or deny attachment when I chose; and where the traditional being knew that his home, his past, and his community were all givens, often to an oppressive degree, someone like me—or Ish, or Madame Nhu—could select even the most fundamental details of our lives.

The other striking thing about Ish, I'd already seen, was that I'd closed both his last two novels without knowing the protagonist's first name; in his most recent one, *The Unconsoled*, five hundred pages of action, or its absence, had taken place more or less in a hotel, in some unnamed foreign town through which a touring artist walks as through a labyrinth in a dream, surrounded by people and passions he can't begin to fathom. The book is a novel about a state akin to jet lag, a nightmare of disorientation and disconnection, and its main character, at some level, doesn't know where he is, whom he's among, or who he is taken to be. Ish deliberately keeps all colloquialisms and local references out of his books, he tells me in his surprisingly open, precisely affable way, because he knows, from eighteen-month promotional tours around his global markets, that most of his readers will greet him in Norwegian, or Mandarin, or Portuguese.

As I listen to him, I think that with this new kind of lifestyle is coming to light a whole new way of writing (and dressing and eating), as Global Souls face their equivalent of the same issue that confronts nations at the end of the old world order. The heroes of many contemporary novels are multicultural foundlings—one typical one, in Bharati Mukherjee's *Leave It to Me,* is called "Devi" now (she was once "Debby" and once "Faustine") and, in search of her mother, finds that her forebear carried six different passports at least; this child of Eurasian parents learns about the mysterious East from a Chinese lover in San Francisco. The person reading such a book, I suspect, will be equally mixed up often (in terms of national name tags) as she listens to "Norwegian Wood" sung in Punjabi (and wreathed in sitars), and dines on French-Korean food from down the street. All that her parents could take for granted, she has to create from scratch.

In a way, it seemed, the central issue before us offshore beings (as before the floating world around us) was how to keep the soul intact in the face of pell-mell globalism; and how to preserve a sense of universality in a world that was apt to define unity in more divisive ways. I think, for example, of the man from the Punjab who picked me up recently at Lester B. Pearson Airport in Toronto, and for whom all the traditional immigrant questions were complicated many times over as members of his family, his community, set up on different continents.

"Here not like home, sir," he assured me, as almost every Indian cabdriver in Toronto did. "Here is no corruption. Indian picture we have here, sir; Indian market. Even Indian street name, sir." (I think he meant Albion and Dundas.) But when I asked him if he felt at home in the adopted city whose praises he was singing, his voice turned soft, and gathered feeling.

"Where you spent your childhood, sir, you can never forget that place. I am here, sir, and I like it here. But"—and I could hear the ache—"I love my India."

I know a little about the Global Soul in part because, having grown up simultaneously in three cultures, none of them fully my own, I acquired very early the sense of being loosed from time as much as from space—I had no history, I could feel, and lived under the burden of no home; and when I look at many of the most basic details of my life, I realize that even though they look hardly strange to me, they would have seemed surreal to every one of my grandparents. Growing up, I had no relatives on the same continent as myself, and I never learned a word of my mother's tongue or my father's (because, coming from different parts of India, they had no common language save that of British India). To this day, I can't pronounce what is technically my first name, and the name by which I go is an Italian one (though often mistaken for Spanish, Portuguese, female), mostly because my parents, realizing I'd be living among people foreign to Indian polysyllables, named me after a fifteenth-century Italian neo-Platonist whose name was easy to spell and to pronounce.

As a permanent alien, I've never been in a position to vote, and, in fact, I've never held a job in the country where I more or less live; I thought relatively little (though my parents were middle-class academics, far from rich) of going to school over the North Pole, and have never had a partner who belongs to the same race. ("Miscegenation is the great hope and future of mankind," an optimistic soul in San Francisco tells me. "It's not possible to hate your grandson.") The son of Hindu-born Theosophists, I was educated entirely in Christian schools and spend most of my time now in Buddhist lands (the Caribbean islanders would call me a "Nowherian"); and, though I spend most of my year in rural Japan or in a Catholic monastery, I've nonetheless accumulated 1.5 million miles on one American airline alone.

A person like me can't really call himself an exile (who traditionally looked back to a home now lost), or an expatriate (who's generally posted abroad for a living); I'm not really a nomad (whose patterns are guided by the seasons and tradition); and I've never been subject to the refugee's violent disruptions: the Global Soul is best characterized by the fact of falling between all categories (and at college, for example, I counted neither as a local, who could receive a government grant, nor as a foreigner, who was subject to a specially inflated fee). The country where people look like me is the one where I can't speak the language, the country where people sound like me is a place where I look highly alien, and the country where people live like me is the most foreign space of all. And though, when I was growing up, I was nearly always the only mongrel in my classroom or neighborhood, now, when I look around, there are more and more people in a similar state, the children of blurred boundaries and global mobility.

I've grown up, too, with a keen sense of the blessings of being unaffiliated; it has meant that almost everywhere is new and strange to me (as I am new and strange to it), and nearly everywhere allows me to keep alive a sense of wonder and detachment. Besides, the foreigner is in the rare position of being able to enjoy the facilities of a place without paying the taxes, and can appreciate the virtues of anywhere without being wholly subject to its laws. My complexion (like my name) allows me to pass as a native in Cuba, or Peru, or Indonesia, and none of them, in any case, is more foreign to me than the England where I don't look like a native, the America where I'm classified as an alien, and the India where I can't speak a word of any of the almost two hundred languages. Enabled, I hope, to live a little bit above parochialisms, I exult in the fact that I can see everywhere with a flexible eye; the very notion of home is foreign to me, as the state of foreignness is the closest thing I know to home.

Yet deeper than such tidy formulations, any number of questions begin to gather, and the fact remains that humans have never lived with quite this kind of mobility and uprootedness before (indeed, the questions themselves may be the closest thing we have to home: we live in the uncertainties we carry round with us). A lack of affiliation may mean a lack of accountability, and forming a sense of commitment can be hard without a sense of community. Displacement can encourage the wrong kinds of distance, and if the nationalism we see sparking up around the globe arises from too narrow and fixed a sense of loyalty, the internationalism that's coming to birth may reflect too roaming and undefined a sense of belonging. The Global Soul may see so many sides of every question that he never settles on a firm conviction; he may grow so used to giving back a different self according to his environment that he loses sight of who he is when nobody's around. Even the most basic questions have to be answered by him alone, and when, on the planes where he may make his home, the cabin attendant passes down the aisle with disembarkation forms, it may be difficult for him to fill in any of the boxes: "Home Address," "Citizenship," "Purpose of Visit," even "Marital Status."

I can answer almost any of these questions from a variety of perspectives, I often feel (depending on whether I'm calling myself Indian in Cuba, or English-born in Burma, or affiliated with California in the Philippines). But though this can be a natural- and useful-enough impulse in response to the question, "Where do you come from?" it becomes more treacherous in answer to the question "Where do you stand?"

Every one of these concerns is, of course, still the province of a tiny minority (and a relatively comfortable minority at that); the most urgent issues in the world today, as the plaintive voices of Davos remind us, are still the same ones they've always been: how to get food on the table, and find shelter for your children; how to live beyond tomorrow. Indeed, one of the most troubling features of the globalism we celebrate is that the so-called linking of the planet has, in fact, intensified the distance between people: the richest 358 people in the world, by UN calculations, have a financial worth as great as that of 2.3 billion others, and even in the United States, the prosperous home of egalitarianism, the most wired man in the land (Bill Gates) has a net worth larger than that of 40 percent of the country's households, or perhaps 100 million of his compatriots combined (according to Robert Reich). The rich have the sense that they can go anywhere tomorrow, while 95 percent of the new beings on the planet are among the poor; I worry about the effects of E-mail and transprovincialism, while two-thirds of the people in the world have never used a telephone.

Not long ago, I flew to Haiti, just two hours from New York City, and, stepping off the plane, I walked into the pages of the Bible. Women were relieving themselves along the main streets and the principal sights on view along National Highway One were tomb-stones. The sidewalks were crowded with people around the Centre de Formation Intellectuelle, but that was mostly because unemploy-ment was running at 70 percent; the sign that said TOMORROW BELONGS TO HAITI was all but obscured by mountains of trash. Most of the adults I saw around me, I learned, had never had a day of for-mal schooling, and the average man would be dead by the age of forty-four. Though only 5 percent of the people I saw would vote in the coming elections, it was unsafe for anyone to go out at night, people said, "because of democracy."

Haiti still remains the globe's rule more than its exception—more and more of the countries I visit are descending into anarchy—and it makes a mockery of the concerns of the Global Soul, as of the air-line's happy talk of "15,000 travellers transcending borders every minute." There are more telephones in Tokyo, it's often said, than on the entire continent of Africa. But these very discrepancies are one of the by-products of the age, and more and more of us, moving between countries as easily as between channels on our screens, are tempted to underestimate the distances between them. My parents, when they traveled to the England that seemed the end point of an educated Indian's destiny, had to travel by boat, through the Suez Canal, or around the Cape of Good Hope, and the two weeks at sea, on the Peninsula and Oriental lines, gave them time to measure the distance between the two countries; now, such shifts are instanta-neous, and it's not always easy to differentiate between traveling from Seventh Avenue to Eighth Avenue and traveling to a place that has no tradition or values in common with our own.

I woke up one morning last month in sleepy, never-never Laos (where the center of the capital is unpaved red dirt and a fountain without water), and went to a movie that same evening in the Westside Pavilion in Los Angeles, where a Korean at a croissanterie made an iced cappuccino for a young Japanese boy surrounded by the East Wind snack bar and Panda Express, Fajita Flats and the Hana Grill; two weeks later, I woke up in placid, acupuncture-loving Santa Barbara, and went to sleep that night in the broken heart of Manila, where children were piled up like rags on the pedestrian overpasses and girls scarcely in their teens combed, combed their long hair before lying down to sleep under sheets of cellophane on the central dividers of city streets. It is hard not to think that such quick transitions bring conflicts, and sometimes illusions that we haven't confronted before, and though I, as a sometime journalist, travel more than many people I know, the planes on which I travel are full of management consultants and computer executives and international aid workers and tribal backpackers who fly much more than I do.

And what complicates the confusions of the Global Soul is that, as fast as we are moving around the world, the world is moving around us; it is not just the individual but the globe with which we're interacting that seems to be in constant flux. So even the man who never leaves home may feel that home is leaving him, as parents, children, lovers scatter around the map, taking pieces of him wherever they go. More and more of us may find ourselves in the emotional or metaphysical equivalent of that state we know from railway stations, when we're sitting in a carriage waiting to pull out and can't tell, often, whether we're moving forwards, or the train next to ours is pulling back.

Thus even those people whose lives haven't changed are subject, at times, to a universe increasingly shaped and colored by the Global

Soul, and the Bangladeshi who's never moved from his village finds
himself visited by images of Hong Kong (on-screen), and videos from
Bombay, and phone calls from Toronto, perhaps, while the Torontonian who's never left the city walks out of his grandmother's house,
only to see signs he can't read and hear words he can't understand,
among people whose customs are strange to him. Never before in
human history, I suspect, have so many been surrounded by so much
that they can't follow.

The temptation in the face of all this can be (as the great analyst of
the modern condition, Graham Greene, saw) to try to lay anchor anywhere, even in a faith one doesn't entirely believe, just so one will
have a home and solid ground under one's feet. To lack a center, after
all, may be to lack something essential to the state of being human;
"to be rooted," as Greene's fellow admirer of Catholicism, Simone
Weil, said, "is perhaps the most important and least recognized need
of the human soul."

In response to the bombardment of data all around us, we steady
ourselves, often, with the consoling sound of a "global village": a
village, after all, in the ancestral sense, is a truer, simpler place
of shared ideals, linked by a common sense of hierarchy and center
(all the things cyberspace, in fact, eliminates)—the village, as even
Muammar Gaddafi writes, in his latest screed in favor of ancestral tribalism, *Escape from Hell,* "is peaceful, clean and friendly;
everyone knows everyone else." There "is no theft in the village"
(as he writes in an earlier book, *The Village Is the Village*). Yet
what we are entering is, in fact, much closer to a global city, with
all the problems of rootlessness and alienation and a violent, false
denaturing that we associate with the word *urban* (the "city," writes
Gaddafi again, "is just a biological worm in which humans live and
die without perspective, without patience. . . . The city kills social
instincts and human feelings"). When the twentieth century began,

scarcely 14 percent of all humans lived in the city; by the time it ended, the figure was roughly 50 percent (and the twenty-first century, UN officials say, will be the "century of cities," with perhaps thirty-three "megacities" rising up by the year 2015). The place we reassuringly call a village looks already a lot like a blown-up version of Los Angeles, its freeways choked, its skies polluted, its tribes settled into a discontinuous pattern—the flames of South Central rising above the gated castles of Bel Air.

Insofar as the global village is a village, moreover, it brings with it all the frustrations that have propelled so many millions away from villages (and into cities): small worlds and narrow horizons, village idiots and ancestral rivalries. Rumors and superstitions fly now across the planet at the speed of light (on CNN, on the World Wide Web), and where the poor have always been able to look, inflamingly, at the towers of the rich, in New York or Rio or Johannesburg, now they can do so everywhere by turning on their machines (more and more of the world may be feeling homesick now, if only for the unreal and unattainable homes they've seen on-screen).

A million people are crossing borders every day, and it's safe to assume that many of them are transporting viruses, or illegal goods, arms or biases: even as I write this, Nigerians are getting onto Lufthansa planes bound for Frankfurt, and, upon departure, disappearing into the toilets and swallowing every page of their passports. On arrival, they will say that they have no documents, and ask for amnesty (and though they will likely be denied it, the six dollars they are given every day while staying in "amnesty hotels" may be more than they could earn at home). To take an almost random example, more than half a million Ukrainians have been smuggled into the West of late, according to the International Organization for Migration (itself a global body), and at least 100,000 of them are living by selling their bodies. The new motto of the Disney Company, as enunciated by the character Hades in the animated version of *Hercules* is, "It's a small underworld after all."

.   .   .

The obvious response to all this is that, much as the Global Soul is
having to find new ways of living with an adulterated or chameleon
sense of self, so the global order is being smoothed down into a tepid
whole. My own experience, however, crisscrossing the planet, suggests that the world is more divided than ever, in part because of our
illusions of closeness. The last time I was in Havana, I was
approached, as I'd often been there, by a young, strikingly articulate,
and well-informed character from the university who seemed (as
almost everyone on that isolated island does) desperate for any contact with America. His brother lived in California, he told me, in a
place I'd never heard of called Tamal; he had a large house and a
swimming pool, tennis courts, and limousines. Please could I, on my
return to the U.S., take back with me a letter for his sibling in the
hope that he might be able to do something to rescue him from the
privations of Havana?

I did so—my suitcase always came back from Cuba crammed with
such entreaties—although I knew, from five previous trips back, that
most of the letters would come back to me with "Addressee
Unknown" stamped on them, or would arrive on the doorsteps of
people who never wanted to think about Cuba again, if they were
even alive (most recent Cuban refugees end up in the most violent
and drug-stricken corners of America). In this case, however, an
answer came back within a week, from Tamal, California. "Dear Pico
Iyer," the brother in the large house wrote (and I paraphrase),
"Thank you so much for sending me the letter from my brother in
Havana: I think of him, I think of Cuba, all the time. I don't know if
he knows my circumstances here, but I am in San Quentin Prison,
here on Death Row. Is there anything he can do, do you think, to
set me free and get me back to the safety of Havana? Please write
me soon."

.   .   .

At O'Hare Airport in Chicago recently—another of the great cross-cultural meeting places of the spinning globe—a Romanian told me how his mother, new to the country, had been baby-sitting her nine-year-old granddaughter, when the little girl said she wanted to watch TV. The old woman said no, the child protested, and the woman did as she would do in Romania: she spanked the little girl.

Instantly the nine-year-old, as a good American, dialed 911 to report a case of "child abuse," and when the father came home, it was to find his bewildered mother (speaking not a word of English) being dragged away by policemen to possible incarceration.

The world we like to think of as united, my experience suggests, looks, in fact, more and more like a group of differently colored kids all sleeping under the same poster of Leonardo DiCaprio, while arguing about whether *Titanic* is an attack on capitalist hegemony or a Confucian parable of self-reliance: in short, a hundred cultures divided by a common language. And though it may not matter if what I call "blue" suggests a different shade to you, it does matter if what I mean by "true" or "soon"—or "hope"—is different from what you do. Saddam Hussein may have requested Frank Sinatra to be played at his fifty-fourth birthday, and his son Uday may run a magazine called *Babel* and a youth television network that debuted with *JFK*, but that makes neither of them any less likely to wage war on Washington.

The CIA still has more employees worldwide than the United Nations, and while some parts of the planet look like a collection of broken shards (Cambodian gangs face off against Hispanic ones in Long Beach), others (I know from spending time in North Korea and Paraguay and Bhutan) are doing everything they can to keep their distance from the Information Planet. "Perhaps science and industry . . . will unite the world, I mean condense it into a single unit," I remember Wittgenstein having written in 1946, "though one in which peace is the last thing that will find a home."

· · ·

If I were to write a fairy tale about the Global Soul, progressing through the revolving doors of empires, I might tell of a young boy who goes to the Cathedral School in Bombay, where he is trained by the British even though they had formally left his native India just as he was coming to life. Already he is an exile many times over—a Muslim, who, post-Partition, ought to be in Pakistan—and does not fit any of the central categories (of Hindu, Christian, Sikh) in the city where he was born (the city where Kipling was born, too, though his famous tale *Kim* tells the opposite story, of a British boy raised by Indians).

This young changeling from Windsor Villas goes on to Rugby School, the most imperial of all Britain's training grounds (where every boy, Dr. Arnold had said, will become "an Englishman—and a Christian to boot"), and afterwards, to King's College, Cambridge (as Sri Aurobindo and E. M. Forster did), and then he starts writing novels, in English, newly enlivened by all the spirits he's brought over from his tropical birthplace, and made magical by the everyday exoticism with which he's matter-of-factly grown up. An archetypal "None of the Above," he can see the strangeness of India through an Englishman's eyes, the strangeness of England through an Indian's gaze; the story of how he and his country came of age at once, as "midnight's children," is voted the strongest "British" novel in a quarter of a century.

The man's freshness comes in savoring the *masala* fusions of our times—in part because he lives them—and in celebrating the end of all the old imperial distinctions of East and West and high and low; he speaks for many of the "translated men" in the new International Empire (as he calls them) because he soars beyond all traditions and religions and lives in the spaces between cultures (his book on India offends the Indians; his book on Pakistan outrages the Pakistanis). Belonging nowhere, he's beholden to nowhere, and, settled in no faith, he underestimates, perhaps, the extent to which many people remain fiercely rooted in an older order, of doctrine and heritage and the past (the more so as they see the old constancies burning down).

His displacement is so great, in fact, that he mocks even the tradition in which he was born, and on Valentine's Day in the year of revolutions (the year the Berlin Wall comes down), as he's mourning the passing of a fellow wanderer, an apostle of nomadism brought down by the new nomadic plague, the word *fatwa* joins all the new terms he's imported into the universal dictionary. The great spokesman of the people who live everywhere becomes literally a man with no address, in a society of one.

The forces that resist what they see as the promiscuous liberties of the Global Soul—responding to the man's celebration of planes and speed with the Prophet's words, "Haste is the devil's work"—pursue their almost medieval cause as globally as their enemy did (killing his Japanese translator, attacking his Italian translator and his Norwegian publisher). And they are as precise and ingenious in their symbolism as any master craftsman of fiction (bombing the World Trade towers in Manhattan, claiming the name GIA in Paris, exploding the Planet Hollywood in Cape Town under the name of Moslems Against Global Oppression). In stalking the defining Global Soul, high and low, they want to make a larger point about the resilience of God and the Word and ancient absolutes, even in a time of flux, and if they are called "fundamentalists," that is mostly because they would call for a consideration of fundamentals—basic human needs and promptings—in an age when many of them are seeming to get lost.

As for the voice of the diaspora, he becomes a kind of phantom, protected by the security forces of the country he disowned. He shows up on late-night TV, at pop concerts, in the rooms of presidents on several continents, but the man who's always taken himself as a symbol of the new world order is taken now, by the old world order, as a symbol. His last book of the millennium is about shifting ground and burning childhood homes—earthquakes within and around the "nonbelongers'" world—and it asks, almost plaintively, underneath its affirmations, "How to find moorings, foundations, fixed points in a broken, altered time?"

In the midst of all this, the Emersonian hope keeps burning: in Davos, one of the scientists I met spoke of the Internet as the makings of a "planetary soul," and when people today quote Chief Seattle's famous dictum—"Whatever [man] does to the web, he does to himself"—they cannot fail to hear an extra resonance. A leader such as Václav Havel always takes pains to stress that the main term to be qualified by "global" should be "responsibility," and that in a world in which everyone's problems are everyone else's, a new sense of community must be formed on the basis of something deeper than soil and higher than interest rates, if our "One World" dreams are not to devolve into One Nation parties.

Besides, many of the figures helping to shape our new world are themselves Global Souls, sometimes by choice (the former president of Mexico spoke fluent Japanese), and sometimes by circumstance (the King of Tonga, I recently heard in New Zealand, though a global descendant of the sky-god Tangaloa, has to spend much of his time traveling from Auckland to Sydney to San Francisco, since the majority of his people live outside Tonga). Technology has made much of local politics global—a typical constituency is likely as polyglot as an Immigration line—and leaders in every field are aware that the possibility exists, as never before, for one bright soul to light up the planet in a moment.

Yet it seems unlikely that globalism will prove any less ambiguous than any other of our dreams. While I was writing this book, I happened to visit the Dalai Lama in his increasingly crowded exile's home in the foothills of northern India (the clocks in the little village showing the time in Israel), and I heard him say, as he often does, that the shrinking of the planet is making visible and palpable what

Buddhists, among others, have always held: that all our destinies are intertwined, and even the meanest self-interest suggests we look out for the ones around us. "Due to the modern economy," he told me, "and also due to information, to education and to tourism and the ecology problem—due to all these factors—now the world is heavily interdependent, interconnected. So, under such circumstances, the concept of 'we' and 'they' is gone; harming your neighbor is actually harming yourself." And your neighbor is everyone alive.

Yet as one trained for twenty years in logic and dialectics, the head of Tibetan Buddhism was not about to settle for a watered-down "global ethics" that is no more than the spiritual equivalent of the lowest common denominator. "If we try to unify the faiths of the world into one religion," he told a group of Catholics a few months before, while expounding the Gospels, "we will also lose many of the qualities and richnesses of each particular tradition"; indeed, for a Westerner to practice Tibetan Buddhism, he said—given that the discipline grew up in response to a culture and environment very different from that of the West—is as strange as putting a "yak's head on a sheep's body." And as his doctrine, long hidden behind the highest mountains on earth, has been translated around the world, the Buddhist monk has himself lived out the fork-tongued destiny of globalism: giving more Kalachakra Initiations for World Peace than all the thirteen Dalai Lamas of six centuries before him, yet having to face questions about why Tibetan Buddhism is so "patriarchal" and why he's not a vegetarian.

In Tibet, in fact, many of the currents of our "small world" hopes come into a compact focus. The accordioning of borders has meant that many of us, even in western Japan or Madison, Wisconsin, have gained access to the rites and teachers of a culture that, in my parents' youth, was as remote as *Lost Horizon;* yet, in the same breath, Tibet itself has acquired a Holiday Inn, a Rambo café, and a hunger for pencils. The singers of groups called Public Enemy and Porno for Pyros cry out for a "Free Tibet," while the Disney Company (rather than the State Department) sends Henry Kissinger as its emissary to

Beijing (and the incarnation of the Tibetan god of compassion, to promote his cause, serves as guest editor of French *Vogue*). Tibet is now on the world's screens, impeccably re-created in the mountains of Morocco and Argentina, while the country itself draws ever closer to extinction. And as its people get cast around the globe, running from their own burning houses, it can seem as if all of us have gained something of Tibet and lost a little of Shangri-la.

In recent years, any number of books have begun to speak of our global future, but very few of the ones that I have seen have spoken of our dreams, of disconnection, of displacement, of being lost within a labyrinth of impersonal spaces. (I, when feverish, find my subconscious clicking round a dizzying sequence of airline codes and flight numbers and departure-board destinations, where once it had spun around the London subway map.) And nearly all of them have read as if they were aimed at political scientists or public-policy experts more than at the neighbors of that Hmong tribesman from Laos who, suddenly airlifted to America, is found dead in his sleep, like too many of his young and healthy compatriots, the victim, doctors can only suppose, of a nightmare so strong that it stopped his heart from beating. It's familiar to hear that the stories on the "Business" and "Technology" pages of our newspapers—about international coproductions and virtual "town halls"—contradict the ones on our front pages (about tribal conflict and "Balkanization"). Yet an even deeper story, and often a richer one, is being played out on the "Personals" page, and it may be the more critical for being the most overlooked.

I thought it might be interesting, therefore, to try to take some readings of how this shaking of the planet felt and looked at ground level to a not entirely untypical global villager making his way through a scrambled world. Instead of consulting experts (who, when questioned with a microphone, speak as if into one), and instead of making special trips to places outside the common domain, I decided to see how these forces crisscrossed, unbidden, in one life, as one (admittedly privileged) Global Soul went about his business, seeing friends, reading the novels that fell into his lap, going now and then on trips for business and pleasure. Though in a much less desperate sense than most of the world's peoples, I, too, had a strong incentive in finding out where I belonged, as, with my house burned down, I'd been stripped of a past, and of any future I'd imagined.

In recent times, I'd found myself thinking more and more of Thoreau's sage reminder that all the new methods of communication in the world don't actually ensure that we have anything more, or better, to communicate (in fact, they may detract from that); and as the millennium approached, with its somewhat illusory sense that we were not just continuing a sentence but turning a new page, I'd found myself meeting, more and more, a statement from a relatively obscure twelfth-century Saxon monk called Hugo of St. Victor:

> The man who finds his homeland sweet is still a ten-
> der beginner; he to whom every soil is as his native
> one is already strong; but he is perfect to whom the
> entire world is as a foreign land.

The sentence was first shown to me by a young friend, of Swedish and American heritage, who lives up the road in California (he'd been sent it, through E mail, he said, by a Barbadian correspondent who'd lived in England and Germany but was settled now in Israel). A little later, I came upon the same piece of wisdom, in an essay on exile by Edward Said, and then again, written out as a poemlike epigraph, by a Chinese Australian in a Kyoto magazine, and then, once more, in bastardized form, among the floating fragments of global wisdom that run along the margins of the latest treatise by the Dutch architect Rem Koolhaas.

Yet the monk's injunction to a higher sense of home seemed to mean something different from the Global Soul's slippery proteanism. For in context, of course, it is a call to the other world: to one rooted in Heaven, the monk is saying, all places on earth will look the same. For those of us not yet ascended, however, the wisdom gives less solace as we sort through the confusion of "postdenominational" temples and self-created traditions.

Looking around the ashes of my home, the day after the fire, I'd recalled that in the Buddhist poems I'd been reading, much of the world's a burning house. Indeed, in the *Lotus Sutra*, a house in flames is a symbol of the urgent confusion in which a father notices his children, so caught up in their latest toys that they hardly notice that the walls around them are in flames. The only way to lure them out, he realizes, is by promising them a cart—using the image itself to save those of us hypnotized by images while the flames burn all our foundations down.

THE AIRPORT

"If you stayed in that airport for one year," she said, beaming like a carhop as we headed up the glittering con-course full of passengers and loved ones looking for partners, "you'd see everybody in the world. And you'd sure see Charley Pride a hundred times at least."

— RICHARD FORD

I started my travels—where else?—in the airport. For many a Global Soul is likely to find that he spends as much time in the air these days (forty days a year, I once calculated) as with the closest members of his family, and so will conduct many of his most essential tasks in a nonplace, an interval of sorts, where there are no rules beyond the IATA regulations, and few people who aren't on the time schemes of distant continents. Many of my most vivid memories of growing up had come from those times when I'd say good-bye to my parents and get onto a jumbo jet as an "unaccompanied minor" to fly to school—leaving behind a shiny, synthetic world with very little sense of past for an ancient monastic realm where we wore morning dress to chapel twice a day and were beaten for stepping "out of bounds."

It is the same transition that every child makes, of course, as he says good-bye to his mother and races towards his girlfriend, yet it is a stranger one, perhaps, when you're traveling between 1441 and 1968, and neither is the place where you entirely belong.

For me, in those days, the airport was a rare interregnum—a place between two rival forms of authority—and the airplane itself was a kind of enchanted limbo in which, a de facto VIP, I was brought soft drinks and nuts and headsets, on which to absorb risqué (to me) movies and *Burt Bacharach's Greatest Hits,* by attractive young women—all on my way to a school where movies and snacks and

Cokes and young women were attractions punishable by near death.
The plane became a high-tech equivalent to the Dickens adventures
we read in class, where the man next to me said that he was a professional football player, and had boxed against Cassius Clay, while the
woman ahead of me in the check-in line turned out to be Raquel
Welch. The entire area around Los Angeles International Airport is,
moreover, where Hollywood re-creates Beijing and Morocco, and
the glamour of my hours there, the sense of unreality, was height-
ened every April as a Brit or two would get on my plane waving the
golden man-shaped statuette he'd won at the Academy Awards the
night before.

In midair, above the Pole, I'd carefully switch the voltage on my
radio, turn my watch eight hours forwards, and move my accent (and
perhaps my attitudes) a little to the right: upon arrival, a surrogate
mother would be waiting for me at the passenger bridge and I would
hand her my papers—my very identity—to carry to the Immigration
area. There I would give my British passport to the British passport
officer, say my good-byes, and be free—alone, for several hours, in a
multicolored swarm of turbans and galabias and record shops and
telephones, lit up by the excitement that attends any child's unmoni-
tored time. Were I to return to school—hours before my classmates,
taking the evening train down from London—I'd have nothing to
look forward to but a drafty medieval room, a regimental matron,
and a one-eyed clergyman; but in the airport, homemade living
room, study, bedroom, and recreation room, I was free.

I think I intuited, even then, that the airport was the spiritual center of the double life: you get on as one person and get off as another.
I had emigrated to California by plane, after all (and seen, for the
first time, my mother's sari as exotic, as faces pressed against the glass
in Reykjavik to look at her), and so had learned that even a routine
ten-hour flight can shake up one's life irrevocably. Later, when I
picked up Caryl Phillips's *European Tribe*, describing how he would
sit through tutorials at the Queen's College, Oxford, and then race up

to Notting Hill to spend evenings with other West Indians, the part
that stayed with me was his confession that, sometimes, loitering too
late in London, and too poor in any case to afford a hotel room, he'd
go to Heathrow and spend the night there (surrounded, no doubt,
by Indians and Jamaicans, the airport always being a suburb of
Empire).

When I heard that a dozen people or more often live, around the
clock, in Kennedy Airport, making the most of the ubiquitous snack
bars, the climate control, the strangers rendered openhearted by jet
lag or culture shock, I was hardly surprised: I'd been doing the same
thing, using my large suitcase as a pillow, and occasionally spending
days at a time in an airport, catching my breath, since my teens.

In recent times, however, airports have become something more
than just an intranational convenience zone, and it is easy to see
them as models of our future. So often we find ourselves in their
accommodating, anonymous spaces, surrounded by the familiar
totems of The Body Shop, The Nature Company, The Sharper
Image—the impersonal successors to the family names of old—
while a man taps away at a laptop beside us and another mutters into
his cell phone, "If there's no emotion in it, it's just a business decision. . . ." The air is conditioned and the plants are false.

A modern airport is based on the assumption that everyone's from
somewhere else, and so in need of something he can recognize to
make him feel at home; it becomes, therefore, an anthology of
generic spaces—the shopping mall, the food court, the hotel lobby—
which bear the same relation to life, perhaps, that Muzak does to
music. There are discos and dental clinics and karaoke bars in airports today; there are peep shows and go-cart tracks and interde-
nominational chapels. Dallas–Fort Worth International is larger than
Manhattan, and Istanbul has a special terminal just to accommodate
"shuttle shoppers" from the former Soviet Union. As I was passing

through San Francisco's airport recently, I came upon a whole exhibition on the history of airports—wheels within wheels—and read that Berlin's Tempelhof used to be the busiest air facility in the world, receiving eleven thousand passengers in 1925. Now Chicago's O'Hare sees that many in two hours.

As a boy, I had often found airports exciting because they were the closest thing around to the starship *Enterprise*, a cut-rate Adventureland, Tomorrowland, and Fantasyland combined, rich in flashing screens and exotic costumes; now you can see the same kind of activity on every other street corner in Paris, or Sydney, or Vancouver. The modern city is a place where everyone's a stranger, so it seems, on his way to somewhere else.

Yet what makes an airport especially curious is that its look-alike settings are the scenes for the most emotional moments in our public lives. People break down at departure gates, I'd noticed as a boy, in racking sobs, and others shout at workers they've scarcely met; many passengers are at the far edge of themselves in transit areas, in mingled states of alertness and discombobulation. So all the most intimate encounters—that girl closing her eyes as she kisses her lost love, that child comforting the mother just widowed, that group of dark-suited worshipers gathering around a departing missionary with their prayers—are played out in a maze of yogurt shops and public-address announcements and crowds waving pyramid-shaped boxes of chocolates that say AMERICA THE BEAUTIFUL.

Part of the pathos and stress of the airport (the leading cause of death at JFK is the coronary) is that lives are being changed irreversibly, and people have nothing to steady themselves with but a Coffee People outlet, a Sky Plaza, and a Smarte Cart that (in Los Angeles at least) speaks seven different languages. All the comforts of home, made impersonal.

Thinking all this—and suspecting that LA, of all places, was the one where people most come to make new lives (40 percent of its residents now are foreign-born, and California receives half of all America's immigrants)—I went to live for a while in LAX.

. . .

As I began to look around Los Angeles International Airport, walking around its terminals as I might a foreign city, I quickly realized that it really does have all the amenities of a modern metropolis. There is a fire station there, and a private hospital next door; the airport has its own $10 million post office. There is an airport police squad, cruising around in Crown Victoria patrol cars, another unit forms a Bicycle Patrol, and the Coast Guard also maintains a station there. There is a movie coordinator at LAX, a tow-truck service and a five person Airport Commission (made up, not long ago, of a Chinese man, a Japanese man, a Hispanic woman, an elderly white man, and an African-American named Johnnie Cochran, Jr.). There is even a public-relations department, one of whose employees told me, casually, "FBI, Secret Service, CIA—everybody's here."

There are 23,000 parking spaces in LAX—the PR person dubbed it "the largest parking lot in the world"—and more than fifty thousand people work in this microuniverse (or almost twice as many as live in Monaco). Everything was more complex than I had imagined, in fact. I thought I knew LAX pretty well before going there—after all, I had formally emigrated to the U.S. there, thirty years before, and had visited every few months ever since; many of my most fateful partings and reunions had taken place there.

Yet when I looked around me, I found myself adrift in a world I could not recognize: even most of the airlines here were ones I'd never heard of—Air L.A. and Croat American Air, and AOM; Carnival and Leisure Air and Express One; Translift and Sun Country and Canada 3000. The previous year, a few people had even flown in and out on Air Evasion.

To get my bearings within this mobile sprawl, I went to consult a Travelers Aid desk in the Tom Bradley International Terminal (or TBIT, as it's exotically called), at 400 World Way, built in anticipation of the 1984 Olympics. Around me, a blond Mexican in a Caesar's Palace hat was sprawled against an Indian swathed in Giordano and

Vuitton, while a Japanese girl in a sari was pushing a lurid copy of the *Bhagavad-Gita* on an African. "Oh, I forgot!" cried a woman in front of me, addressing two very bewildered-looking Home Stay visitors. "In Japanese, *yes* means *no!*"

The friendly volunteers at the Travelers Aid desk assured me that I could request help in more than one hundred languages, from Tajik to Pashto and Pampango to Waray-Waray. But the miscommunications around me suggested that more than translators were needed: "Remember me?" someone was asking plaintively, and someone else was saying, "It is not a request, but can you spare some money today?" A group of Cambodians in Long Beach Unified School District shirts were bumping against black-clad security men who looked uncannily like ninjas.

Airports say a lot about a place because they are both a city's business card and its handshake; they tell us what a community yearns to be as well as what it really is (much like the people inside them, often, who are dressed up for the occasion, and worn ragged and bare by the experience). YOUR IMPRESSIONS BEGIN HERE, the sign in Bangkok's arrivals terminal announces, and governments often cannily turn their airports into showpieces, with landscaped exit routes through Potemkin settlements, designed to disarm the disoriented newcomer. Osaka's $15 billion Kansai International Airport is the largest building in Japan, its mile-long terminal the only manmade structure (other than the Great Wall) visible from the moon; Hong Kong's new $20 billion facility boasts the "largest food court in the world" and a 140-store Sky Mart; even the unremarkable Kenyan town of Eldoret (the hometown of President Moi) now has a $90 million international airport.

LAX, however, is unlikely to thrill people who've dreamed of it from afar. It is a flat and centerless mess with no real defining principle or heart—just a mass of gray, gray terminals around a central international building that is no longer large enough to accommodate all international arrivals. Eight satellites, you could say, in search of a sun.

As I walked around this microcosm of LA, I was taken aback to find deserted Eastern Airlines counters (with all the defunct airline's destinations still painted on the wall) in place, and goods on sale from a World Cup that had finished long before. Huge Pan Am Clipper Cargo hangars sat disinherited around the perimeter, and ten of the twelve car-rental phones I tried were broken. Yet the *AMC Gram* I found (an Air Mobility Command newsletter) at the edge of one terminal proudly, even patriotically, announced, "LAX—Leading and Excelling Daily," and the postcards in the gift shops (made in Korea) declared LAX to be "one of the busiest and most beautiful air facilities in the world." The place resembled, in that way, many of the city's most famous residents, clinging to outdated five-by-seven glossies of themselves while the face-lifts and Gucci-leather skin told a sadder story.

At one point, while I was staying in LAX, I had to go to Melbourne for a weekend for my work, and I found myself passing through a rapid succession of air facilities. The new airport in Osaka, with its talking telephones and fifty pinball machines in the departure area, showed off its own telephone card and T-shirt and hand towel, all featuring its own Olympic-style mascot (and tourists came from all over Japan to inspect this modern wonder of the world); in Auckland, I happened upon a beautifully silent Scriptorium in the transit area, with writing desks for last farewells, and a quiet, clean chapel and Theaterette. LAX, by contrast, seemed mostly to offer two enigmatic tortoises in front of Gates 111 and 113. The copy of *Business Traveler* I read on the plane back placed LA among the five worst airports in the world, in terms of Customs, Facilities, and Conveniences (its only consolation being that JFK placed dead last in all these categories).

In recent times, its rulers have given the international terminal a theme-park makeover, so that foreigners can walk through a neon-quickened blur of L.A. Sports and Euro Coffee, Sushi Boy and a Warner Bros. store (all in a concourse called El Paseo); yet still it was clear that LAX told more about LA than it would like to, with its

public-address system, on perpetual loop, telling the thirty thousand
international passengers who arrive each day, "Attention, travelers!
You are *not* required to give money to solicitors. This airport does *not*
sponsor their activities. I repeat: you are *not* required . . ."

Airports are always a little like dolls within the larger dolls of the
city, like the ads for a My Twinn product in Denver's new Stapleton
Airport—its terminal made to resemble the snowcapped mountains
all around—showing a picture of a little girl holding a machine-made
replica of herself: INDIVIDUALLY CRAFTED TO LOOK LIKE YOUR
DAUGHTER. Thus Shanghai, true to stereotype, has People's Liberation Army soldiers guarding its gleaming corridors (under Master
Card Global Service signs), and liveried attendants who present you
with a baggage cart upon arrival, then promptly ask for payment. Rio
has a famously husky transvestite announcer whose breathy invita-
tions to final calls have often caused whole groups of mesmerized
Japanese businessmen to miss their flights, while Dum Dum, in Calcutta, in order to assure itself of maximum chaos, has all international
flights, it seems, touch down at 2:00 a.m.

Orly, near Paris, has an art gallery, and San Francisco obligingly
pretends to be the place we're hoping for by including a Grateful
Dead corner, a cybershop featuring cutting-edge Bay Area graphics,
a Hairport, a funky b-zinc shop offering books on Krishnamurti and
Jung, and fourteen quirky corridor exhibitions at any time, on such
unlikely themes as platform shoes and Ashanti stools. LA, by contrast, offers VAC8ION mini license plates and tilting mugs that say
CALIFORNIA: A NEW SLANT ON LIFE, amidst $12.95 Best Actor
statues and Beverly Hills Confection Collections. Much of what I
saw on offer was the kind of thing you'd find anywhere in America—
U.S. Army patches, mock-Elvis gold records, magnets representing Tanzanian stamps commemorating Whitney Houston. Yet in its
particulars, LA was selling beaches and movie stars and cash—that
whole anomalous mix of leisure and affluence captured by the curious term *entertainment industry*.

At the time I was staying in LAX, Malibu had just been washed into the ocean, Hollywood Boulevard was more run-down than Tegucigalpa, and in parts of LA, only 11 percent of the people over the age of eighteen could read; but in the simplified transaction of images in which the airport traffics, the departure terminals were still selling L.A.'S THE PLACE posters and postcards of the Disney trinity announcing LIFE'S A PICNIC IN CALIFORNIA. It had also shrewdly identified the consumers most ready to spend handsomely on a piece of the California Dream. JCB credit cards from Japan were accepted in many gift shops, and WELCOME signs (in Japanese) were plastered often on their windows. Daruma dolls sat amidst miso soup and *onigiri* in the coffee shops, and one of the only non-Crichton or -Krantz offerings on display among the books was *The Japanese Visitor's Guide to Silicon Valley*. An Osakan arriving here— and paying ninety-five dollars for some Teriyaki Beef Jerky—might reasonably have concluded that he'd never actually left home.

The other item that greeted me everywhere in the airport were magnets with one-hundred-dollar bills painted on them. In some gift stores, there were mugs designed to look like rolled-up hundred-dollar bills, and in others, lighters that resembled hundred-dollar bills. It was a poignant thing to see Filipinos, say, with the ten-dollar bills they'd saved up over months, buying one-hundred-dollar bills to take back to their brothers, or others, who'd found life hard here and were returning home in disappointment, buying key rings that said LIFE'S A BEACH.

What makes the airport special, though—something different from any souvenir store in Universal City or Warner Bros. store world-wide—is that it is a gift store with culture shock; the product, in its video arcades, its hotels, and its cocktail lounges, of a mixed marriage between a border crossing and a shopping mall. And the confusions of any shop where people are surrounded by signs they can't read and people they can't follow are amplified in this place where so many customers are from somewhere far away, and so many of the shopkeepers are recent arrivals with a shaky hold on English. Things get lost in translation in airports, and the whole cross-cultural drama is stirred up by the fact that many of the people in airports are in something of a dream state.

As I was looking at some macadamia nuts in a gift shop—the closest thing we have, an airport suggests, to a One-World currency—an Indian man, with a fresh copy of the hard-core magazine *Variations* (its cover half-concealed for discretion) under his arm, rummaged showily through his pockets, then asked me for some change in Hindi (I assume it was Hindi, of which I speak not a word, though it included the English word *change*).

"I'm sorry," I responded, not very companionably. "I don't speak Hindi."

"You're not Indian?"

"I am Indian, but . . ."

At that, he shuffled off, and the cashier wearily turned to another Indian, this one with a very shy bearing, and cried, "Clearasil? You want that for your face?"

A Frenchman was speaking his native tongue to another startled, though friendly, worker, trying to explain that he wanted his Hershey bar wrapped. ("A souvenir," he said, switching to English. "A remember. From the war. The GIs used to give this same chocolate to me. I was four years old.")

Meanwhile, Soldiers of the Cross of Christ Church were shaking tins by escalators, priests (or at least men dressed as priests) were approaching strangers with requests for money, and a sweet Brazilian girl (with a NONPROFIT, NONSECTARIAN badge that apparently allowed her to operate here) was pulling copies of a book called *Renunciation* out of a brown paper bag. Airports everywhere are places where hustlers try to sell displaced foreigners taxi rides, tours, and girls; in LA, I was amused to see, they were largely peddling salvation.

The most conspicuous characters in the departures terminal, though (partly because they were so much in possession of themselves), were tall, dark, extremely well dressed men in sober suits and ties who were circling around with clipboards, like UN diplomats on the loose. I saw one of them sidle up to a chic Taiwanese girl, who was clutching a copy of *Mademoiselle*, and flip open his folder to show her horrifying pictures of bodies being mutilated in Iran. I saw another accost two terrified-looking Japanese girls in BORN TO BE WILD California T-shirts and offer them evidence of Shiite torture. I saw them detain a blond girl and ask her (always urbanely and politely), "Excuse me. Where are you from?"

"Here," she said. "But Denmark originally."

The Iranian addressed her in fluent Danish, corrected her Californian inflections, and then, in her mother's tongue, said sadly, "Good-bye, Danish girl."

As soon as she walked away, he turned to me. "Excuse me. ¿*Habla español*?"

Traditionally, of course, what makes the airport unique (though now it is more and more common on every sidewalk in many cities) is that no one knows where anyone is coming from (in both the Californian and the global sense), and no one really knows where anyone is at. I spent one day walking around LAX with a blond Angeleno friend, and saw one Korean matron sweetly compliment her on her command of English, and another mujahedin (with who knows what intent) ask her if she were Indian.

Upstairs, where a group of students was gulping down "Dutch chocolate" and "Japanese coffee" and translating *school* from English to American (while learning—the hard way—that *soliciting* loses some of its cachet as it crosses the Atlantic), a large man was nuzzling the neck of his outrageously pretty Filipina companion, and a few Brits were staring, with undisguised skepticism, at an ad that said that seafood was "cheerfully served at your table!" (Only in America, they were doubtless thinking.) Women dressed as nurses rattled tins, others announced, "We serve the youth in getting off drugs," and a shady man slipped from table to table, depositing on each one a key chain attached to a miniature globe. Whenever some unsuspecting victim picked one up—This really *is* the "Land of the Free," he might have been thinking—the man suddenly appeared at his side, flashing a sign that said I AM A DEAF and requesting a compulsory "gift" of a dollar.

On my last trip back here, I now recalled, I had cross-questioned a Skynet computer in Osaka about what to expect in LA. "Guard against theft in the arrival hall," it had advised me. "A thief is waiting to take advantage of you." Elsewhere, it had offered, "Be on guard when approached by a group of suspicious-looking children, such as girls wearing bright-colored shirts and scarves." Meanwhile, on TV monitors all around, amateurs had acted out minidramas of all the horrors awaiting unsuspecting Japanese at the other end—friendly strangers slipping them poisoned orange juices, room-service waiters pushing them to the ground, con men posing as limousine drivers, and just typical foreigners not specifying currencies when they made out a credit-card receipt.

Everyone, in fact, is on alert to some extent when he goes to the airport, and it is that sense of free-floating apprehension that all the life-insurance companies (and their spiritual equivalents) hope to turn to profit. "People are scared here," a security guard told me as we inspected the X-ray machine he was supervising (security checks being a favorite place for criminals, who seize advantage of the general commotion, and the guards chattering in Tagalog while the passengers fret in Hindi, to whip bags off the belts). "Because undercover are working. Police are working. Three hundred and fifty police are here. You could be undercover, I could be undercover, who knows?"

Ten rival surveillance companies work the Bradley Terminal alone, and the arrivals hall seemed constantly to buzz with the whines and beepings of their paging devices and walkie-talkies. Everywhere, people were patting their pockets to make sure they had their IDs on them, or wondering if their valuables were on the far side of the planet. "You can't say, 'Don't go there,'" an English-woman was telling a Mrs. Chang at the information desk. "The only thing we can say is, 'Don't go out at night. Watch yourself!'"

"Attention travelers," the announcements went on and on. "You are *not* required to give money to solicitors. This airport does not sponsor their activities. I repeat . . ."

Airports, in fact, are charged zones, where we are regularly reminded to observe our mothers' wisdom not to accept offers from strangers, and where the guidebooks tell us that most of the waiting taxi drivers are waiting to take us for a ride (no part of urban folklore, this was the issue covered on page one of the *Airport Press* magazine I picked up in LAX). These private anxieties are reinforced by all the public ones that gather around these places, famously "sensitive" areas where photographs are often prohibited, and khaki-clad sol-diers patrol the tarmac, while, over to one side, a whole shadow world of stealth bombers and camouflaged helicopters, on covert operations, sits beside the bright official comings and goings of tourists. The airport is the place that is closed during coups, and the airport is the place where troublesome dissidents (like Ninoy Aquino) are sometimes shot; its dark lexicon of arteries and black boxes and manifests is made even darker by the images we carry with us of hijackers on the tarmac, and black-masked antiterrorist squads (the Unabomber, when jealous of the attention Timothy McVeigh was receiving, threatened to blow up LAX).

Almost everyone knows these days that she is twenty times more likely to die in a car crash than in a plane (and, in fact, three times more likely to die when an asteroid hits the earth), but still each of us brings more fear to an airport than she would to a cigarette or a

Toyota or a tab of ecstasy. For every time a plane does crash, it is instantly front-page news—three hundred killed, not one—and all our Icarian fears, our sense that there is something not quite right, something inhuman and hubristic, about taking ourselves into the heavens, are rekindled. The KIA of Kennedy International Airport used to be said to stand, James Kaplan writes, for "killed in action," and on the one occasion I took a tour of LAX with a public-relations official, she took pains to try to point out the skid marks on the tarmac that designated one of the highlights of the airport's history (a hideous crash).

The other quality that ups the stakes in airports and places them in the rarefied company of luxury hotels and upscale shopping malls is that they are among the only sites in public life where immortals rub shoulders with the rest of us, and everyone is subject to the same rules (even Michael Jordan has to go through customs and even Queen Elizabeth has to deplane). The airport is not so dangerous as a typical inner-city Greyhound station, or Port Authority bus terminal in New York, say, because it doesn't attract so many desperately poor people; yet it is more dangerous than any of those places for the same reason, which is that scores of rich people pass through, amidst the rest of us, tourist and terrorist, Olympian and Everyman, all thrown together into the same promiscuous mix.

Airports do what they can to segregate the privileged from the rest of us (indeed, the whole point of Business Class, a relatively new invention so popular that it has given rise to Executive Floors in hotels, and Gold Card lines at car-rental agencies, is that, if you pay two thousand dollars more, you can separate yourself from the riffraff for every step of your fifteen-hour trip, checking in at a separate line from them, waiting for your flight in a separate lounge, and then eating your nuts without being bothered by their cries, an expensive form of detachment nicely mocked by Virgin Airlines' cheeky name for its top-flight seats, "Upper Class"). Once upon a time, England did not even accept "tourist-class" airline passengers (thus prompting the growth of Shannon in Ireland).

Yet for all such measures, terminals still speak to the anxieties rife in our borderless world, in which every kind of soul is thrown together in the Immigration line, and "affordable luxury" claims to make exclusiveness the right of all (lofty Harrods now sits next to a Metropolitan Museum of Art gift shop in Tokyo's second-tier airport, while Wolfgang Puck offers Express pizza service in LAX; in one issue of *Los Angeles* magazine, the best bookstore in all of ten-million-strong, eight-area-code greater Los Angeles was pronounced to be the Waterstone's in Terminal 1, "the very model of a small bookstore"). Thus airports offer the privileged every luxury except the one they really need—full privacy all the time—and so become the site of many of our tabloid sightings; Deepak Chopra is twiddling his thumbs next to me at the Silver Wings taco bar and Nicolas Cage is racing down the sidewalk to make his flight outside Terminal 4; once, in Terminal 2, I came upon a whole array of men in suits and girls with cornrows and kids with backpacks standing in front of a man with a beeper under his Warner Bros. T-shirt—a group of regular people, in short, acting as regular people in a movie.

The airport evokes, in fact, the very image one sees so often in the deeply poor cities of the world—in Port-au-Prince or Addis Ababa—where security posts and tall barbed-wire fences and armed guards separate those on the ground from those lucky enough to be flying in or out. The stranded ones peer through holes in the fence at the blessed ones able to be part of the global village.

In LAX, such signs of exclusiveness were most noticeable in the private terminal run by MGM Grand (or, since it traffics in distinctions, the "general aviation facility" run by MGM Grand), which stands by itself a long way from the rest of the passenger terminals, out amidst the warehouses along the Imperial Highway, which local workers know by the name of "Cargo City."

On the afternoon I visited this last word in privacy, with its gold-fixture sinks and carpeted toilets (linked to a 5,005-room hotel in Las Vegas, and a thirty-three-acre theme park), it was to find it completely empty save for one morose Pakistani guard sitting above a

motionless security belt. He'd been here for only four days, he told
me, but already he'd seen displays of Croesan wealth beyond my
imagining. Once, a 727 had flown in and disgorged exactly one passenger; another time, a plane had landed with only twelve on board.
"All big shots come over this terminal," he said, with more solemnity
than pride. "You and me, small potatoes like us, we cannot come
here."

The final aspect of the security issue at LAX (which again reflects a
world in which more and more of us are on foreign ground, surrounded by different values) is that of customs: if much of the public
officiousness at airports is about guarding passengers from criminals,
much of the rest of it derives from the fact that the passengers are
themselves often criminal. The largest cash robbery in American history, at the time, was pulled off at JFK (Lucky Luciano actually died
at an airport—on his way to meet a Hollywood producer); and in
LAX, during my sojourn there, four Chinese men were apprehended
as they tried to smuggle in whole gallbladders of Asiatic black bears,
testicles of musk deer, rhinoceros-horn powder and tiger-bone plas-
ters—$2 million worth of aphrodisiacs, all drawn from endangered
species.

It has been known for people to try to smuggle fig trees on their
persons into the Promised Land (the trunk hidden under their
pants, the branches underneath their shirts), and in Japan it's not
unusual to hear of mobsters trying to smuggle Thai girls into the
country, sometimes in their check-in bags. Cities like Bangkok
famously see scores of Nigerians catching flights for Europe with
entire inflatable balloons of heroin in their stomachs, and, in
response to such scams, Singapore nearby precisely announces to all
visitors on its disembarkation card, "DEATH for drug traffickers
under Singapore's law."

In the Departures Hall of TBIT, therefore, I wasn't wholly taken
aback to find two large glass cases announcing TRAVELER BEWARE

amidst the milling Iranians. Inside was a motley assembly of rhinoceros-horn cans, whales' teeth, ivory Buddhas, heads of dead toucans, leopard skins (with heads attached), and a crocodile hand-bag belonging to Lai Ching Hsing of Beverly Hills. All this seemed a useful-enough caution, though it did go a little oddly with the Pandamonium display on the other side of the hall containing battery-operated pandas, panda Valentine cards, and a mannequin, chic behind a panda mask.

And in Osaka Airport, not far from the massage chairs rented by the hour, and a machine on which you can make business cards, I came upon an entire "CIQ" room that helpfully tells aspiring crimi-nals everything they might want to know about their chosen profes-sion. In one small case alone in the comfortable room (boys sprawled out around it, waiting for their flights) were replicas of paint thinners and diet pills, peyote buttons and "black mollies." There were sym-bols of Valium and "microdots," "pink ladies," "red birds," and "yel-lows"; and as I pored over the selection of roaches and "rainbows" and PCP black tar heroin, I realized once more that the airport was teaching me about worlds I hadn't known existed.

"You could be undercover, I could be undercover, who knows?"

The defining paradox of the airport, though, is that it offers all these amenities to people who don't really want to be there, and tries to divert people whose only attention is on when they can get out (the Sheremetyevo-2 transit zone in Moscow's airport actually merits a paragraph in the UNHCR's book, *The State of the World's Refugees*, because at any given time up to twenty people are being held in its detention quarters). You can swim in a rooftop pool in Miami, I had read, or play in a meta-miniairport in O'Hare (complete with its own air-control towers and baggage claim areas); you can visit a micro-brewery in Bangkok, or explore hiking trails in Kuala Lumpur. Yet all these diversions feel a little like the images in Plato's Cave (designed to keep people away from the world of flesh).

The language of airports has become the language of our private lives, as we speak of holding patterns and living on autopilot, fly-by-night operations and getting bumped. Yet the language we meet in airports is rigorously impersonal, all passive tense and "congestion-related flight delay." We move from pedestrian walkway to terminal to concourse; we pass booth personnel and "Personal Assistance Training" rooms and "interior cosmetic upgrades." The whole act of flying sensualizes us, but in an anonymous space, with the result that we're lost in a free-floating state of temporary intimacy. Part of us is thinking of the "romance of travel," as the ads for Singapore Airlines have it—the scene from *Emmanuelle,* or the Dating Channel on Virgin planes, whereby you can contact attractive strangers on your seat monitor (there are masseuses in Virgin's Upper Class, hairstylists in its Club House lounge); yet the rest of us is conjugating "exit row" and "flotation device," "gate lock" and "dwell time" and "safety procedures."

I thought of all this as I walked and walked the long corridors of LAX, labyrinth leading into labyrinth, and uniformed personnel outside Jody Maroni's Sausage Kingdom wearing name tags on their chests (BABY LEE REYNOLDS, NARITA WEISS). I recalled the eerie first sentence of Kathryn Harrison's memoir of her love affair with her father—"We meet at airports"—and I thought of the friend who told me how, on an Aeroflot flight once, a stewardess had invited him into a private room and given him a white-tablecloth meal and a taste of cross-cultural romance, high above the miles of snow and darkness in Siberia. When they landed, she waved good-bye, and he realized he didn't even know her name.

Departure boards clicked over with their never-ending list of initials, digits, codes; passageways led to escalators that brought me into junk-food El Dorados where a robotic male voice next to a cash register intoned over and over some New Age chimes: "Spirit Worlds," "Dolphin Sounds," and "Piano Moods."

The white zone is for loading and unloading only. No parking. Mr.

Al Sharpton, Mr. Al Sharpton, please report to the white courtesy telephone. Mr. Al Sharpton, to the white courtesy telephone. Please maintain visual contact with your personal property at all times. All unattended baggage is subject to immediate removal.

Once, rousing myself from a daze, and not really sure of whether I was coming or going, I heard, "John Cheever. John Cheever. Please contact a Northwest representative in the Baggage Claim Area. John Cheever, please contact a service representative in the Northwest Baggage Claim Area."

It could have been true, for all I know; people take on strange identities in airports.

And so, half-inadvertently, not knowing whether I was facing east or west, not knowing whether it was night or day, I slipped into that peculiar state of mind—or no-mind— that belongs to the no-time, no-place of the airport, that out-of-body state in which one's not quite there, but certainly not elsewhere. My words didn't quite connect, and the world came to me through panes of soundproof glass. I felt myself in a state of suspended animation, five miles above the sea—sleepy, light-headed, unsure of how much pressure to put on things. I had entered the stateless state of jet lag.

By now, like more and more of us, I'm no stranger to this no-man's-land, a realm of spaced-out dreaminess where something in one doesn't engage, and something else comes loose, so one is left either skating giddily, heart wide open, on the surface of oneself or feeling mysteriously clogged somehow, heart-high in mud. Every few weeks, quite often, I fly from Japan to California, and find myself revved up, speedy, all adrenaline as I touch down, with my mind turned off and my defenses flung open. I write wildly emotional letters to people I've hardly met, and get shaken and moved by every film I see, as if truly under some foreign influence (the wonder drug of displacement). On the way back, I end up at the other pole, reluctant for days to get out of bed, with every book or thought I entertain seeming leaden. My words have not caught up with me—it's as if they are pieces of luggage that the airline has misplaced and sent on by a later flight—and it is only slowly, day by day, that I come back into focus, until, at last, perhaps a week after I've returned, I wake up one morning (at a normal hour) and realize that I'm reassembled, intact, here.

All this, of course, is nothing more than a matter of biorhythms and "circadian rhythm upsets," as they say, and is only an accelerated, compacted form of that process whereby we feel differently, and occupy different moods, at 8:00 a.m. and 3:00 p.m. A "morning person" stays awake and throbs all night on jet lag, and doctors reassure us that moroseness and even cataracts and high-frequency hearing loss are to be expected from this constant crisscrossing of time lines. But what is interesting—in part because so new—are the less calculable effects of this modern whirl, or the ones it's still too early for scientists to gauge. Humanity today is facing all kinds of sudden jerks it's never known before, and many of us embrace this phenomenon—the definition of possibility—without knowing what the consequences will be. The average person today sees as many images in a day as a Victorian might have in a lifetime; but compounding, and confusing, this are the shifts in place and mind we experience that Sigmund Freud and Oscar Wilde could not have imagined. We wake up, orphaned, in West Hollywood and go to sleep, surrounded by our parents, in medieval Kathmandu; we zigzag across centuries as if they were just settlements in a village.

As I wandered through the long gray terminals of LAX for day after day, and through departure lounge after departure lounge, I realized how many of the people around me were sleepwalkers, too, on edge, wound up, trying to bring the twilight zone inside them in sync with the hazy sunshine all around. I saw people, opened up, pouring their life stories out to strangers (and other people making new life stories with the strangers they began embracing); I saw people reaching out to one another with the jangled camaraderie of survivors at sea. I saw people slip around disappointment and hide their relief behind strong makeup. "People get ugly here," a woman who'd worked as a Travelers Aid volunteer for seventeen years told me. "I no longer think of travel as very pleasurable. It's really only travail." Those around her, over and over, likened the airport to a hospital, where people break down or through, in extreme states of exhaustion or emotion.

Time itself plays strange tricks around the airport, as we routinely wake up in Tokyo today and arrive in LA last night. Everyone's looking at his watch in departure lounges, but all the watches show different times. People tap their fingers, stretch their legs, pace restlessly back and forth in terminals; they also run in them (like O. J. Simpson in the Hertz commercial), hurdling obstacles and brushing past strangers who stare at them listlessly from their different worlds. Airports are among the only places in our lives where we sometimes have to wait for six hours, or eight, or even ten; where we are actually paid off for waiting with free hotel rooms, or offered two hundred dollars in cash if we will voluntarily wait another three hours. Events are bunched up weirdly (like the people suddenly primitive, pushing their way towards the counter), and time slips and stretches as in the final eleven seconds of a basketball game, which takes fifteen minutes to play out on TV.

I think sometimes we become children again in airports, irresponsible and without stewardship, of course, as I was as a nine-year old in Heathrow; but also spoiled and denied and restless and bemused all at once. One of the odd things about airports (like every other modern convenience) is that the instruments we make to serve us always hold us hostage, and many of the people in gate lounges are clearly frustrated because they're at the mercy of forces they can't understand or control—red-eyed, bored, waiting to be transported.

In our worst moments, in fact, it can seem as if the airport is an anthology of modern ills—we munch fast food in a transit lounge amidst the beeps of Mortal Kombat machines and the anonymous props of a motel, the sleek shops and cold screens undermined somehow by the paper cups and sniffling noses, the sense of people at loose ends. Neil LaBute's audaciously heartless independent movie, *In the Company of Men,* about two young executives on an out-of-town trip who decide not to take with them the most fundamental rules of humanity, begins, perfectly, in a departure lounge in some Nowhere International late at night. A land of fluorescent lights and empty hotels, garment bags and shoeless men in suits. The nighttime start of a journey into an amoral zone where we are not ourselves, and so anything is possible (the film's most brutal scenes of calculated heartbreak take place in a borrowed hotel room).

Airports can be vertiginous places because we have nothing to hold our identities in place there; the most fundamental things are up for grabs. Heathrow, writes John le Carré, referring to a Russian spy, "is one of Checheyev's favorite places. He can take rooms there by the half day, he can rotate hotels and fancy himself anonymous." Gander Airport in Newfoundland is famous for only one reason: it is the place where for years people became someone else, as Cubans and other Communists, briefly touching down for refueling, would race across the tarmac or hide in bushes, effectively saying, I am no longer who I used to be. My new self starts today.

One day in Kyoto, staying at the Holiday Inn, I returned to LAX in a dream, and found myself taking the shuttle bus round and around, looking for a hotel in which to stay. The other people on the bus were all disheveled immigrants, looking for a job, and speaking not a word of English, and so all of us went round in circles, archetypal residents of that running in place that becomes part of the airport state of mind.

In LAX, as the days went on, I found myself gravitating towards the center stage of this area of transformations, the Arrivals Hall in the International Terminal. Planes themselves are often backstages of a kind, where we can see women hastily applying lipstick and checking themselves out in mirrors as the pilot says, "We're beginning our descent" (while men often stash romantic keepsakes in the innards of their briefcases as soon as the pilot announces, "Flight attendants, prepare for takeoff"). But the fascination of the terminals themselves is that they become a public forum for the most private of transactions. In poor countries, the center of poignancy is usually around the departure gates, where a prize student takes off into a new life, leaving tens of friends and relatives sobbing behind him. In a place like LAX, the center of intensity is the arrivals area, as people who've been dreaming all their lives, often, of the place they've seen on-screen (in the *Santa Barbara* soap opera I saw for the first time in an Indian Airlines terminal, or the *California Dreams* sitcom shown on the government educational channel in Japan) meet, for the first time, the American Reality.

I took to spending more and more time, then, making myself at home in the airport, in front of the huge mural of Desertland, which dominates the first floor of TBIT, and it was easy to feel as if I were watching people extending their hands across centuries, or chasms they hadn't known to exist before. Most of the souls around me, waiting for arriving planes, looked to be recent immigrants, dressed to show off their ease in their new homes, and gazing towards the customs door as towards some fragment of their past; and most of the ones walking out were probably the same people a few years before. The only currency common to both sides of the fence was America, as the arrivals, very often, came in loaded high with Schwarzenegger videos and John Cougar Mellencamp tapes, dressed in cowboy hats and 49ers jackets and all the symbols of America that mean most when you're a long way away from it. And the people waiting to greet them, in many cases, were now Americans in a deeper sense, so that Chiang Hsieng found his niece called herself Cindy now, and had a ring in her nose that glinted as she rubbed herself against that surfer from Berlin.

"Is there a lot of heavy people in Germany?" a sleek Russian blonde called Natasha asked her German friend from California. "Look how they walk the same way. So military."

Next to her, Dr. An, from Monterey Park, was waiting for the flight from Kuala Lumpur, with a yellow rose in his hand, and a copy of a dental magazine, and a young wife from Sri Lanka was circling around with three cases on a baggage cart, wondering whether this was how her marriage would end up.

A little Filipina girl came out of air lock with Fred Flintstone in one arm and a panda in the other, and two lanky giants loped out in Aerial Assault sneakers, fresh from playing some exhibition games in Mexico. People shuffled up to one another, faces crumpled, so that it was clear that this was an antechamber of a funeral; other people clapped, bought eighteen-inch Mylar balloons, and wildly waved the flag of Mexico. An old Japanese man came in and said, "*Tadaima!*"— the ritual greeting used when one arrives back home (a grandson dutifully replied, "*Okaeri!*"); a Thai girl filed out in thigh-high boots with a sandy-haired son whose name she couldn't pronounce. Some people came out with the spoils of war, like Odysseus from his travels: new mothers for their children, fresh business cards from Shanghai, ways of saying *sorry* in Korean, macadamia nuts from Oahu. Others came out with next to nothing, Mexicans in trainers that said UNIVERSITY OF SEÑOR FROG'S DRINKING TEAM, Southeast Asians with logos that declared, for some reason, THE VERY LAST VIKING.

Every few minutes, the whole area (like LA itself, it was tempting to think) was made over by the latest wave of newcomers, as, in a single hour, planes disgorged passengers from Taiwan, England, the Philippines, Mexico, Austria, Spain, Costa Rica, Germany, and Guatemala. And each of them brought a new mood and rhythm to the terminal—mornings, the blue blazers and white shirts around the early flights from Tokyo; afternoons, a flood of tropical colors from the Hawaiian Air arrivals. And what was waiting for all the new entries—a distilled version of their future—were Indians wagging

heads, Iranians kissing one another smackily on the cheeks, Oki-
nawan honeymooners in color-coordinated outfits, and girls in hot
pants who looked very much like the ones you didn't talk about at
home. The most startling initial surprise, surely, for many immigrants
in LA was that they were arriving in a land full of other immigrants
who looked nothing at all like the Robert Redford and Michelle
Pfeiffer they'd seen on TV; the land of mom and apple pie was a
place of tacos and *udon* and Wiener schnitzel.

I think this shock of discovery—a feature of our global village—is
especially acute in LA, just because the city is the world capital of
illusion, a kind of terminal of dreams where so many people come
expressly to "arrive" (more than half of all passengers here come for
pleasure). When we think of London or Paris, say, most of us imagine
the Houses of Parliament or the Eiffel Tower; some image—from a
Monet watercolor or a Hardy novel read in school—that stands in
front of us imposingly. When we think of LA, often, we think, by contrast, of backdrop: beaches and bikinis and palm trees and sun. There
is a sense that we can fit ourselves into its 2-D scenes, as seen in *Bay-
watch* or *E.T. The Extra-Terrestrial,* and that what it is offering is less
history than lifestyle (which is available to all). Perhaps the greatest
danger of our global community is that the person in LA thinks he
knows Cambodia because he's seen *The Killing Fields* on-screen, and
the newcomer from Cambodia thinks he knows LA because he's seen
City of Angels on video.

And as I stood among the chadors and tribal flags and Mickey and
Minnie balloons in Terminal 4, I felt I could see how transitions that
had looked so easy at home suddenly gaped huge. A Confucian
couple from the countryside near Kwangju comes out into the bright
light of a culture where people take courses in "parenting" and
regard old age as an embarrassment to be covered up. An Indian
woman exits with her hand in that of her husband, and he drops it as
soon as he sees his friends from Intel, leaving her to walk behind and
get coffee for the males.

A man leads out his young bride from Chiang Mai (young enough to be his daughter, his son thinks, with a variety of emotions, and dark enough to be his housemaid), and she sees a Buddha statue in that ad for Clinique.

So many of the new arrivals in LAX were coming, clearly, with memories of centuries-old rivalries in their heads, or of thirteenth-century mullahs, and they were arriving in a city that traditionally is as forgetful as the morning, where World War II was mostly a back-drop on a studio lot and people thought of themselves as works in progress, in the middle of a thirteenth rewrite. The airport seemed a kind of abolition of history, for people who sometimes had little else.

And, more than anywhere I knew, the terminal seemed a place where no one knew whom she would meet, even if it was a sweet-heart she had kissed good-bye three weeks before, or a daughter she had protected every day for twenty years. And though this has been true of ports and stagecoach stops for centuries, it has surely never had an intensity or speed akin to that of the modern airport, where Henry James dramas are played out to an MTV beat. If airports have some of the exhilaration of bars—strangers here for an hour—they also have much of the poignancy of bars: a pretty Korean girl dressed in tiny shorts and a halter top sits alone in a deserted Baggage Claim area, waiting to be claimed, I guess, by a friend who never shows; a Vietnamese man, lost, tells officials he has friends in Orange County, but when the friends from Orange County are called, they say they know no one from Vietnam.

"Michael, is that you?"

"Sorry, I didn't recognize you."

"You haven't changed at all."

"Nor you. It was just—just, I guess, the clothes."

We can make games and adventures out of this strangeness, go to love hotels where the beds are shaped like airplanes, or the Arty Space Airport Bar that graces Kyoto's entertainment district; we can relish the slippery glamour of a place where everyone can be anyone for a while. But the quality that underwrites all of this is vulnerability, the exposedness we feel whenever we're in a place we don't understand, but compounded many times over when we've just descended thirty thousand feet.

One LA psychiatrist, a local woman told me, counseled women to work around their shyness by going to LAX to practice boldness. "Pick a nation whose people you find attractive," she told them, "and go to the arrivals gate at a time when people from that place are disembarking. Then stare every eligible male in the eye for a full thirty seconds—they'll be disconnected anyway, and you've got the home-court advantage." I imagined these men disembarking, completely at a loss, and issuing into a hall where lots of single women were staring at them for a full thirty seconds, and I thought that one LA myth, at least, might prove to come true.

It was strange, I thought, as I roamed the Arrivals area, that the airport was the place I thought of as my home from home, the site of some of my most resonant childhood memories; for many of the people around me, especially the ones who'd just deplaned, it was clearly a zone of uncertainty and excitement, all the alien tinglings that attend any entry into a new life and a new world.

In W. G. Sebald's determinedly melancholy, death-haunted vision, an airport becomes, quite literally, a terminal zone, "like an ante room of that undiscovered country from whose bourne no traveller returns," as people sit in chairs in bright and sterile spaces—the hospital again—and, one by one, disappear as their names or departures are called out; yet for many of those coming to LAX, it surely marks their first encounter with a provisional kind of heaven, and a release from a longtime containment. To try to appreciate better what it could mean to such a migrant, I took a flight in from Osaka and tried to imagine myself a newcomer arriving in the place he'd always dreamed of.

The first rule for ensuring a happy reception in LA is to arrive after nightfall, when the city settles into a shining grid of buzzing energies, laid out with the well-ordered mystery of the back of a transistor radio (in the metaphor of Thomas Pynchon's that hypnotized us in high school), or the field of lights panned across in a hundred LA movies. "Flying in at night," I read Jackie Collins declaring in *Los Angeles* magazine, while I was staying at the airport, "is just an orgasmic thrill."

By day, however, the sight is less transporting: the city announces itself, most often, through a thick layer of brown haze as a mess of dun-colored warehouses comes into sight, and dirty ribbons of freeway clotted with trickles of slow-moving cars—a no-colored blur, really, without even the lapis ornaments (of swimming pools) that light up the residential areas of Johannesburg or New York.

My own plane hovered down through the haze and landed in front of a hangar that said T ANS RLD AIRLINES, and a sign welcoming us all to TOM BRADL Y INTERNATIONAL AI PORT. The air-control tower, not reassuringly, was swathed in scaffolding.

As we filed into the terminal, the first thing to greet us was a row of Asians seated on the floor under a sign warning us of a twenty-thousand-dollar fine for bringing in the wrong kinds of food. We walked through long, bare corridors, rode escalators, made our way round hallways and along more gray, anonymous passageways, to more escalators (one of the major causes of accidents at airports, for people who've never seen moving stairways before). There were no signs of welcome or greeting (though later I would come upon a bland portrait of Mayor Riordan, surrounded by some multicultural children, in Terminal 5), and the faces waiting to welcome us looked almost as disoriented as our own.

A woman called Noriko directed me towards an Immigration desk and a man called C. Chen stamped me into the republic; another man, one Yoji Yasaka, transferred my luggage to a domestic terminal. Around us, in the free-for-all chaos of the Customs Hall, beagles were sniffing busily (in coats that said AGRICULTURE'S BEAGLE BRIGADE on one side, and PROTECTING AMERICA'S AGRICULTURE on the other), and a voice on the PA system was calling out for one Stanley Plaster; on a bulletin board, there was a letter from a child (bewildering, surely, to a person just arriving from Guangzhou) that began, "Dear Taffy, We liked your show. You are cute, smart and a good sniffer. . . ."

The minute I stepped out into America—walking past a large armed guard seated behind a desk and protected from the natives by ropes—I saw a sign being waved at me for a "Mr. T. Ego" (a limousine driver was doing his thing). A whole crowd of Japanese officials, with cell phones slung around their shoulders and faces whose hardness showed how far they had come from Japan, flourished signs that said JET TOUR, BEST TOUR, LOOK JTB. Behind them was the entire Cook Islands Dance team (complete with oars), and a troupe of seventy-seven girls, JTB stickers neatly on their sleeves, sitting in formation on the floor, their identically sized bags parked in perfect rows beside them.

SAFETY AREA. DO NOT BLOCK, said a yellow line on the floor, and the yellow tape cordoning off other areas came with the unpromising initials DOA.

"Don't be Fooled!" cried the signs behind the Information booth. TAKE EXTRA PRECAUTIONS TO HELP US INSURE THE SAFETY OF AIR TRAVEL. Outside a bar, more warnings prohibited the removal of beverages from the premises.

To me, of course, none of this was unexpected (and I knew that LA was no situation comedy); yet I wondered how it would seem to someone who had risked imprisonment or death to come here, or who had saved up for thirty years for this sudden, unanticipated blur of security officers in Elsinor Airport Services uniforms, and people shaking tins on behalf of America's Hopeless. In the men's room, when I entered, I saw a chilling gangland message scribbled across one wall—SHARAZZ SPIRIT LINE—and when I came out, it was to hear a woman on the public-address system saying, over and over, "Paging a representative from the U. for Understanding program. A representative from the U. for Understanding program . . ."

In the whole vast expanse of the TBIT Arrivals Hall, there was only one snack bar to cater to the five thousand people who passed through every hour, and it was offering only nine items, of which five were identified as "Cheese Dog, Chili Dog, Chili Cheese Dog, Nachos with Cheese and Chili Cheese Nachos." On the other side of the main doors, a panel told us we could rent a Payless or a King Cobra car, and stay in the Grand Hotel Cockatoo or the Banana Bungalow (FREE TOAST, it offered inscrutably. FREE BED SHEETS, FREE MOVIES AND PARTY and BASKETBALL COURT).

Around us, the voices echoed over and over, in Spanish and Japanese and English that sounded like Spanish or Japanese, "Maintain visual contact with your personal possessions at all times" and "The white zone is for loading and unloading of cars only. No parking."

Outside, on the sidewalk, I was greeted by a Van Stop, a Bus Stop, a Courtesy Tram Stop and a Shuttle Bus Stop, all elaborately coded with swirling colors and diagrams, the Shuttle Bus alone tracing circuits A, B, and C. I went to the Shuttle Stop and found myself confronted with forty-nine different offerings, from the Great American Shuttle to the Apollo Shuttle, the Movie Shuttle to the Celebrity Airport Livery, all waiting to take me to Vegas or Disneyland. Koreans were piling into buses that said TAEGUK AIRPORT SHUTTLE, which would take them to a Koreatown decorated all in Hangul script, and men in robes were disappearing under the Arabic lettering of the Sahara Shuttle to be taken to who knows what desert tent. All around, disciples of Louis Farrakhan, unsettlingly natty in their dark suits and bow ties (the Nation of Islam headquarters is just down the street), walked up to newcomers and asked for a dollar "contribution" for their magazine, called, with unlikely wit, *The Final Call*.

THIS TERMINAL IS IN A MEDFLY QUARANTINE AREA said the first sign to greet me as I walked. STOP THE SPREAD OF MEDFLY!

Across the street, in the parking garage, I walked into a chaos of sirens and beepers and alarm systems ringing, passengers zapping their car-door openers, antitheft devices wailing constantly, and a voice intoning behind me, "Do not leave your car unattended. Unattended cars are subject to immediate towaway."

If I left my car here for thirty days, it would be impounded, I read; if I lost my parking ticket, I'd be liable to a sixteen-dollar fine. If I parked my car in the wrong zone, I'd have to pay fifty-six dollars. The man at the parking kiosk—a Tigrean, as I could tell by his tribal scars—held up fingers to show how many dollars I owed, on the safe assumption that I would not speak English even if he did.

I suspect that many visitors, by this time, might be half-unwillingly recalling that LA was the place where they'd seen that white Bronco on the 405 freeway nearby, and that man in the speeding car beaten up by police officers; and I think that many of the "homeless" and "tempest-tossed" invited here by Emma Lazarus might be coming to realize that the "last resort" of which the Eagles sing points in more than one direction.

Such thoughts would hardly be stilled by the building that stands at the very heart of LAX, its talisman and crowning trademark, the 136-foot parabolic arch Theme Building, as it is called, on 1 World Way, that "reflect[s] a futuristic vision" (as I'd just read in an airline magazine). These days, alas, the structure that must have looked all the rage once upon a time sits like a stranded jet-age beetle in the middle of the parking lots, symbol of a future that's already distant past. Pictures of Saturn's rings and Jupiter and its moons greet you as you enter, and a plaque laid down by Lyndon Johnson announces its status as an icon of American idealism, just as the Vietnam War was setting all that aflame.

Upstairs, in the Cultural and Historic Monument, there are a few Host International offices, and a Theme Restaurant, where a few desperately merry waiters serve cheeseburgers and nonalcoholic wines to a few sallow diners who look as if they've truly landed up at the very end of the road. HELLO ALL THE NEW PEOPLE OF LAX— WELCOME, says the bright graffiti in the elevator, but when I visited, there weren't many new people in the "gourmet-type" restaurant, and they didn't look as if they were very welcome.

"Does the building revolve?" I asked a waiter.

"Now it will," he said chirpily, setting down in front of me a soft drink.

"That guy, Iglezi—what's he called?—he was here once," a man from the reception desk was saying in the distance. "John Travolta, he asked me a question."

Recently, the "landmark building" was refurbished, so that the Theme Restaurant became the Encounter Restaurant, and its waiters were decked out in "*Star Trek*–influenced uniforms"—but still it looks like something from your grandfather's science fiction nightmares, the Jetsons' second home, and its ambiguous new title can only be equivocal about what encounters will ensue.

As you begin to pull out of the airport and onto Century Boulevard, a grand eight-lane thoroughfare that runs like an Everystreet through a long line of minimalls, tower blocks, and fast-food joints, you might be forgiven for thinking you've ended up in the definitive Malled City of the future. The streets are called Avion and Aviation, Airport Boulevard and Concourse Way, and they are filled with FOR RENT signs and anonymous houses, billboards for Nissan (LUXURY FOR THE PRIVILEGED MANY), and pictures of Las Vegas replicas of the Grand Canal. As you edge along, towards the Christopher Columbus Transcontinental Highway and the Howard Hughes Parkway—the phantom campus of the University of Phoenix commuter college is just up the road—you can easily recall that you are in a place, as local writers estimate, of 2,000 street gangs, 40,000 minimalls, 20,000 sweatshops, and 100,000 homeless residents.

The people who stay in this nowhere zone—as I did for a while—
seem to linger in some kind of never-ending layover between the
half-life of the airport and the graves of Forest Lawn a few miles
down the road. They stay—as I stayed—at the Marriott, the Sheraton, the Hyatt, and the Holiday Inn (the whole Hyatt chain started in
a coffee shop near LAX); they listen—as I did—to AM 530 Airport
Radio, available around the clock, and enjoy "happy hour" spreads
at the Proud Bird bar, where you can listen to air-control tower
messages on headphones at every table. At the Adult Boutique next
to the Airport Hilton (the only shop I've ever visited where you have
to pay—fifty cents—just to enter), the businessmen of all five continents were silently inspecting Womb Brooms, Double Dongs, and
Wind-Up Dirty Old Men; next door, at the LIVE NUDES outlet, girls
multiculturally called Sunni and Cinnimin and Trixie and Cherokee
were offering private lap dances to a pair of phlegmatic Filipina
matrons, and some Singapore accountants who looked pretty much
bemused to be paying $14.25 for a compulsory Coke, while a
Dancer's Salad went for only $2.10.

I suppose none of this is any more impersonal than the trappings
that attend any transit area or orphaned district catering to those
from out of town. Bored, adrift, and far from home, every trader
since Phoenician times has looked for the same ways to assuage his
loneliness.

But there was something special about the amorphous orbit
around LAX that marked it as the province of the airport. In the
Gateway Sheraton, while I was staying—not far from Flight Avenue
and Sky Way—one room downstairs was given over to the ringed
confessionals and linked hands of a spiritual healing group called the
Lighthouse, whose leaders had apparently realized that this was fer-
tile ground for lost souls. The hostesses were dressed up in Hal-
loween masks at Zeno's Bar, and nearby another room was reserved
for the Institute of Certified Divorce Planners. At the beginning of
Michael Tolkin's mock-Fundamentalist LA story, *The Rapture,* the
last word in decadence is embodied by the swingers who haunt

LAX's look-alike hotels and bars, on the prowl for one-night thrills and other amoralists passing through.

In the room upstairs, next to my Gideon's Bible and *The Teaching of Buddha*, there was a magazine for tourists that advertised "Beautiful Californian Girls" ("Show Your Hotel Key for a 50% discount"), and "Beautiful Dancers," to be found in the "California Happenings" section, right next to "Psychic Consultant" ("She is 75 per cent accurate. . . . Mention Inn Room magazine ad for $20 reading (Regularly $50)"). The side doors in the hotel were locked at eight o'clock every night, and one could not even get the elevator to move without a room key.

Part of this, again, was simply because airports are danger zones, magnets for people in flight, quite literally, or anxious to move on, and airport hotels are notoriously meeting points for under-the-counter operators talking, in low whispers, of import-export, extradition, the shipment that's just come in (which, comically, in the movie *Get Shorty*, is surrounded by "a zillion DEA agents" masquerading as regular people in the Bradley Terminal). The airport hotel gift shop was full of leopard-skin women and men with gold rings fingering mugs in the shape of five-hundred-dollar bills, and again I was in that classic modern venue: the tower block ringed by jungle. One wrong turn round LAX (as depicted in Lawrence Kasdan's *Grand Canyon*), and you can be in the midst of lawlessness.

"Be extra careful in parking garages and stairways," said my hotel room, in its official tone of bureaucratic nervousness. "Always try to use the main entrance to your hotel, particularly late in the evening. . . . Never answer your hotel room door without verifying who is there."

Yet the biggest shock of all, ultimately, for the newcomer who's issued forth at last into the place that calls itself a World Gateway Community, is that many of its brightest hopes look most feasible

on paper. In its early days, California had more languages (all Native
American) than all of Europe, and even now the archetypal home
of the mestizo routinely refers to itself as "a global crossroads city"
and a "modern Alexandria"; in the *Airport Annual Report* I picked
up, the LA City Council was a glorious rainbow coalition of people
called Woo and Goldberg and Yaroslavsky and Alarcón and Ridley-
Thomas.

Yet the black men making money along Century Boulevard were
doing so with T-shirts protesting O.J.'s innocence, and the writing on
the rest room wall in the International Arrivals Terminal said "Yes on
Proposition 187. Mexicans go home." California was the place where
affirmative action had just been repealed, and where the state university was forever embroiled in a debate about reverse discrimina-
tion. Airports more readily issue entry permits than welcomes; and,
as a policeman at JFK told James Kaplan, with surprising nakedness,
"We hate every ethnic group here. When the Third World flushes, it
comes through the International Arrivals Building."

Almost the minute you exit from the airport, along the main artery
decorated with banners hanging from the lampposts, celebrating the
town's favorite Dodgers (at the time Nomo and Mondesi and Piazza
and Karros, in case you'd forgotten multiculturalism), just past the
signs for Postal Road and International Road, you come upon a large
fortresslike structure that announces itself as the United States Post
Office, Worldway Postal Center, Los Angeles, California 90000. The
place, big enough to house an embassy, is open around the clock, 365
days a year, and for certain immigrants, just getting off the plane,
must seem like a model of all the convenience and abundance
they've come here to enjoy. Yet outside its entrance, when I visited, a
clean young man with piercing eyes and short blond hair had posted
himself, and was delivering a furious harangue to anyone who'd listen (and many who wouldn't).

Henry Kissinger, he was yelling, "is the Bürgermeister of the New
World Order, the poster boy of the March of Crimes." Galileo,

Bertrand Russell, the IMF had all conspired against the American way, partly with their notions of a larger order. NATIONALIZE THE FEDERAL RESERVE, the signs on his table cried out, and JAIL THE TRILATERAL COMMISSION.

"We ruined the UN Population Conference," the clean-cut La Rouchite was shouting out. "Jail Ollie North, that son of a Bush." He took pains to dress well, answer questions politely, and carry himself with as much dignity as any Mormon missionary (or the Farrakhan agents down the street); but for a Laotian or a Palestinian or a Salvadoran who'd just arrived here in search of a peace not available at home, he must surely have served as a reminder that global unity looked easier, as Bette Midler sang, "from a distance."

And as my days at LAX began to stretch into weeks, and I found myself sinking into that nether state that marks the amphibian, the geographical equivalent of jet lag, I noticed something else about the airport: I was running into names here I'd never seen before—Hoa and Ephraim and Glinda and Hasmick, women called Roccio and blond Lorenas; in Terminal 5 alone, one day, I came upon an Ignacio, an Ever, an Aura, and an Erick, all in a single Host cafeteria, and many of them speaking native tongues I could not begin to decipher. Down the street and up the pecking order a little, at my hotel, I was helped at the reception desk by Viera from Bratislava (as her name tag, like those in Las Vegas, identified her), and Faye from Vietnam; Isabelle from Guatemala City, Khrystynne from Long Beach (by way, I'm sure, of Phnom Penh), and Moe from (unaccountably) West LA. Many of the people who arrive at LAX, so full of bright expectations, never really leave the airport, I was beginning to see, and find that the skills they've brought here are reduced to the simple ones— speaking Khmer, or knowing how to handle boisterous Croatians— that are most in demand around the airport. As is the immigrant fate everywhere, qualified doctors and professors at home find themselves janitors and bellboys, patronized by schoolboys as they struggle with their fourth, or seventh, tongues.

Darkest of all, they are surrounded by the people they came all this way to flee, not just the other exiles from impoverished countries with tangles of their own but the very people who drove them from their homeland.

One day, in the Airport Sheraton, I asked my Ethiopian waitress how she liked LA. Well enough, she said in elegant, reticent English; she'd actually been here now for seven years. She must miss her home, I said, knowing that the shopping centers of LA are thick with places like the Homesick Bakery.

She nodded sadly; she missed it bitterly, she said.

"But I can't go home."

"Why not?" I said, still smiling.

"Because they killed my family. Two years back. They killed my father; they killed my brother." "They," of course, referred to the Tigreans, the friendly man down the street holding up fingers to show me how much I owed, the gracious woman collecting litter as I walked along the fourth-floor corridor.

THE GLOBAL MARKETPLACE

Birds in flight, claims the architect
Vincenzo Volentieri, are not *between*
places, they carry their places with
them. We never wonder where they
live: they are at home in the sky, in
flight. Flight is their way of being
in the world.

—GEOFF DYER

In Hong Kong recently, staying with one of my oldest friends from English high school, I found myself in a flat furnished almost entirely with suitcases (a PRIORITY label around the handle of one, the stickers of hotels all over another). A Hewlett-Packard desk jet printer sat on the desk in the guest-room, and next to it I found some stationery from a Marriott Hotel, and a few postcards of the Imperial Hotel (in Bombay, in Bangkok?—I couldn't really tell). Nearby were some pictures of Macao and some personalized stationery (for someone I'd never heard of) made up by the Oberoi Hotel, Bombay. Next to the bed, a Dragonair systems timetable; against the wall, a travel iron, together with some guidebooks.

My old friend Richard and his wife, Sharon, were as kind and individual a couple as I knew, but they'd set up their flat—like the city around them—for people passing through. So there was a box for a Worldwide Power Adapter in the room where I slept, a set of Chinese Standard Version 3.2 diskettes, and a box of matches from Rick's Café down the street (where expats could collect a partner for the night). And everywhere, there were suitcases. When I arrived, two MBAs from Los Angeles, who'd just flown over for the weekend (on our hostess's unused frequent flier awards) moved out of the guest room and into the functional living room.

Now, as I joined them to discuss dinner, I let the fourteen-hour difference from California seep through my woozy system. We could order room service, I was told, from a hotel with 565 rooms next door, or from one with 604 rooms next to it; we could order food from the other hotel in the complex, which had 512 rooms. Around us, in the distance, sat the last sad remnants of British rule: the Happy Valley Racecourse, the Noon Day Gun, the Craigengower Cricket Club. Beneath us, in the area known as Admiralty, were the trappings of the new Empire—a four-story shopping mall (called simply—definitely—the Mall), where shiny signs pointed towards the Atrium, The United Center, One Pacific Place and Two.

"The thing about this place," Richard said to me as I slipped in and out of time zones, "is that you've got a miniairport on the ground floor, where you can check in for all Cathay flights. There's a Seibu department store on Level Two, where you can buy everything you want. My bank's next to the elevator, and the Immigration Office is next to my office. You never really have to leave the building."

When I went into the guest bathroom to splash some water over my face—I hadn't yet come down to earth—I found some Thai Air hair treatment next to the sink, and a bottle of La Quinta Resort and Spa moisturizer. There was a Delta business class toilet kit nearby, as well as a British Airways towelette and some Princess Cruises French formula shampoo. Otherwise, nothing whatsoever, except for some toothpaste from some Imperial Hotel.

There was maid service, should I want it, and laundry service, too; there were DO NOT DISTURB signs to hang outside the door. The place was run by the Swire Group, the venerable old British hong that had provided new Eastern lives for many of our schoolfriends, and here had constructed a kind of Club Class Lounge three hundred feet above the ground. A permanent hotel.

"It's an odd life you lead here," I said to Richard, whom I'd always thought of as a Victorian district officer transferred to a digital age. "It is," he said, not without some glee, and, with that, he proceeded to pull out his phone bill for the month just past. It was only one of the five he paid every month—and the smallest, as it happened—but still it came to seven hundred dollars. "I have twelve telephone cards," he said, fishing them out, one by one, from his wallet. "A Singapore Telephone card, an AT&T calling card, and an MCI—three AT&T's, actually—as well as an ETI—you know, an Executive Telephone International. Also, of course, a GSM phone with two SIM cards"—he drew out his mobile and showed me how he could slip the cards in and out, depending on whether he was in Asia or Europe. "And three Kallback services, with the appropriate cards."

I was tempted to gape, except that I had just paid almost a week's salary for my monthly telephone bill, not to mention another bill for the cell phone I'd gotten for my mother, another for a Kallback service, another for my phone in Japan, a few more for fax machines in Japan and California, as well as overseas on-line surcharges. An unlikely fate for two friends raised on Latin hymns.

"I don't know how you keep up with all this."

"I don't have to. I just charge everything to my AmEx card."

"For which you get miles?"

"For which I get miles enough to send Sharon around the world every month. Look"—and with that he spread open his wallet so I could inspect a colorful assembly of members' cards—from the Red Carpet Club and the Passages service, for Marriott Miles and Singapore Airlines. He had a Europlus and a Priority Passenger Service card, as well as the customary guarantee that he'd never be turned away from a seat on Marco Polo Class.

"The thing is, I always carry at least five plane tickets with me everywhere I go, so I can use segments sometimes." He drew out a stash of half-completed, worn, and folded plane tickets, for almost every itinerary he might take tomorrow: Hong Kong–London, Hong Kong–Madrid, Boston–Tokyo, London–Boston. He had courted his wife, I recalled, by flying around the world—London–San Francisco–Tokyo–London—virtually every weekend for two years, and still was without doubt one of the least ambitious and acquisitive people I knew: on expense-account trips, he'd been known to stay in youth hostels.

"I just switch back and forth," he said, knowing that he was talking to someone similarly trained in living in midair. "It saves the company a lot of money. In fact, I probably pay less for flying First Class than most people pay for Business Class." After getting off the thirteen-hour flight from London, Richard usually took the A2 bus home.

At that point, bulky envelopes began to emerge from his briefcase—one after another, till I'd counted twenty-seven—and I saw that every single one of them was stuffed with telephone cards, coins, and tokens for the twenty-seven countries he was likeliest to find himself in tomorrow. "Bus tickets for Amsterdam," he said. "That's the best way to get around there. Phone cards for Japan. Pesetas for Madrid."

"And you can still keep working wherever you are?"

"Absolutely. I have voice mail in Japan, Hong Kong, and Boston, and I can check my messages from anywhere. The only trouble is, I don't have a mobile modem, so I can't collect my E-mail in a car."

"But you're never in a car!"

"That's true. I'm more often in a plane than in a car. Some flight attendants recently were working out that I fly more than they do."

We paused a little while I took in the SIM cards. "But you're right," Richard continued. "We don't have a car anywhere. We don't need one. I don't even have an office, really. I'll show you when I get back from overseas."

The thing to stress here is that Richard is by no means extravagantly rich, and certainly no jet-setter; he's just an extremely hardworking international management consultant in a global market that asks him to move as fast as it does. He's also one of the most human people I know, loyal and affectionate and strong enough to root himself in something other than the circumstances of his life.

But he works—more and more of us do—in an accelerating world, for which the ideal base of operations was this international Home Page of a city. There were four cinemas in the Mall where we were sleeping, more than twenty places in which to eat, and fully ninety-seven boutiques (Gucci, Guess, Valentino, Vuitton; Boss, Hugo Boss, the Armani Exchange). There was access to the MTR subway, to the Far East Finance Center, and to a car park. There were the great department stores of Britain, Hong Kong, and Japan. "A world of delights," as the literature announced, "under one roof."

On the plane coming into the old city airport, I'd flipped through the in-flight magazine and found a kind of mobile emporium of goods to allow "flexecutives" like Richard to take care of business in midair. There were ads for Sky Tel alphanumeric paging services and for World Cell pocket phones, for credit card–sized "PC companions" and "voice file portable IC chip recorders." As I scribbled down on a piece of paper the details of teleconferencing speakers with satellites and digital cameras with built-in PC cards, not to mention a Card Scan Plus 300 for scanning cards into your "Personal Pilot," I felt, as I did more and more often these days, as if I'd left my language on another continent. In any case, most of these devices would probably be out of date by the time we hit the ground.

I could order any one of them, I read, in my "Airborne Office," by credit card, using the Airfone nearby, which could also be used for sending faxes, taking calls, and charging everything to an En Route credit card. The airline was about to install ATMs in its aisles, and even in Economy Class, the *Entertainment Guide* for my personal video system was a glossy magazine sixty-four pages long. You could live on the plane, I realized, or on the phone—or, best of all, on the phone on the plane. The declaration of John Self, the transoceanic creature in Martin Amis's mid-eighties novel *Money*—"I am a thing made up of time lag, culture shock, zone shift"—needed only minor updates now—to "jet lag, shell shock, paradigm shift." The "thing" part could remain.

"The Indians here, they are having a hard time," said the German next to me, catching my eye with a shrewd glance, his eye having fallen on my disembarkation card (Indians living in Hong Kong would soon be given British passports with a crown on them, but no right to live in Britain). "They are like stateless people now."

I fingered my old British passport, heartbreakingly close to a Hong Kong one, but minus two extra words that mark all the difference between freedom and incarceration.

"Sometimes the Indians are third-generation," he went on, "but the Chinese won't take them, the British won't take them. Things will be strange under the new management."

"That's all right," I said, writing off the Indians with the blitheness of one born in Britain. "They're used to getting on everywhere. They know how to make a living out of displacement."

"I know," he said, nodding seriously. "I, too, am so cosmopolitan now. I do not care where I live. Anywhere, it is the same: you can do business."

At that point, the pilot gave his mellow-voiced, BBC-worthy announcement of the time and temperature awaiting us on the ground—which we could follow on the Airshow Channel—and the cabin attendants prepared for landing, the vessel itself a perfect model of the old colonial order (cool British male at the helm, and women from ten Asian nations dishing out the drinks).

We descended between tall apartment blocks, almost entangled in lines of washing, and touched down.

When I arrived at the desk in the Immigrations area, I handed an official my passport. He looked at it, looked at me, looked at it again. A superior was called over, and he, looking at it, asked to see my ticket, my alien registration card, my Time Inc. ID. Then a third man came over, and led me to an "Interview Room," where I sat down under a sign that informed me of my rights "under custody."

I could make a single phone call, I read; I could contact my solicitor. I was, for the moment, an alien resident of limbo.

A fourth official came into the cell and, pulling up a chair across from me, looked at my face, flipped through my passport, and peered some more at my pinkish-colored green card. Why did I choose to live for twenty-nine years in a country not my own? he asked.

Because I liked America as a base, but never began to think of it as home.

This is not normal, he said, to live for almost all your life as an alien.

However, he could find nothing officially wrong with my papers, except for the fact that my face didn't match my birthplace, and people who looked like me were stateless. Finally, releasing me with ill-disguised unease into the colony of transients—the Customs Hall decorated with a pangolin, a monitor lizard, and other replicas of endangered creatures—he got up to attend to two young Germans in the next booth, whom I heard being told to wait for the next plane home, to be deported.

In Richard's apartment, the wonder of his phone cards and his plane cards exhausted, I retired to my bedroom, half-dazed and half-electrified (jet-lagged, in other words), and tried to will myself to sleep. But one sleeps strangely in such a state, in fitful, violent fragments, and my dreams unraveled like action movies, till I jerked up into wakefulness, after a month's worth of images, only to see that I'd been out for hardly more than an hour.

The clock beside the bed read 2:23.

I flicked the remote beside me, for what was here known as "terrestrial television," and stock-market listings came up on Channel 4. Listlessly, I flipped through Pearl TV, Jade TV, Phoenix TV; through

CNN International, BBC World, CNBC Asia. I caught Asian music videos on Channel V, some intimate Kanto drama on NHK-1, a Cantonese show on ATV-Home. I decided to walk off my confusion in the darkness.

Slipping out of the apartment, I went down in the elevator to the lobby, where two security guards were watching me on rows of monitors. Outside, through a set of electric doors, I passed into an open glass elevator and descended into the Mall below, the names all around the same ones that I'd seen on the other side of the planet that morning (Florsheim, The Body Shop, See's Candies).

I took an escalator up to the second floor, and walked through the brilliantly lit corridors of the empty arcade—Timberland, Lacoste, DKNY, The Athlete's Foot. Signs led me up steps and out into the night, to a sixty-one-story hotel.

Inside the lobby, the clocks showed the times in major centers of the world, while machines flashed and hummed in the Business Centre. Outside, in a small banyan-tree garden, two lovers (made of concrete) embraced, a bag of potato chips (also made of concrete) between them.

Looking for something to ground me—or simply to sustain me—I began walking down the main, deserted street, till I came to Lockhart Road, where heavy bass rhythms were thumping out of the Express Club and what looked like Moslems were gathered outside a pita and kebab stall called Midnight Express. A pretty young Filipina in a Dallas Cowboys jacket sat on the stoop of the New Pussycat club, while other of her compatriots, flouncily done up in pillbox hats and gold-chain bags, clucked and fluttered past noisy holes called the Lady Club, Hot Lips, and Venus. Upstairs, in a loud Western bar, where I tucked into a burger, a man in a jacket and tie was running his hands along the bare arms of a small dark girl with a baseball cap on backwards, while a five-a-side soccer match unfolded on-screen.

A few hefty British traders in gray suits were wailing, "I would do anything for love," in time to the record, at the bar, pumping their fists and steadying themselves against one another's shoulders.

Back out on the street, as I tried to walk off my restlessness, a man bumped into me, slipping out of a 7-Eleven with a package of Pro-Fil condoms in his hand; another, in a straggly leather jacket, was clutching a chubby new girlfriend to his chest and roaring, "But she's in England—thousands of bloody miles away!"

I passed the Duke of Windsor Social Services Department, a large skyscraper with a neon sign for TOEFL (Test of English as a Foreign Language) at its top, a rat scuttling across a vacant lot. In a small business hotel, I found a Japanese girl in a very short skirt, nursing a Heineken, while a young man in golfing pants, holding a glass of wine, whispered to her from the far end of the same small sofa. UKIYO-E, said the sign by the elevator button. FLOATING WORLD.

It was getting light by the time I returned to the room where I was staying, and the phone was ringing—from New York—while faxes continued to chug in through the night. I found a copy of *Time International* lying around, and opened it to see pages of classified ads at the back—for Offshore Companies and Second Passports, for EU Residence Permits and Call Global telephone cards. I could enter a green-card lottery through the magazine; I could apply for Canadian citizenship. I could even get goods from the Counter Spy Shop. The overseas edition of *Time*, like the Sky Mall catalog on the plane, suggested (with its ads for "Camouflage Passports" and "Satellite Decoders") that the future was just a video war conducted by other means.

Outside, though, the day looked warm and sunny, and, still in some cloudless afternoon state from California, sixteen time zones away, I decided to go out to take in the scenery. People talk these days about how the world is turning into a Microsoft and McDonald's uniculture, but every empire has always tried to remake its image around the globe, and when I went out into a place like Hong Kong, even now, I was almost instantly in boyhood again, in some tropical rendering of Berkshire.

Taking a tram (with "Cathay Pacific" written all over its sides) down to the Bank of China, I got out and started climbing the steep concrete slope to the Citibank Plaza—Hong Kong's Central district was a web of such anonymities—when suddenly I saw the towers of an Anglican church down the street. I walked along to its entrance, stepped inside, and instantly I was in England, on a gray November morning, being prepared for a war—or an Empire—that never came. It hardly mattered that birds were chirping in the rafters here, or that fans were waiting to turn above the pews; I hardly noticed the signs in the parking lot speaking of a VEHICLE IMPOUNDING ZONE. The circulars pinned up with thumbtacks, the "collects" fluttering from green baize notice boards, the hymnals lined up higgledy-piggledy along the pews, and the grand organ ready to strike up another chorus of "Almighty, Invisible, God Only Wise" made the years, the miles evaporate.

It was a space as generic in its way as any Burger King, I thought; I could have been standing outside the Supreme Court building in Singapore, or along the Avon in the tree-shaded parks of Christ Church: the Empire had meant that children singing of "a green hill far away" were all thinking of the same place. Standing in this mock thirteenth-century Gothic cathedral, I could have been my father, in Bombay in 1937, reciting a borrowed litany—except that his world was made up of two cultures that he knew, while I, at this moment, was between two homes (California and Japan) that were quite strange to me.

In recent times, in fact, when our family got together, the discussions we had were about whether it was better to fly from Los Angeles to Bombay via Frankfurt or via Tokyo, and how best to convert PAL videotapes into U.S.-compatible ones; our local issues had to do with green-card applications and student visas, and which international phone company offered the best rates for Bangalore. A hundred and fifty years before, Tennyson and those around him had seen the railway as both the force of history and the death of neighborhood; now the jumbo jet made all such thoughts antique.

Outside my bedroom, as I returned to sleep, huge cranes were moving clumps of earth, to construct a new British embassy for the postimperial order.

The next morning, when I awoke—my body only slowly following my mind—the clock showed 4:00, 4:45, 6:00, though inside my stomach it didn't feel like 4:00 a.m. or 6:00 p.m. or any time I could recognize. For hours, my dreams had organized themselves around the sounds of transmissions coming in from around the globe. And all through the night, the phone by my head had kept ringing, though every time I picked it up, all I could hear was the shrill tone of a fax, or, in one case, a friend of mine, from the far side of the world, calling and calling my name (to be answered by a sharp mechanical whine).

On TV, one channel was showing a live image of the lobby, and another some still life of an apartment building. O. J. Simpson was on one channel, and on another the London Monarchs were playing (American) football against the Rhein Fire. Somewhere a woman was talking of rape.

I called up a Chinese friend whom I'd first met in Nepal (where he'd been working on an Anglo-Italian film about the Buddha), and his Japanese-American wife picked up.

"What time is it in California?" she asked me sweetly.

"Four p.m.," I said, looking out at the early light.

Already, behind the TV screen, workers were moving poured concrete on the forested hillside to erect the future.

· · ·

Basil suggested we meet at the Foreign Correspondents' Club, on Lower Albert Road, in the heart of the area still known (on the maps) as Victoria, and when I opened the heavy institutional doors, it was to walk into my school again, decorated in the local style known as "Anglo-something." The notices on the board offered club ties and cuff links and umbrellas; the crested letter paper reminded members to place their orders soon for mince tarts with rum butter and sliced smoked Scottish salmon: this part of Hong Kong belonged to Graham Greene's Abroad.

All around the slightly dusty dining room, wooden boards listed the names of club officers through the ages much as, at the Dragon School in Oxford, they'd listed the winners of prized scholarships to public school.

But the characters living and working within this museum case belonged, more and more, to the Empire that had made all this redundant. Basil, coming in stylishly from the ferry—having dropped his daughter off at school—and ordering breakfast for us in Cantonese, was just off the road after spending most of the year past traveling around the world with a member of Monty Python's Flying Circus; he was now about to spend a few months photographing hotels around Asia. His wife, an expert at finding Philippine settings for Hollywood movies set in Vietnam, had just found a Bhutanese boy in Hong Kong to act as the Dalai Lama in one of the latest international productions. Thinking of his daughter's schooling, as his Chinese compatriots moved in on Hong Kong, Basil was wondering whether to move his clan to Singapore, to Seattle, to San José in Costa Rica.

We had much in common, if only because we'd both grown up with a sense of half-belonging everywhere (Basil had been cast around the world by his exile family); we spoke of our faraway English schools—and the (Kenyan) schoolfriend Basil had met by chance in the Rangoon market—as if one of us was not Chinese, and the other was not Indian. Occasionally, worn Chinese waiters in

stained white jackets—identified by their name tags as Carson or
Edmond—dropped off on our table plates of baked beans and fat
sausages, or triangles of toast. Scholarly old women and pink-faced
colonial types resettled themselves with their faded copies of *The
Times* in thick leather armchairs.

"Hong Kong," I said, "must have been a lot more English when
you were a boy."

"A lot more Chinese, too," said Basil.

After finishing breakfast, I made my way down the steep sidewalk,
past the New World Centre, to Queen's Road Central, walking up tall
flights of stairs, through passenger bridges, in and out of a never-
ending web of walkways, across access buildings, up ramps, past a
whirl of foreign faces until, quite without meaning to, I found myself
in the Worldwide Building, which stands at the heart of Central,
between Alexandria House and the Prince's Building.

Inside was as poignant a network of little shops as ever I have
seen, and, shaken out of my imperial daydreams, I was brought up
against the force of a much more urgent form of wistfulness. The
Worldwide Building is a virtual monument to the fact that a world
with a hundred kinds of home will accommodate a thousand kinds of
homesickness. Its shops—stalls, really—were brightly emblazoned
with names like Filipino Shop and Worldwide Filipino Club and
Little Quiapo and Romance Boutique, and on every side were
young women from the Philippines, most of them in tight jeans,
with gold crosses above their Hard Rock Café and Planet Hollywood
T-shirts, at home in this Little Manila. The signs on the storefronts
told them when they could catch a Filipino star on ATV-World, or
how to "Apply for Peso Loan" or convey Tele-Money to their children back home. Posters of the beaches of the Philippines were
hung up in the windows, and smiling Filipinos invited you to BRING
A FRIEND TO THE PHILIPPINES; stores were stacked with "Legal

Love Romances" and offers of "Christian Song Love Song Karaoke,"
and they were called Your Shoppe and Fanny and Friendly Remittance Company.

I felt drawn into this world for all the ways it contradicted everything around it—a Trojan horse, it seemed, of romance and sentiment and devotion; of escape, really—and all the ways it grounded
what my time in Pacific Place suggested: the lucky go around the
world to find the props of home available round the clock; the less
lucky stand at the service entrance staring through the railings for
any piece of home common to Makati and Manhattan.

In some of the shops were piled precarious towers of jars, containing Phil brand purple yam jam and sweet jackfruit and sugarplum; in
some, there were greeting cards offering "Christ Is Born Today" and
letter-writing paper with "Remember to Pray" on every sheet. There
were signs offering DOOR TO DOOR REMITTANCES TO CAGAYAN
DE ORO CITY, and others listing all the ships sailing to Manila; with a
few adjustments, I could have been in a Vietnamese shopping mall a
friend from Da Nang had introduced me to once in Melbourne, or
any of a hundred minimonuments to Iranian/Guatemalan/Korean
plaintiveness in LA.

The girls were everywhere, no taller than my shoulder, mostly,
holding hands, staring at Panasonic radios or National blenders in
the windows, counting out coins to get "Talk-Talk" cards to call back
home. At one of the remittance centers, the line was eleven deep—
as if outside a U.S. embassy—and young women were chatting about
four-year-old tyrants who dragged them into Kentucky Fried
Chicken, and children a thousand miles away. The windows of the
cashiers' kiosks were plastered over with handwritten messages on
scraps of notebook paper: BECAUSE FULL NO MONKEY BUSINESS
AROUND OUR SHOP or NO BUYING-SELLING OF PESO. A Lebanese
trader in the next booth had pinned up signs that said WANTED
URGENT: 3 HOUR PER DAY. GOOD LOOKING. BELOW 25 YEAR and
WANTED GOOD-LOOKING POLITE HONEST.

. . .

The Filipinos who live and work in Hong Kong—130,000 of them in all, most of them rented mothers and vicarious housewives—tend to get lost in all the official equations involving Empire and Emporia; "domestic outsourcers," as the chilling euphemism has it, they tend to fall between many of the publicized categories in a city that conjugates all the ways one does not belong, as expat or exile or refugee or stateless person. They've come here by choice, after all, to support the families they've been forced to leave at home, and, like Filipino nannies and nurses and go-go dancers everywhere, they belong to a kind of unofficial economy, which provides the human services that the official world likes to delegate. I'd seen Filipinos running most of the stores and security checks at San Francisco Airport and spinning the roulette wheels in Reno; in Osaka's airport, I was used to seeing Filipinas from the local bars perfectly imitating the inflections of fourteen-year-old Japanese girls as they giggled their good-byes to the gangsters who kept them, and boarded planes with stuffed animals in their arms. In Hong Kong, gathering around the fifty-story glass towers, they could seem the most visible and voluble inhabitants of Central, stuck in the throat of the global metropolis like a piece of the global village.

The next day in the paper I read an article headlined DEATH-LEAP MAID COMPLAINED OF SHOUTING, and describing how a local professor had slept through the night while her Filipina maid, on only her fifth day in the city, had thrown herself out of a twelfth-floor window ("Police found a pair of scissors and a chopper lying on the maid's bed"). The professor told investigators that her worker seemed happy, and protested, "I had no time to shout at her as I was always away till nine o'clock." Another incident to get filed next to the numberless cases of Filipina maids attacking their employers and molesters in Singapore and Arabia, where local values were not always made for pious Catholic girls from Asia.

Here in the Worldwide Building, though, the women were smiling, mostly, as they snapped up copies of the souvenir *Filipinos in Hong Kong* yearbook, and sparkled back at Instamatic cameras as they flashed. You could almost hear them preparing stories for the sweethearts back home, or anxious parents, about the city where there were more Rolls-Royces per capita than anywhere else in the world, and where even a spot in the local cemetery could cost eighty thousand dollars. Study Bibles, wedding dresses, cream for removing stretch marks; a sign near Best Friends Jewelry saying NO PRETENDING FRIEND.

I suppose one reason I had been drawn here was the same reason that had pulled the Filipinos: namely, that it was the rare city that had been built up almost entirely by people from abroad, and so had become a kind of Platonic Everyplace, the city-state as transit lounge: for foreign businesspeople at least, Hong Kong felt like a hyperconvenient luxury hotel, a shopping mall–cum–conference center–cum–world trade center where there were no taxes, few real laws, and no government other than the freest of markets. English was spoken, even minor credit cards were accepted and, just around the corner from me, there were three 7-Elevens and a Circle K, open at 4:00 a.m. Entering Hong Kong could feel a little like going on-screen, into a world buzzing with options and graphics, itself a kind of rough diagram of the digital city of the future.

The place meant something very different for the Chinese who swarmed through its back streets and outlying villages, of course, but for outsiders at least, the perpetual colony remained a curious artifact: less a capital of empire, increasingly, than an empire of capital, which, with a survivor's versatility, had managed to change identities to fit the shifting of history's tides. In the nineteenth century, the "little England in the eastern seas," as the future King George V called it, had been the definitive Victorian outpost, facilitating the narcotics trade of Empire, and in the twentieth century it had turned

into a Cold War listening post, at the heart of the American Century
(and briefly occupied by the Japanese). In recent years, it had come
to look like the next (postnational) century, a city without citizens in a
world where ideology was obsolete and economics trumped all. The
central question raised by the handover to China was whether this
hybrid nest of Global Souls could pull the Middle Kingdom into the
twenty-first century before the Celestial Empire pulled it back into
the nineteenth.

And unlike most places, which grow organically into themselves
and settle into their grooves as a person does, Hong Kong had based
its identity on everything it wasn't. For generations of British FILTH
("Failed in London, Try Hong Kong"), it had simply been an alternative marketplace where black-sheep sons could find the opportuni-
ties unavailable to them at home (not least in the company of pretty
Filipinas); for the Chinese who'd poured in after the ascent of Mao,
making it by some counts the fastest-rising city in history, it was a
perfect counter-China, as free of politics as the Mainland was
drowned in it. For the Filipinos who came here, it represented a job
market unimaginable at home—especially with so many foreigners
around, in need of domestic help—and for the more than 200,000
Vietnamese who had fled here on boats, it was simply—irresistibly—
not Vietnam.

And what was the result of all this willy-nilly multiculturalism?
Pure mishmash, till I felt, sometimes, as if I were in a city whose local
tongue was Esperanto (or "fusion culture," as *Concierge*, the magazine of the Hong Kong Hotels Association, more optimistically put
it). Wasabi Mousse Caviar and Crème Brûlée flavored with lychee
and pomegranate and mango; Matins in Mandarin at St. John's
Cathedral, and Holy Eucharist in Pilipino; "HK/British system when
addresses given in English script," as my map carefully informed me
(distinguishing between ground floors and first floors), "American/
Japanese and also the Chinese system when address in Chinese characters." Hong Kong was the portmanteau city par excellence, identified by people called Freedom Leung and Philemon Choi and Sir

Run Run Shaw—the perfect site for "market-Leninism" and all the
other improvised hyphens of the age.

The latest artifact of Hong Kong, the superfashionable new movie
Chungking Express, came at one much as the city did, in Mandarin
and Cantonese and Urdu and Japanese and English all at once, giving one the jostling, indecipherable sensation of being on any of its
mingled streets, and serenading one with a synthetic blast of "masala
music," Canto pop and "California Dreamin'." Named for one of the
city's most infamous hotels for transients, it played out its quick-
change scenes in all the classic Hong Kong locations—the convenience store, the fast-food stall, the check-in area: cities click by on
departure-boards, Indians surrender their passports for cash, and the
camera whirls back again and again to CD player and Coke machine,
boarding pass and tiny toy plane. The three main female characters
are a Chinese woman in a blond wig, a girl who works at a late-night
junk-food outlet (that calls itself Midnight Express), and a Cathay
Pacific stewardess who likes to make love to the sound of a safety
announcement.

Now, as I walked behind the New World Centre—New Worlds
were everywhere in Hong Kong—I saw a Chinese man kissing his
short-skirted love, eyes wide open as his briefcase banged against her
back. A group of Sikhs was seated in a circle on the ground, enjoying
a picnic amidst the debris of McDonald's containers and old beer
bottles. An African was lying flat out on the pavement, his Chinese
girlfriend brushing him tenderly with her hair.

Not far away, in one of the many new blue-and-gray high-fashion
movies shooting in the colony, Vivian Wu was playing a Japanese girl
who gets her British boyfriend to write on her back in French, English, Japanese, and, finally, Yiddish. The Italy France Japan Fashion
Square was open till 2:00 a.m. around the corner and the Harbour
City mall invited one to "Go around the world in one day" by sampling its six hundred shops. Everywhere, I felt, a crush of multicultural props offering one goodies that answered every need except for

the ancient, ancestral ones that convenience and speed could not wish away.

When I arrived back in my friends' apartment, my hostess (herself long a stateless soul of the more ancestral kind—when her family had been displaced, for the second time in forty years, by the Iranian Revolution, she found herself alone in London, thirteen years old, with nothing to protect her but some papers that said, not very ringingly, "Travel Documents: Citizen of the World") was nowhere to be seen. When at last she returned, quite late, from the office, we turned on the TV to see when Richard would be back (Kai Tak arrivals were shown on Channel 6). That didn't help, though, because neither of us knew which country he'd be coming from.

When at last he did come in, off the plane from Tokyo, he was hungry and tired, and the number of places where we could eat was diminishing quickly. "Anywhere," he sighed, "so long as it's not a hotel." Hotels, though, were the most convenient option—so close and yet not closed—and so, sometime after 11:00 p.m., we found ourselves in the sixty-one-story tower block next door.

"How are things in the office?" Richard asked his wife.

"Everyone's getting frazzled," she said. "Having to work till six o'clock every morning."

"Oh well," said my friend, always a kindhearted manager. "I'll go in and tell them to go home."

It was long after midnight then—8:00 a.m. for me; who knows what time for him?—but Richard got up before dessert was served and went to tell his workers to stop working.

The next morning, when I followed him to his home from home, I found, as he had warned me, that he really did have no office other than his head; his only workspace, as the Asian head of a booming American company, was a tiny desk jammed against a window, with a map of Tokyo posted to his wall and a laptop somewhere under a pile of faxes from Coca-Cola Vietnam (transmitted, I couldn't help but notice, by AT&T Easy Link Services Australia, Ltd.).

I also couldn't help but notice, as an unbeliever, that most of the messages he received seemed to have to do with the difficulty of receiving messages—the state-of-the-art communications facilities seemed to be adept at communicating communications mishaps. "Resend" reverberated around the office, and "abort." "Your call is being diverted," said his phone; "Your call is being transferred."

"Can you print out my itinerary?" Richard called out to a secretary, and when it came juddering out, I counted 139 border crossings in the previous year alone.

"I don't know how you keep up with all this."

"Nor do I," he said cheerfully. "Last week I went to the airport to fly around the world, and simply changed my mind and came back home instead."

"Sharon must have been surprised."

"She was shocked."

Richard had had to petition for special dispensation from the Foreign Office, he told me, to carry two passports simultaneously—he went through their pages so quickly; his money was deposited in some offshore account in Jersey, and he paid taxes everywhere and nowhere.

"You can call me in Hong Kong," he said, showing me his Global Access number, and speed-dialing his secretary to fix up a breakfast appointment with his wife, "and get me in eighteen different countries." When he got onto his dollar account in Hong Kong, though, and the thirteen countries where he'd be in the next thirteen days, I began to feel a little seasick.

To anyone who hadn't known him for thirty years, I thought, to anyone who hadn't seen him with his family, or read his warm and funny letters, Richard could seem like a creature out of science fiction; yet I kept thinking of the two portraits in his mother's house of ancestors who'd served as governor-generals in India. On the other side, his grandfather had been Dean of Durham Cathedral, and his father a knighted civil servant who'd devoted all his extraordinary talents to Queen and country. Here, again, the same pattern as in the city all around us—service to the Church of England, and then Her Majesty's Treasury, turning into a roaming job for an American consultancy whose international clients just happened to be everywhere ("ex-patriots," as the Freudian misspelling had it).

Richard and I had lived in the same house at school (and when his parents had moved to Washington, we'd been the only students in the school returning for holidays to America); we'd been to the same university, in the standard English way, and when I'd gone across the Atlantic for graduate school, Richard had suddenly shown up in the same university two years later. Sometimes I felt that our main formal ties were global ones, and our destinies twinned as those of actual neighbors might have been once upon a time (I went to Japan, and Richard showed up as the head of his Tokyo office): it was as if we were riding parallel horses on some cross-cultural merry-go-round, always about to meet up at the next departure lounge.

"It's funny," he was saying now, giving me his access number in Kazakhstan. "I've just closed five bank accounts and I've still got six more. We don't live in a normal world."

A little later, I would hear the same line delivered in almost exactly the same context by the Saint, in the ludicrous movie of the same name ("I don't have a name, I don't have a home," the postmodern hero mumbles as he switches from an Australian to a Russian to a South African and then to a Southern self in the film's opening scenes). Before I could respond, though, Richard was off to Singapore.

Outside, as the lunch hour approached, the whole amped-up, fast-forward, quick-cutting music video of a city seemed to be going into overdrive, and I felt myself all but overwhelmed by the press and

push of bodies, signs, beepings as I threaded my way through crowds
ten times denser than in jam-packed Tokyo. I climbed a flight of
stairs to a central walkway, linking tower block to tower block, and
walked along a pedestrian bridge leading to a mall in which a moving
staircase transported me to another walkway, and then down a ramp
into another overpass, with people streaming everywhere in all directions all at once, out of Kodak Express, into Maxim's Express,
through a While-U-Wait color photo stall, into a place that sold *Time
Express* (my employer turned into a monthly in Chinese).

Sometimes, in this Universe Express, I felt like a digit spinning
round in some calculator, a unit clicking over amidst a whirl of bar
codes, area codes, and tracking numbers. Asked to identify myself,
I'd press in my PIN number, or my password, key in my fourteen-
digit World Phone number, or the sixteen digits of my Visa card:
"What is the city over the mountains / Cracks and reforms / and
bursts in the violet air / Falling towns / Jerusalem Athens Amsterdam / Vienna London / Unreal." I could be in Toronto, in Wellington, in Sydney; I could be at home.

This sense of abstraction, of moving through a city of ideas and
images where the faces faded into the background and the people
became units in some higher (and unseen) equation, was intensified
by the allegorical nature of its names. The Chinese like to name their
buildings after sturdy Confucian ideals, and when these are translated into English, they give main streets, often, the feel of a modern
pilgrim's progress, as one walks past the Sincere Insurance Building
and the Efficient Building, with buses that say DOUBLE HAPPI-
NESS and PROSPEROUS HOLIDAYS on the side, streaming past Filipinas and their grinning Englishmen, taking out their Happy Meals.
On the same block, the Wesley Hotel, with the Methodist Book
Store attached; down the little alleyway next to it, the Lofty Virtues
Publication Centre.

Even the certificate in the elevator I entered was signed by one
Yu-Wing Law, whose signature looked like "U.U. Law."

In order to steady myself in the midst of such impersonalities, I stopped off in a mall and put through a call to a cousin who'd recently moved here with her family. They too, like so many now, were half-inadvertent internationalists, the husband living for years at a time on ships, my cousin recently moved from Sharja, in the Gulf States. Her parents were currently in Zimbabwe, having moved down from Nigeria. From her window, she said, she could watch the ships sailing across the world, carrying bodies to every continent; her own daughter had spent each of her six birthdays in a different country.

As I waited for the elevator up to their apartment, I caught sight of a bulletin board by the parking lot.

"I am a Filipina maid with release paper, looking for a job. I worked with the same employer for four years. Be released due to financial problem."

And "I am hardworking and can tackle all the household chores like cleaning, washing, cooking and marketing, and can also take care of children."

There were notices of Ikea goods and Habitat side lamps—the mobile props of people moving on; one ad was soliciting a new home for some puppies. Most of the little scraps of paper, though, were handwritten messages strikingly similar to the ones in the Worldwide Building, and ending, nearly always, "Thank you for your kindness and consideration."

That night, with Richard away and Sharon in the office, I went down the street to Wanchai, the area where foreign Hong Kong relaxes after work. The savory old domain of Suzie Wong and her sisters had been radically refurbished for a multinational age, and most of its habitués now were not would-be artists sketching Hollywood back-drops, but traders used to foreign homes. The street gleamed with new establishments made for every kind of business: Joe Banana's, Carnegies, Big Apple, open all night, often, and spilling out blond party girls and tie-loosened stockbrokers into the early hours; "pubs and discos" called Neptune and Strawberry, with sliding entrance fees posted outside their entrances ("Lady $50; Guest $100; Armed Forces $100; Non-Member $300") so that the boys on bar stools could decide whom to let in and keep out, whom to call "Guest" and whom "Non-Member"; the more discreet and elegant nightclubs down the streets catering to a more punctilious kind of expense-account being, called Kitty Lounge and Club Cherry and with a large neon sign of a geisha above them (the Wall Street Bar was in Kyoto Plaza); and, most conspicuous of all, jammed into Lockhart Road between streets named after forgotten dignitaries—Fenwick and Fleming and Jaffe—gaudy little bars called New Makati, San Francisco, Waikiki, some of them with video monitors at their entrances so you could inspect the goods inside without pulling back the thick velvet curtains.

The dancers, on almost every stage, in skimpy bikinis and smiles, were Filipinas, and the deejays, very often, were American or Australian; the customers were in many cases Brits, murmurously talking of Unilever in their suits; and the ones behind the cash register were nearly always Chinese. The global marketplace in mufti, practicing supply and demand as ever, though with need inflected differently than in the daylight hours; the age-old transaction—unchanged since Maugham or Kipling—whereby the Third World gets its own back on the First once the lights go down.

The next day, at lunch, I would hear the aftermath: "He came over here straight from Oxford, to work for Jardine's, a bit wet behind the ears, father this classic cold-fish type who was a fellow of some Oxford college. She was thirty-five, a mother many times over, from the Philippines. He only wanted to be loved, of course. Never really had a girl before. Now they've got a child, so there's more to be broken up if they do break up."

Englishmen sipped thirty-dollar drinks in the Firehouse and spoke in the language of school again (travel always a shortcut for

moving back in time). "Get a look at those legs!" or "Even the wedding ring looks good on her." A girl got up on tiptoes to wipe the lipstick off her customer's mustache, so he could return intact to the
missus. Another, pouting, turned her back on a man in a shabby
jacket, who sat alone at the end of the bar, looking at her. Men in
striped shirts and silk ties talked about closing prices and what might
be a reasonable opening bid.

I didn't have the heart for much more of this, and as the night
wore on, I knew, the smiles would grow more plaintive, the ones that
said, Be kind to me, please, and I'll take good care of you bouncing
against the ones that said, How ever did my need bring me here?

I'm sure the girls in thigh-high boots and G-strings were still circling
lethargically to "You can ring my be-e-el, ring my bell . . ." when I
woke up the following morning, in my hotel-room manqué, where
Phil Donahue was discussing extramarital affairs on Channel 8 and
another channel showed the building's lobby. There were 282 British
Airways flights to Europe, the morning paper told me, and article
after article talked of "astronauts" and "parachute children" (in other
words, Hong Kongers affluent enough to acquire second homes
abroad). There is a putting green in Palm Springs Airport, the *Asian
Wall Street Journal* told me, and a Massage Bar in Seattle. In Frankfurt Airport, you can go bowling or do your dry cleaning or see a
porno movie. There is even a whole book—*Stranded at O'Hare*—
that tells you where you can find a Russian-speaking nightclub
between planes.

I went out into the fresh subtropical morning, and stopped off in
the Pacific Coffee Company for breakfast. Like more and more of
the service industries in the heart of Hong Kong, it was staffed by
"white coolie" waiters from Britain and Australia who'd taken over
the menial jobs in Hong Kong now that the lines of power were
being redrawn. As white sons of Empire danced attention on

Chinese customers, I picked up a daily paper and read, "Being almost British is like being homeless" (next to a picture of a Chinese schoolboy in a British uniform); another paper featured ads for "Submissive Expat" and "Decent-Looking Chinaman."

It was such a vertiginous world here, sometimes, the American Restaurant serving Peking food, and Ruby Tuesday offering "authentic American food at genuine American prices." Whenever a new customer walked into the place, I never knew what kind of voice would come out of her—Roedean, or University of Michigan, or pure Kowloon—and she, of course, was no less in the dark with me, not knowing whether to expect South London or Silicon Valley or Calcutta. Cabbies in Hong Kong used walkie-talkies so that passengers' requests could be translated into Cantonese at HQ, and at the cinema, where I chose my seat by pressing my finger on a computerized hologram, Chinese-speaking Indians pointed me towards the auditorium. The Grupo de Teatro Macunaima, the paper informed me, was performing *Little Red Riding Hood* in "Gibberish."

"I begin to feel increasingly at home in big cities," Kazuo Ishiguro once told me when I asked him if he felt himself a foreigner everywhere. "Perhaps because big cities have become the place where people of different backgrounds tend to congregate." I think I know what he meant, though he, of course, is 100 percent Japanese, just as I, who'd seldom been in India, was 100 percent Indian.

Almost everyone who lives in Hong Kong—6 million of its 6.2 million people—is 100 percent Chinese, and yet, I realize, I have written all these words without very much acknowledging that Hong Kong is a Chinese place. To this day, many local businessmen pay more than $1 million for auspicious license plates, and even the managing director of Cathay Pacific moved his office four floors because of a geomancer's warning. In one temple alone in Hong Kong, there are 12,500 Buddhas, and on the streets of Kowloon there are 350 jade vendors. Two-thirds of the land in Hong Kong is parkland, and much of it is a bird-watcher's paradise.

And yet the fact remains that a foreigner can spend days—the better part of years—in Hong Kong and hardly take this in. If you fly Connoisseur Class, if you stay in a fifteen-thousand-dollar-a-month apartment like my friend's—if you're a Global Soul thrown this way and that by the global marketplace—you dwell in a kind of floating International Settlement where you never have to worry that 98 percent of the people around you can't understand a word you say. The word for foreigner in Hong Kong, *gwei-lo*, famously means "ghost."

I notice, too, that I've written all this without really making mention of the fact that Hong Kong has passed back to the Chinese. When I returned to the city after the change of management, it was to find that its puckishness—its nose for turning everything to profit—hardly seemed dented at all. The new cathedral of "Long March Chic" was the store Shanghai Tang, right at the heart of Central, with its motto of "Merrily Opened by Chinese," and its photos, just past the Sikh doormen, of Margaret Thatcher and Prince Andrew kowtowing before its Hong Kong owner; the PRC sign I came across late one night in Causeway Bay was for a People's Republic of Chic store offering 50 percent discounts until midnight. Club 97 had just changed its name to Post 97, and, riding on the Mid-levels Escalator one day—the Hong Kong contraption that climbs all the way from downtown to the mountainous suburbs, through a series of twenty connecting moving sidewalks—I bumped into a Red Star Café, opened the day after the handover and bright with campy Mainland videos and mock-propaganda posters (HEY, GIVE ME A RED) amidst its "Revolutionary Chinese food."

An old schoolfriend's son was still going back to school in England on the "lollipop special"—soon to leave from what Norman Foster had called his "horizontal cathedral," a new airport as large as

Heathrow and JFK combined—and another cousin of mine had arrived here from Bombay, by way of Houston (and soon to be transferred to Cape Town). And at the luxury apartment complex in Repulse Bay where I waited to go up to a twenty-seventh-floor party, the sign said "MANY YEARS EXPERIENCED WORKING IN HONG KONG. I HAVE WORKED FOR ONE EMPLOYER FOR TEN YEARS."

A few months before, the Black Watch (having played at a special banquet for sixty of our school's alumni nine hours before) had struck up the melancholy strains of "The Day Thou Gavest, Lord, Is Ended" as the HMS *Britannia* set sail for the final time. That same morning, the outgoing governor had taken the new British prime minister—in what sounded like a carefully diplomatic vote for the kind of future the British favored—on a tour of Pacific Place.

On one of my final afternoons in Hong Kong, I drove out to the farthest edge of the New Territories, not far from the Chinese border, to see how the Vietnamese boat people were faring. There were very few left here now—a far cry from the days when sixty thousand had been here, and twenty thousand had been kept in virtual cages, awaiting screening at the Whitehead Detention Centre—but what that also meant was that those who remained were the "hard cases," in the apt phrase of the UNHCR official who briefed me. "Someone once said you never notice the rock when there's a flood," he said. "But when the water passes, you see the rocks below."

The rocks, in this case, were mostly drug addicts or convicted criminals who, as official undesirables, were not claimed by third countries, and not welcomed back by Vietnam. They lived now in long rows of numbered two-story blocks, out at the end of a long expressway, in a scrubland of lychee trees and tall housing blocks where Hong Kongers from villages and boats had been resettled. As my UN escorts carefully pointed out, their "open camp" was scarcely any different from the "temporary housing" of many of the local people, and many of the refugees, though not officially assimilated into Hong Kong, had regular jobs, especially in the construction industry, and especially helping to build the new airport nearby. Some of them even made a living by selling their refugee passes to real citizens, hungry for "refugee benefits."

The camp was by no means squalid. Because of the age-old racial differences that all the bureaucracy in the world could not paper over, it was divided into two areas, one containing Vietnamese refugees and the other "nonnationals," which is to say ethnic Chinese from Vietnam who had been more or less pushed out by the Vietnamese government. Tall fences separated the two areas of blue shacks. But on both sides of the barrier there were cheerful schoolroom doors, brightly painted over with Santa Clauses and dancing bunnies and happy tigers, and when a Vietnamese interpreter led me round, he took pains to point out a piano room, friendly with Seven Dwarfs and Hello Kitty details, and even a computer room. Couches had been put out in the dust between the barracks, to make the place feel like home, and residents had even set up noodle shops and impromptu cafés. One woman had put up a table outside her small room where she sold pomelo and sugarcane and caramel corn, and outside nearly every room was a rusty washing machine with modern clothing (Santa Barbara Polo and Racquet Club) fluttering nearby.

"We used to have a lot of violence," the Durable Solutions officer from India who was showing me around said. "Even murders. It was sad: children were being used by their own parents as couriers—for drugs. But now we've installed the Gurkhas, things have been much better." A nice imperial irony: the Nepali hill tribesmen who'd so long been a fiercely loyal part of the British army, based in Hong Kong, were now working as private agents for Jardine's Securicor; they waved at us as we passed, their small blue security kiosk covered with a huge poster of Princess Diana and her sons.

As everywhere in the colony, there were signs all over reading POISONOUS RAT BAIT, but there were also signs, in Vietnamese and

English, saying THE FUTURE IS IN YOUR HAND. The UN was eager now, I was told, to instill in the refugees a sense of self-sufficiency— not, in short, to look after them too much—but there was still a bright clinic run by Médécins sans Frontières and staffed by friendly Filipinos and young locals. "Our hope," an official told me, "is that soon the children will be reciting classical Chinese poetry."

The only trouble was that there was no end in sight to the problem of the refugees' official identity. Some had had the chance to leave a few years earlier, but, gambling that they could get on better here, had chosen to stay on, only to find the doors close behind them. A few women had married out of the prison of the detention center, only to find themselves living with junkies or hardened criminals. Even schoolchildren in Hong Kong had protested the presence of Vietnamese kids in their classes, feeling that the British were slam- ming the door on refugees from China while letting in those from Vietnam.

Yet the biggest problem of all was simply—insolubly—money. Though the first wave of boat people, in 1979, had generally been fleeing war and uncertainty at home, the second large wave, around 1990, had not been fleeing Vietnam so much as seeking out affluent Hong Kong. Ironically, they were coming only because of relaxed travel restrictions and greater freedom at home. And when word got round that the UN was paying $360 resettlement allowances to every refugee who agreed to go back to Vietnam, more people came here in order to be paid to go back home. The $360 they could get for being professional exiles was higher than a whole year's salary.

The UNHCR, formed as a temporary agency in 1951 to deal with the refugee emergency in Europe at the end of the war, had received mandate after mandate to keep going. It now had offices in 115 countries, and the number of refugees, just 2.5 million in 1970, was up to 27.4 million, having doubled in just the past eight years. Refugees, a UNHCR official told *Time*, "are one of the growth indus- tries of the '90s."

The woman selling pomelo smiled sweetly at us as we inspected her goods, syrupy Vietnamese music floating out of the shacks and, here and there, used needles on the ground around us. She'd been here for eight years, she said through Tom, the Vietnamese interpreter who'd chosen to come back from Canada to work with refugees, and she was very much happier than in Whitehead (where people had lived four or five to a bunk, and behind five or six security posts, with nothing to separate them from the next family). But she was still a resident of limbo.

"I am wondering when I can leave Hong Kong," she said, searching out my eyes "My mother is very old. My girl is sick all the time—ever since the screening center she has headaches." She looked at me with hopefulness. "My husband has relations in San Francisco."

My handlers, at this point, tried, understandably, to cut the discussion short, but, before they could do so, the woman wanted to ask a question. Where did I come from? England, I said.

"England is fine," she said, looking up at me expectantly.

Back in my room, I picked up the book I had been carrying round with me, *L'Enracinement* (translated as *The Need for Roots*), by Simone Weil. For most of her thirty-four years, the French Jewish Catholic had taken pains to live no better than the peasants and factory workers around her, and so, during the war, while in England, she had been asked by General de Gaulle to write a report on the possibilities and responsibilities of the French after they were liberated. Anticipating the death of certain fixities, she had written, "No human being should be deprived of his *metaxu*, that is to say, of those relative and mixed blessings (home, country, tradition, cultures, etc.) which warm and nourish the soul and without which, short of sainthood, a *human* life is not possible."

Such issues, inevitably, were on many minds after the Chinese handover. "What are the values we stand for? And what is the social

fabric that ties us together?" the new chief executive of the Special
Administrative Region, Tung Chee-hwa, had asked aloud at the Asia
Society. The Universal Declaration of Human Rights, which I
reencountered several times in the UNHCR literature, said, simply,
"Everyone has a right to a nationality."

Richard and Sharon, I knew, were solid and inwardly rooted
enough to live with any change; now, in any case, they live in London,
with a son, as firmly grounded as anyone I know. But what of the others who don't have their gift for adapting, the ones I knew who called
their own answering machines several times a day, to be greeted by
their own voices, or were crowding in, even now, to Jolly Air Cargo
and the Pansy House and San Tropez to send remittances back to
Manila? I thought of the friend who'd called me up once to say, "Yesterday I was driving towards the Hollywood sign, and I had a cell
phone in one hand and a laptop in the other. And I thought, What am
I doing? Who is this? It's not even like I had anything to say."

That same friend had once flown so many miles that he'd won the
ultimate frequent flier award—thirty days of unlimited flying around
the globe—and had told me of a dream he'd had under jet lag which
was "not a 'Where am I?' dream, which you'd expect, but a 'Who am
I?' dream. I couldn't remember who I was."

It was no surprise to me that nowadays he was spending much of
his time (as I was, too) on retreat in a monastery.

My last day in Hong Kong, I celebrated my birthday together with
Richard (born on the same day of the same year—my global twin), as
we had done almost every year for a quarter of a century, in small tea
shops in Berkshire, in Cambridge, Massachusetts, in the Oxford
Motel in San Francisco. Now we went to one of the restaurants in the
four-hundred-dollar-a-night hotel next door, to find the largest
transoceanic buffet I'd ever seen, while Richard's clients in Indonesia
called on the cell phone and his wife disappeared to check on the
man who was checking on the hard drive.

"I really don't need to exist in real time or real place at all," my friend concluded, putting the phone away. "Probably the strangest thing is when I'm sitting right here, and Sharon's over there"—he pointed to a chair across the table—"and I leave a message for her by calling her voice mail in Boston."

"Because you can be more specific?"

"Yes. And she can listen to the message repeatedly, and take down a lot of concrete information."

A little later, I had to get up to go to Bombay, where a cousin of mine was getting married.

"You know where you can find me," Richard said.

"I do. I can call you up from anywhere."

"Eighteen countries," he reminded me. Just in case, though, he gave me his number in Tokyo and his office number in Tokyo. He gave me his fax number "at home," his fax number "at the office" and his home and office numbers in Hong Kong. He gave me his fax number in both places, an 800 number for his voice mail, his mobile number, his mother's fax number, his office fax number in London, and his E-mail address. He even gave me a toll-free number for calling his voice mail from Japan.

Somehow, that left no room in my address book for his name.

THE MULTICULTURE

I can't be Japanese and I can't be Western—but
I understand both. I am double-binded, but—
and this is perhaps most important—I am also in
a position that generates a great deal of energy
and creativity.

—ARATA ISOZAKI, describing
    his "schizophrenic eclectic"
    brand of architecture

The first time I ever flew into Toronto, coming from San Francisco, I felt as if I were flying east in the classic sense, into somewhere ancestral, with nearly all the passengers around me chattering away in some Chinese tongue as they moved from one suburb of the Chinese "world-city" to the next. The woman next to me brandished a passport on which was written "Ministry of Foreign Affairs," and spoke not a word of English; every time the cabin attendant came round with drinks, she whirled around to the younger women behind her—a daughter-in-law, I presumed, or perhaps a niece—and asked her to request hot water on her behalf (or to find out whether the water was boiled); meanwhile, around us, some member of the family or other would pop up every now and then, whip out an expensive Olympus camera, and snap photos of the others, the startled purser, or herself.

I watched my old neighbor as she looked and looked out of the porthole, and I wondered where she was going, and what future awaited her: a new home, perhaps, in another alien colony, and surely a different place from the one that awaited her English-speaking relatives.

I, for my part, was on my way to Cuba—in the archetypal way, I was coming to Toronto not for itself, but for the other worlds it opened up—and when we disembarked, I noticed that most of the faces pressed against the window in the arrivals area were from

India. The Visitors' line at the Immigration desk stretched all the way into the corridor, people fanning themselves with a rainbow of passports; the line reserved for Canadians was next to empty, save for a small Indian family, a Chinese girl with fuchsia hair, and another Chinese girl deep in a volume entitled *Conversational French.*

"Sir, please, welcome to Toronto," said a turbanned man as I stepped out of this western Heathrow, throwing open the door to his Aerofleet car and half-bowing before he disembarrassed me of my bags. "Sir, kindly watch your step; I hope your stay in Toronto may be a pleasant one." We headed off into the dark, the screech of Hindi film music turned low on the radio, the billboards looming at me with their Hangul script, and the man told me how they had *gurdwaras* now in Toronto, and places where you could follow all the news from home. When he'd arrived, twenty-two years earlier, he'd felt like the only Sikh in town; now there were 23,000 from his community here.

"I can't believe how much I feel at home here, too," I said as we eased towards the universal lit-up huddle of skyscrapers, the antique word DOMINION gleaming on the top of one, and I pointed to the crown encircling the numbers on the green interstate signs, the exit ramps leading to Kipling Road and the Queen Elizabeth Way. "Very nice city, sir," my self-appointed guide assured me. "Very clean, very safe. Nobody here, he is from Canada. So nobody can say, 'You could not be here. You cannot come!'"

There were kilometers on the odometer, I noticed, and "litres" outside the gas stations, and as the man dropped me off, wishing me well, as if he really did hope I would find a new life here, I saw that every word of the sign in front of us—HARBOURFRONT THEATRE CENTRE—was spelled differently from the version of America where I now lived.

The next time I found myself in Toronto, it was to go to that very Centre—I was one of more than three thousand international writers who've traveled to what is now the largest literary festival in the world. The Harbourfront Writers' Festival, partly founded and run for all its twenty-five years by Greg Gatenby, a vigorous evangelist for Canadian writing, takes care to invite participants from every continent, every year, as if to remind us that Canada can be a confluence of rivers; indeed, while politics and economics take care of the external details of the new world order, writing (Harbourfront tells us) can actually give the global village a face, a voice. Though the huge modern hotel in which I was staying posted up an Innkeepers' Act, protecting itself against damage done by a "horse or other live animal or any gear appertaining thereto" and though the signs at traffic lights still read, quaintly, PEDESTRIANS: OBEY YOUR SIGNALS, there were "Jamaican Beef Patties (spicy)" at the deli across the street, and "Indo-Canadian sweets" flavoring the fragrant streets.

"We're all displaced here," said the woman from Australia who greeted me as I walked into the Harbourfront Hospitality Suite; her own first name was Spanish, she explained, and her last name was from Hungary, though she'd been born, in fact, in Italy, and was on her way now to India. "Australia's better than it's ever been," she went on, thanks to its recent influx of Russian cabbies and Filipina nurses and venture capitalists from Hong Kong.

"That's right," piped up one of our official hosts, with an enthusiasm I'd never expect to find in Britain. "The new immigrants here have made our city, too, more international, more alive. Sometimes the old people object because the white-bread areas are full of samosas. But it's good: cosmopolitanism has made the place more tolerant. When my parents were growing up, you couldn't get a drink in a hotel."

It was the same sentence, almost verbatim, that I'd later hear in Wellington, and similar to one I might deliver to a newcomer in London; it echoed, in reverse, the kind of sentences you hear in Bombay, where, suddenly, respectable young girls can enjoy drinks with American stockbrokers in MTV-crazy bars. Yet what was different about Toronto was that everyone, in Harbourfront at least, was speaking of books as the new unlegislated power, hymning into being a new cross-cultural order, and many of these novels (which were invariably the most striking and unprecedented that came my way) took Toronto not just as their setting, but as their inspiration. A few blocks away, Marshall McLuhan had written of how electricity—communications technology, as it's become—could bind us all together in a new kind of global community; yet Canadian literature (which had mostly to do now with Italian priests and Zoroastrian landladies, Japanese grandmas and the uncertain affiliations of Egypt before the war) offered an even more emancipating vision of a new kind of gathering: the city as anthology.

Back in my hotel room, I turned to the local phone book and was surprised to find ten "Iyer"s listed in its pages, and thirty-nine "K.Kim"s (the "Lee"s alone took up thirty-six columns); at dinner the next night, I looked across the table and saw Michael Ondaatje, a central figure in the Canadian literary renaissance (his ancestors English and Singhalese and Dutch), handing me a copy of the international magazine he brought out here, in which Salman Rushdie said, nicely, that if he could have been anything other than a writer, he'd "always wanted to be an actor." So much around me was familiar, but in unfamiliar ways, as if different corners of my life—an Indian grandmother and a Californian girlfriend—had been brought together into the same small room. People used the word *thrice* here, in the same sentence in which they'd speak of "triples"; the airport, I'd noticed on the map, gave out onto American Drive on the one side, and Britannia Road on the other. "Toronto used to be this no-man's-land for various Indian tribes," my host explained to me as we sat among the tropical buildings along Queens Quay West, overlooking the chill gray lake. "The name Toronto comes from an Iroquois word that means 'meeting place.'"

The hope of a Global Soul, always, is that he can make the collection of his selves something greater than the whole; that diversity can leave him not a dissonance but a higher symphony. In Toronto I wondered whether the same could be true of a Global City. And I felt, at another level, an instant kinship with this place where people seemed to speak a language I could understand. For even as it presented itself in the self-deprecating tones of Europe, it was going about the classic American task of making itself something new; its hopefulness felt earned, its buoyancy nuanced, like that of one who had struck off on his own en route from the Home Counties to Illinois.

I could hear, now and then, the sound of a onetime colonial township insisting on itself a little—"I'm not anti-American, but I wish people would understand the difference between us"—and I could understand how a land that was shadowed by an empire to the east and an empire to the south would flinch a little at the fact that Saul Bellow and Neil Young and Pamela Anderson (and even Wayne Gretzky) were all taken to be American.

Yet what surprised me was that this not-untypical unease was expressed with a good humor I wouldn't expect to find in England, and a sense of irony (which means a chastened sense of history) I wouldn't associate with America. In Toronto, I felt, there were ghosts as well as prospects.

The first time I ever met the word *multiculturalism* was while reading an essay of Jan Morris's, about Toronto, from 1984, in which she described meeting the word herself for the first time in a city that seemed to be built around it. The singular promise of Canada, for her, lay in the fact that it was no Promised Land, had no torch-bearing statue, no vision of a City on a Hill nor constitution guaranteeing the pursuit of happiness. Canada seemed to her a vast and all-accommodating open space, "all things to all ethnicities," with

"Canadian nationality itself no more than a minor social perquisite, like a driving license or a spare pair of glasses." Ever acute, Morris had begun her piece with the image of a single clamorous immigrant woman pushing her way through an airport arrivals area filled with classically buttoned-up Torontonians; Toronto for her was a "limbo-city" and "a capital of the unabsolute," not unlike the "Sacred City" of the "Church of the Last Purification" I'd read of in V. S. Pritchett, from which anodyne missionaries issued forth to tell small English boys that there was no "Evil" in the world, only "Error."

As the years went on, however, I started to run into *multiculturalism* more and more, much as I began to bump into Toronto at every turn, often in the least expected of contexts. "There are forty thousand South Africans in Toronto," a South African told me over lunch in California one day; the largest congregation of Goan Christians (outside Christian Goa) was in Toronto, I was told by a Goan Christian in New York. "Ya, all the Russians go to Toronto," a Russian émigré shrugged, with a massive show of unsurprise, as we had breakfast together in San Francisco; and even in Manila's airport, on a sultry tropical morning, I noticed box after box being sent to York (Ontario) and Hamilton, and passport holders adorned with maple leaves.

Historically, "Toronto the Blue" (as Margaret Atwood called it) had always seemed a friendly and hospitable tabula rasa for the second sons of Empire—the next best thing to England for many a bright student from Bridgetown or Madras, the nearest thing to America for those from Haiti or Somalia. And in the way in which cities (like people) become what they are perceived to be, it had become more and more a magnet for refugees who knew nothing more of it than that it was a magnet for refugees. So "New Canadians" from Rwanda and Bulgaria and Afghanistan joined several other groups of fugitives who didn't even show up on many charts: Americans who'd come here to escape the Vietnam War (and colored the city now with their impenitent idealism); 300,000 Anglophile refugees from Montreal, in flight from Quebec's violently anti–English language policies; and others (from Palestine, say) who'd simply learned that it was easier to pass immigration tests in Canada than in the United States. One day, I even heard that Phan Thi Kim Phuc, the nine-year-old girl whom much of the world saw running down a country road, her mouth open in a scream as she fled her napalmed village in Vietnam, was settled now in Toronto, and, with a kind of Canadian aptness, working for UNESCO. "I am happy," she'd said, looking past the third-degree burns that still disfigured her body, "because I'm living without hatred."

And the astonishing thing about this flood of foreigners was that it was all happening so quickly— as recently as 1971, 97 percent of all Canadians had been of the traditional kind, of European descent (with the rest mostly "aboriginals," as the Canadians call them); yet already, in scarcely a generation, the number of "visible minorities" in Toronto and Vancouver (to use another local coinage) had climbed above 30 percent. What this meant, in effect, was that seven of every ten of the immigrant beings I noticed on the streets were burdened with no memories of civil rights battles or (as the local paper pointedly put it) of "violently entrenched racism"; their memories were of cricket games on Queen's Park Savannah, or family gatherings in the New Territories, or (as it also happened) racial massacres in Jaffna.

And Toronto, with a self-consciousness and earnestness less common in more settled places, had decided to seize on this fact of postmodern life to make itself something half-imagined. Paris and London and New York were all highly international, too, of course, but all of them, in their different ways, were too old, too amorphous, or too preoccupied with other matters to adjust very much to their latest immigrants; Toronto, by contrast, with less to lose and a less sharply defined sense of itself, had embarked upon a multicultural experiment with itself as guinea pig. Accepting newcomers from developing countries as readily, it claimed, as from Europe, and spending hundreds of millions of dollars to encourage them to sustain their different heritages, it was daring to dream of a new kind of cosmopolis—not a melting pot, as people in Toronto politely reminded me, but a mosaic.

There were still many problems, inevitably, as Toronto and Vancouver raced into a polylingual future while the villages only forty-five minutes away still lingered, undisturbed, in their white-bread, Protestant, nineteenth-century pasts; and I could catch a sense of alarm as much as of pride in the local paper's claim that "Toronto is far past the level of diversity that any European country would tolerate." High Tory clubbishness meant that many parts of the city still remained multiethnic, rather than truly international, and one stubborn legacy of its Old World roots, locals told me, was an intractable sense of class divisions. Yet the fact remained that the most multicultural city in the world, by UN calculations, was also the "Queen City" of a country that had placed first, for five straight years, in the UN's Human Development Index, which ranks 174 countries for quality of life. And the "most cosmopolitan city on earth," as a local columnist called it, was also, statistically, the safest city in North America. It all raised the possibility, exhilarating to contemplate, that a city made up of a hundred diasporas could go beyond the cities that we knew.

During my early days in Toronto, I found myself spinning through cultures as if I were sampling World Music rhythms on a hip-hop record. Every day, I'd wake up early, and hand my laundry to the woman from the Caribbean who guarded the front desk of the Hotel Victoria with an upright demeanor worthy of a Beefeater. Then I'd slip around the corner to where two chirpily efficient Chinese girls would have my croissant and tea ready almost before I'd ordered them. I'd stop off in the Mövenpick Marché down the block—run almost entirely by Filipinas (the sisters, perhaps, of the chambermaids in the Victoria)—and buy a copy of the *Globe and Mail,* which nearly always had news on its front page of Beijing. Then, not untypically, an Afghan would fill me in on the politics of Peshawar as I took a cab uptown, consulting an old-fashioned newspaper that (with its Grub Street column and its "Climatology" section) seemed to belong to Edwardian Delhi.

For a Global Soul like me—for anyone born to several cultures— the challenge in the modern world is to find a city that speaks to as many of our homes as possible. The process of interacting with a place is a little like the rite of a cocktail party, at which, upon being introduced to a stranger, we cast about to find a name, a place, a person we might have in common: a friend is someone who can bring as many of our selves to the table as possible.

In that respect, Toronto felt entirely on my wavelength. It assembled many of the pasts that I knew, from Asia and America and Europe; yet unlike other such outposts of Empire—Adelaide, for example, or Durban—it offered the prospect of uniting all the fragments in a stained-glass whole. Canada could put all the pieces of our lives together, it told me (and others like me), without all the king's horses and all the king's men.

For me, the notion of a Commonwealth had never made much sense before, except as a rather random grouping of subjects in the servants' quarters who had nothing in common except their bosses above. But in Toronto, I began to have a sense of a new, postmodern Commonwealth, to which Empire could come to atone for some of its sins and (as retired power brokers do) to make a kind of peace. a vase that is put together out of broken pieces, as Derek Walcott says, is a memento put together with love. And as I went about the city, I heard how the mayor's own car had been towed to make way for a Ukrainian festival, and how the cricket teams of India and Pakistan, so violently opposed that they could not play on their own home turf for ten years (for fear of riots), came to Toronto every year and held a five-match Sahara Cup at the Toronto Cricket, Skating and Curling

Club. The matches were seen by four thousand excited émigrés in the stands, but broadcast live to 200 million furious partisans at home.

One night, I had dinner with a young Canadian writer called Guy ("named," he said, with a touch of self-mockery I was coming to see as indigenous, "by English-speaking parents who dreamed of a beautiful bicultural future"), and he told me that many people felt that Toronto was much closer to Sydney or Singapore than to Detroit. Guy himself had lived in the Australia of his father's youth, the New Zealand of his mother's family, and the England that was the putative home of all of us; but he'd returned to Toronto as a place where the different empires (British, American, International) cohabited in a more familiar way, perhaps.

And I, suddenly, for the first time in twenty years, recalled how close I had come to being a Canadian myself, as our family gathered around the dinner table in distant Oxford and discussed whether we should move to Manitoba or Winnipeg (the names themselves sending icy winds shuddering through the English spring); the first time I ever set foot in Canada, I was ten years old, visiting the World Expo in Montreal, and carrying a mock passport from pavilion to pavilion to be stamped by nations whose names I'd never heard before. In those days, sitting in the backseat with my portable Scrabble set, I'd have noticed that all the letters that make up the name Toronto (though the same is true, of course, of Seattle or Atlanta) are the least valuable on the board. But put them all together—as it's easy to do, because they're all so common—and you collect a fifty-point bonus.

One Sunday in Toronto I went up to Bloor Street, at the center of town, and, taken by the sound of hymns from a nearby church, I wandered into the Toronto Korean United Church, as it was now called (it had once been the Bloor Street United Church, a sign outside explained). Inside, a tall, pale woman in clerical vestments was talking mildly, but with conviction, about the need to resuscitate the place of women in the Bible, and rescue the book from its "patriarchal" provenance. None of the faces along the pews was Korean, but a picture of Minister Sung Chul Lee watched over us all, with a scroll beside him in Hangul.

Walking out—having been greeted and welcomed by the minister—I noticed that I could also visit, along the same block, in the heart of downtown, a Baha'i Centre, a Covenant Christian Church, a Jewish Community Centre, or (more relevantly, perhaps) a Communiqué Language Training Centre Interamerica. Instead, I passed onto a side street and came upon a large yellow building with golden deer seated on its roof and prayer flags fluttering above a wall-sized picture of the Dalai Lama. Inside this Tibetan Buddhist Centre, I learned, a Bhikkuni was offering a Dharma discourse on "Refuge"—she'd been born in Kenora, Ontario, I read, and grown up with a great passion for Jesus; but then she'd trained as a gestalt psychotherapist and now she was a member of the Ontario Multifaith Council of Spiritual and Religious Care.

Such a clamor of faiths, on one busy block, raised questions about how much real unity was possible, or even desirable; and the city's patchwork quilt of Little Indias, Little Maltas, and Greektowns prompted some to see it as no more than a World Expo writ large, demeaning ethnicities by turning them into theme-park curiosities. Yet for me there was a sense of excitement in being in a place where people were discussing, semipermanently, the nature of community, and Founding Fathers were quite literally drafting a multicultural Constitution.

I was learning new words in Toronto, I realized, among people on every side trying to come to terms with foreignness: a "landed immigrant," I found out, was a newcomer who has yet to become a citizen, and an "allophone" was a Quebecker whose first language was neither English nor French. "Barrel children" were Third World kids whose parents, living away from them in North America, sent them barrels of supplies to support them, and a "middle power" was what Canada called itself, as a country old enough to have a sense of limits yet young enough to be still carded.

And though people still talked about the shocking threats to their complacency—when Air India flight 182 had been bombed out of the air in 1985, the assumption was that the attack was partially funded by Sikhs in Canada, anxious to get back at Hindus in India (and the prime minister of the day sent his condolences to Rajiv Gandhi, although 90 percent of the "Indians" on the plane were now Canadians)—there was still an intoxicating sense of possibility.

"I think you'll find there's a more sophisticated level of discussion on the subject here than you'll find anywhere else in the world," a Muslim from South India told me over lunch as he dazzled me with discussions of the permutations of multiculturalism (from Prometheus to Procrustes). As if to bear that out, he told me how his own children (already fluent in English, Urdu, and Tamil) were going through French lycée here; and how, during the Gulf War, he'd been able to follow the unseen battles through reading the responses of Kuwaitis and Israelis and Iranians and Iraqis, all gathered on the "Letters" page of the *Toronto Star.* I felt as if I were seeing one of the grand inflatable spheres I'd come across in the gift shop of the Royal Ontario Museum—"Globals," as they were nicely called—being turned around and around to catch new scintillations of light.

One bright spring morning in Toronto, I rented a car with "second-generation air bags" (the only second-generation things in the whole city, I was tempted to believe) and drove out to Scarborough to visit what I took to be a typical local school. There is no inner city as such in the metropolitan area, which means that poorer recent immigrants are generally to be found in housing blocks all across the "megacity," their malls liquid with the flowing loops of Singhalese or signs for such quintessentially Torontonian places as Global Pet Foods. L'Amoreaux Collegiate had fewer than a thousand students in all, I was told, but seventy-six different languages could be heard along its hallways, and more than 70 percent of its students spoke a mother tongue other than English. One of the most popular courses in the school, in fact, was English as a Foreign Language.

I walked into the Market Square, which is the central gathering place of L'Amoreaux—bright green and orange and yellow hives converge there—and I felt as if I were in an Olympic Village. Head scarves and bangles and saris surrounded me, *salwar kameez* and tokens whose importance I couldn't gauge. On one side of the hall, lanky West Indian boys were sitting against a wall, long arms wrapped around their tall, dark girls; closer to the center sat a flock of Sri Lankan girls, chattering in a cloud of colorful silks and exotic scents. A teacher was calling out some name on the public-address system that I'm sure nobody could make out, and the pictures of class officers along the walls told a startling story of an all-white student body splintering dramatically, in the last few years, into the colors of a prism.

Around me, among the dozens of students milling around, I could make out only three white faces; they belonged to the most recent immigrants, I learned, mostly from Eastern Europe. These days, it was the Caucasians who were most in need of help with English.

A school in Toronto, at the end of the millennium, I quickly found, was nothing like a school as I'd conceived of it; the largest percentage of the students here was from Sri Lanka, and most of them lived with uncles or distant relatives, their parents having sent them away from home to escape its civil war; the second largest group probably came from Hong Kong, and they lived, often, in expensive condos, by themselves, protecting the escape hatches their nervous parents had acquired (on allowances of two thousand dollars a month). "I remember once going into school on the day of a blizzard," a teacher told me, "when all our classes were canceled, and I got a call from a parent. 'Oh, yes,' I said. 'You must be worried about the snowstorm.' 'Snowstorm?' he said, and I realized he was calling from Hong Kong!"

On a typical day in L'Amoreaux's Market Square, someone was observing African Heritage Month by offering *mehndi* (or traditional decoration of hands) at lunchtime, and someone else was giving a talk on Eid-ul-Fitr. Many students and teachers were dressed in red, in honor of the Chinese New Year, and a video was showing Toronto's first-place finish in the Dragon Boat Races in Hong Kong. I thought back to my own high school in England—entirely male, all dressed in black, fluent in the Apostles' Creed, and assuming that everyone came from the same small section of society—and I realized that I'd never learned what *mehndi* meant; I knew about Eid only from a four-year-old girl in London, who'd passed on to me what she'd learned in nursery school. The teacher with the Irish name who was showing me around seemed to know much more about Tamil customs than I, with my Tamil surname, did.

"Do you make any concessions to ethnic food?" I asked, as we went into the lunch hall.

"Oh, we have kosher, *halal*, all those kind of things," she said. "But the universal language, I think, is french fries."

After lunch, I went into the library, where the poster along the wall that said CANADA THE GREAT was hardly visible for the more scenic shots of Colombo, Mogadishu, and Hong Kong. The library had just requested sixty new books, I saw on a list, most of them at the request of students, and very few of them were ones I had heard of (*Drew and the Homeboy Question, The Roller Birds of Ranpur, An Anthology of Somali Poetry*). The Chinese students all loved Dickens, the librarian told me, because they'd "done" him already in Cantonese; but it was students of all races who'd requested *Black Indians* and *Black Jesus and Other Stories, The Black Canadians* and *Black Women for Beginners.*

Even the problems here belonged to a different universe from the one I'd inherited, and I could see why the staff (seventy-five of the seventy-six pictured were white) had to call in detectives and "liaisons" from a variety of immigrant communities to lead workshops on "Multicultural Youth at Risk." Not long before, one of the school's most promising graduates had been gunned down in a nearby mall, apparently by one of the many Tamil Tiger groups that ran guns and drugs out of pizza parlors here and occasionally tried to recruit in the school; sometimes a Sri Lankan girl came up to her, a teacher said, and reported that a boy had called out to her, "Do you want to go out on Saturday?" She'd been taught—strictly taught— never to speak to a male other than her future husband.

Fathers, in fact, had been known to pull their daughters out of the school—and to face down school authorities with all-male posses— after they'd found out that their girls had gone out on dates (not, generally, with boys from other ethnic groups, but, more disruptively, with boys from their own groups of a different social level). And often, I was told, children couldn't come to class because they had to accompany their parents to a loan officer or an immigration lawyer— as the only English speakers in the household, they'd had to become the effective bosses in dealing with foreign officialdom.

Often the same girls who'd been taught never to answer a question in public could tell you every last detail of how a guerrilla ambush worked, or how you got your own back when your father was killed by a neighbor's gang.

For a certain kind of independent-minded kid, I thought, the reigning gospel at a place like L'Amoreaux could be so insistent (MULTICULTURAL/ANTI-BIAS, advertised the bookstore that supplied the library; next week the teachers would be attending a Multicultural Health and Wellness Symposium organized by the Multicultural and Equity Education Committee) that they might

find themselves fervent uniculturalists. And the mothers called Sunshine coming in to address Gender Equity and Leadership Panels,
the workshops on "implementing antiracist strategies in the classroom" belonged to worlds I couldn't follow. Yet when I thought back
to my own high school again—where even Catholics and Jews were
so exceptional that they were given special exemptions from chapel
(there were fewer than 20, I think, among 1,250 of us)—I realized
that someone like me was speaking a language as outdated in
Toronto as the ancient Greek principal parts we used to recite in our
pajamas.

The kids in the cafeteria, I'd noticed, were all conspicuously
locked into their own ethnic groups—the Jamaican boys playing
dominoes at one table while the Chinese students observed what
looked to be a "Chinese-only" code at another, the "Indians" breaking down into their own elaborate quilt of Hindu and Muslim and
Singhalese and Bangladeshi. But at least many of them knew the
words to the National Negro Hymn, sung out in assembly, and had
the chance to enter an essay competition on "Ways to Invite Strong
Multicultural Relations at L'Am" (essays were accepted in Chinese).
And when, in future years, they heard neighbors cry, "*Kung Hei Fat
Choy*," they might just possibly remember that this was how the
principal had greeted them as she'd handed out Chinese New Year
candies.

Just before leaving the school, I went into the staff room to give
my thanks, and the teachers made sure I came away with a copy of
the oversized, Technicolor calendar the school puts out every year,
featuring students from sixteen different ethnic groups (from Peru,
Iran, "First Nation" tribes) posing in their local dress and offering
recipes for indigenous dishes. It was the perfect thing, the teachers
said, to take back to insular Japan.

Toronto's status as a seasoned veteran of multiculturalism derives in
part, of course, from the fact that it belongs to Canada, which has

been trying to define itself from birth. And through the kind of happenstance that does not seem coincidence, the city had long been home to a disproportionate number of the thinkers who had advanced farthest in imagining a world without borders. It was in Toronto, famously, that Marshall McLuhan invented the very notion of a global village, and, in his idiosyncratic way (which sometimes stumbled into clairvoyance), said that Canadians were especially "suited to the Third World tone and temper as the Third World takes over the abandoned goals of the First." And it was in Toronto that McLuhan's colleague in the English Department, Northrop Frye, had risen above all nationalities—having mastered the literatures of the world—to chart an Olympian map of human consciousness, and explain how all of us participate in a kind of universal imagination, in which our longing for winter and spring corresponds to sighs and rebirth.

After Jane Jacobs completed her definitive autopsy of the modern city, *The Death and Life of Great American Cities,* in New York, it was to Toronto that she decamped, to try to make her theories live (the local government encouraging her in her efforts to devise a downtown of diversity in which supermarket and office block and residence and Russian teahouse would sit side by side, and so preempt the flight to suburbia that had led to what Glenn Gould, another Torontonian, called "1984 Pre-Fab"). And now Toronto's latest writers were taking the mix into the twenty-first century, and into the soul, like Emerson's Poet who "stands among partial men for the complete man, and apprioos us not of his wealth, but of the common wealth."

Yet as much as Toronto's identity was formed by being Canadian, it was equally determined by the fact that it wasn't Quebec. And as its longtime rival and neighbor only five hours away by car had noisily agitated for its own nation, and a state of fortress uniculturalism, Toronto had been pushed even further towards becoming a multiculture of the future (not least because of all the Quebeckers who now migrated there). "Here is peace country for all the world," an Iranian in Toronto once told me, summarizing the ideal image of Canada's relation to the world; yet now, 7 million of the country's 29 million citizens were threatening to withdraw into a different past and to fashion what they called (with typical uncertainty) a "sovereign Quebec inside a united Canada."

Thus the discussion of how best to matchmake cultures—the terms of separatism and federalism—were on the front pages every day, and every other Canadian, at the breakfast table, seemed to be addressing the issue of whether to make a stew, a salad, or an alphabet soup of the neighborhoods around them. Montreal, the largest city in French Canada, was threatening to secede from the secession, so as to ally itself (for economic reasons) with a country whose language it claimed not to speak, and Francophone immigrants to Quebec were complaining they were being cheated of the chance to learn English. Anglophone newcomers to the French-speaking province found themselves, quite literally, neither here nor there, and First Nation tribes were saying that if Quebec could have a separate territory, so could they. For many recent immigrants, who'd come all the way to Canada to leave civil wars behind them, the global debate here had thrown them into the middle of a struggle more civil, perhaps, but certainly no less divisive.

One day, at lunch with a couple of television executives, pursuing a vision of Toronto as the new World City, I learned that one of them (speaking with an accent I couldn't begin to place) was an English-speaking refugee from Montreal. He had, moreover, lived in England for a while, and—so we discovered—studied in the same college as I, at almost the same time. England, he told me later over drinks—almost amused, I think, to be saying this—had been his version of the New World, his way of escaping a Canada to which his family had imported far too many memories.

"Growing up," he said simply, "it was just too hard to bear." His parents were from Hungary—Jewish—and had come here only because they survived the camps of World War II. "So I had this past," he said, "which was a giant wound, and with which I didn't really feel a connection, and my parents were always trying to instill that very identity into me. They sent me to Orthodox Jewish school in Montreal; they talked to me in the very language that had almost been the death of them. So I became an Anglophile: I can still remember, at the age of eleven, reading *The Times* of London and learning about Oxford. For me, I think it was a way of creating a new identity."

"But when people ask you where you're from, what do you say?"

"Oh, the usual hesitations and qualifications." (He'd learned that much in England, I thought.) "Usually, I don't say anything at all. It's like when people ask, 'Are you happy?' I'm completely speechless."

Yet I could tell that he turned these questions around and around in his mind, like the sheets he needed to make himself comfortable in to sleep.

"Sometimes, of course"—he looked up for a kindred spirit—"I just lie.

"But I can still remember, vividly, going to become a Canadian citizen," he went on. "I was nine, and I had to swear on some book—because we were Jewish, it couldn't have been a regular Bible." And then the oppression of an upbringing that belonged to another world—one not just abandoned but destroyed—and his parents, through the press of memory and sorrow, forever lost in the culture that had tried to kill them. "I felt as if I were a living memento mori of some sort," he said almost helplessly, in this congregation of blue tattoos."

His mother had been forced to work for nine months in Auschwitz, he began telling me, as the bare-midriffed girl in the trendy bar around us switched the channels on the TV. His uncle had survived with false papers in Budapest, only to be "liberated" by the Soviets to work in Soviet labor camps. His relatives were exiles two times over by the time they arrived in this land of foreigners.

"My uncle escaped by jumping over a wall and getting on a boat to come to Montreal. But now he's getting older—he's in his eighties—and all his dreams are of that time, and how he failed to save his mother and father. When I go to visit him, it's all he can talk about."

My new friend had gone to England, he said, to fight free of that prison of memories, though he had found, not surprisingly, that the Old World is not very open to people writing new destinies for themselves, especially if they're Jewish and coming from the colonies; he'd come back here, and tried to escape again, by moving from Montreal to Toronto.

He looked so much like my image of a classic Canadian that I realized, with a start, all the stories I was missing, and all the pressures that an "invisible minority" suffers in part because they're not written on his face; few people would extend to him the kind of allowances they might to a newcomer from Kigali or New Delhi.

"I suppose ultimately you're a cosmopolitan," I said. "I mean, you don't really identify yourself with any of the places where you've lived."

"*Rootless cosmopolitan,*" he said with a trace of bitterness. "That's the term they used to derogate the Jews. You know, that whole sense that they had no homeland except in money."

Before he left, though, he said something else, in his searching, slightly melancholy way. "There was only one time I found a home—just once: in a dream.

"I used to keep having this dream of running, running, at nighttime, down a country lane, and being scared. And just this once, I was running down a dusty road, and there were hedgerows on both sides, and then I must have jumped over or something, because I found myself in a deep valley.

"There was a camp there, a tribe of some sort. And I thought—in my dream—This is what it means to be at home. This is what the feeling is."

. . .

Writers, of course, by their nature, draw upon the past—it is, almost literally, the inner savings account from which they draw their emotional capital. But in Toronto, this force of memory had a particular charge because, for so many of its newest novelists, the past lay across the globe, and some of them had come here expressly to abandon it, some to play out its sentences in new surroundings. How much you imported of your previous life, how much you left behind—that seemed, in many ways, the central question Toronto raised (and with an intensity even stronger than in America, where so many of our "immigrant" tales, from Amy Tan, say, or Philip Roth, are the work of second-generation foreigners).

A writer like Rohinton Mistry, for example—for me, the sovereign Indian novelist of our times—lived, to all intents and purposes, in the Bombay of twenty-five years ago, even though he spent his nights in a suburb of Toronto. He'd been here for more than half his life now, having migrated to Toronto to work in a bank at the age of twenty-three; and yet, in some fundamental way, this gentle, modest soul had never really unpacked his bags. All his fiction was set in a particular corner of Bombay in the 1970s, and he could see that corner more clearly, no doubt, for not being distracted by the Bombay of the nineties. Some Torontonians doubtless felt that Mistry should not count as a Canadian, though Greg Gatenby, ever the fervent advocate for Canadian identity, told me he'd recently written an outraged letter to The Times of London, after it had referred to "the Indian writer Rohinton Mistry, currently living in Toronto."

Mistry might not be writing if he hadn't come to Canada, Gatenby protested patriotically; he'd been given grants by the Canadian government and first been published in Canada. He'd even received his first break, while at night school, in a University of Toronto writing competition—enjoying the New World's penchant for offering second lives. He'd met his wife (like himself, from the tiny community

of Bombay Parsees) in Toronto, and even, by chance, found the suburb where he lived now filling up with tandoori houses.

"There are many Canadian writers who are happy to celebrate and
talk about their ethnic backgrounds," said Gatenby, "but they do so
from a Canadian perspective." A young writer like the Sri Lankan–
born Shyam Selvadurai could never, he said, have written about gay
life in Colombo if he had stayed there. Canada was his liberating
force. Besides, "the immigrants who are still living in the Old Country while they're here don't like Mistry or Nino Ricci. These writers
will tell you that they get their most welcoming reception from outside their community."

Ricci, in fact, had just completed a trilogy of novels explicitly
describing how the sins of the Old World seep across the blank
spaces of the New, like blood across a sheet. The hero of his tale—
Vittorio Innocente—is an Italian emigrant whose mother dies while
delivering an out-of-wedlock baby on the passage over (the postmodern version of the classic foundling), and so he arrives in Canada
an orphan. In the last book of the set, Vittorio (now Victor) finds
himself driving around a city of the displaced, in his father's Oldsmobile, unanchored and slipping ever closer to his half sister, till the
shadow of classical incest rears up on bright and secular College
Street.

Going back to the sleepy village that his mother had fled under a
cloud, he finds that the past can't be put to rest because it's been lost
in translation, or rewritten by other hands. His life is condemned to a
"double foreignness" between the "near-odourless newness" of
Toronto and an ancient stench he cannot shake.

Reading Ricci's haunted novel—Catholic priests suddenly looming up on him like specters from the past—I thought that if the
essential question that America asks of every newcomer is, "What
will you do with your future?" Canada adds to it the more difficult
one: "What will you do with your past? How much will you abandon
everything that's made you what you are, and become a Canadian

(whatever that may mean)? How much will you drown your past in a sea of thousands of other pasts?"

The ache of immigrants everywhere—themselves a kind of fiction—was complicated in a place that made the Faustian compact central: give up what makes you special, and you can gain a whole new world.

If you visit Toronto on the printed page, you will soon find that, for many of its "visible minorities," the city is too much a part of the Commonwealth—too close to Britain and Australia and South Africa—in all the worst ways: so attached to its own white past that it refuses to make room for more colorful ones, or, under a semblance of tolerance, encourages only their exotic elements ("Racism with a smile on its face," as the black Canadians call it). "Is the warmth I does miss," says a Trinidadian in Neil Bissoondath's sharp, sad collection of immigrant tales, mostly set in Toronto, *Digging Up the Mountains;* another says, "Everybody's a refugee, everybody's running from one thing or another," though in the fiction of V. S. Naipaul's nephew, almost none of the "wanderlost" from the "urchin nations" ever ends up anywhere. Bharati Mukherjee, in "The Management of Grief," writes witheringly of "Multiculturalism" experts with "textbooks on grief management" trying to put into boxes the feelings of Indian women recently widowed after the bombing of the Air India plane, and stranded in a country where they've never handled money before or (being well brought up) spoken their husbands' names aloud. (Writing of the insults and indignities she suffered there, Mukherjee fled Toronto, with her partly Canadian husband, for Atlanta, of all places, and then New York and California.)

"Something is very awry in this beautiful country, where the cauldron of race relations is boiling over," I read in Cecil Foster's *A Place Called Heaven*, though I couldn't help noticing that never once in his 321 pages did the Barbadian novelist acknowledge that the

"Canadians" he was so broadly condemning are now often of Indian or Chinese or Peruvian origin (and his attack on multiculturalism was written with the help of Multiculturalism Canada and the Canadian Arts Council). The very "Heaven" he invoked in his title was a reminder that "Heaven" had been a code name for Canada in the Negro spirituals of the nineteenth-century—the "North Star" spoken of by Martin Luther King, the new life waiting for blacks at the end of the Underground Railroad—and it made me wonder if Foster was simply accusing Toronto of not being Utopia.

In the classic works of multicultural beings—those of Rushdie, say—Global Souls are seen as belonging to a kind of migratory tribe, able to see things more clearly than those imprisoned in local concerns can, yet losing their identity often as they fall between the cracks. A Global Soul is a ventriloquist, an impersonator, or an undercover agent: the question that most haunts him is "Who are you today?" But in many of the Toronto novels that are flooding through the literary world now, such visions are placed in a more positive light by being set in the context of a whole city made up of such free agents.

In Anne Michaels's radiant novel *Fugitive Pieces,* Toronto is an "active port"—a New World Athens, in which "almost everyone has come from elsewhere . . . bringing with them their different ways of dying and marrying, their kitchens and songs," and it is a place where the very words of English allow a survivor of the Holocaust to enter "an alphabet without memory." As one of her protagonists—a translator, of course—dutifully re-creates his study in Zakynthos, he knows that some of the rooms around him are looking out on Maharashtra, and others are plastered with pictures of St. Lucia. Each, in a sense, is importing his own past, but the whole they are making is a brand-new kind of future. Even the palindrome they flourish like harlequins—English is their new toy as well as their chance for a new identity—looks towards a hope: "Are we not drawn onward, we few, drawn onward to new era?"

. . . .

My friend from Hungary (who sounded neither Hungarian nor
Canadian nor, really, English) had told me that it was important for
me, if I was interested in globalism, to make a trip to Honest Ed's, a
landmark in the history of Toronto immigration. It was a block-long
superstore that sat in the middle of Bloor Street like a homemade
Kmart, pulling in immigrants from around the city with its absurdly
inexpensive deals perfectly tailored to an immigrant's needs (Ed
Mirvish had been known to sell a whole island once for $2.19—even
less in American dollars—and a cruise for two for $1.99).

When I arrived at the place, hectic with carnival slogans and handwritten signs all over its exterior—WHITE SLICED BREAD 29¢; 900
GRAM BAG OF WHOLE GREEN PEAS 39¢—its turnstiles were
already spinning with customers early on a Sunday morning (sometimes, I'd been told, there were traffic jams at 4:00 a.m. around the
discount palace, in honor of one of its all-night sales). Virtually every
square inch of window space, on all the walls that looked out onto the
street, was plastered with old newspaper clippings and yellowed photographs reciting the legend of "Honest Ed." Immigrants everywhere are the ones who run stores for other immigrants, in a kind of
oral tradition whereby yesterday's newcomer knows exactly what
today's or tomorrow's will need (international phone cards, tax
advice, pieces of luggage, and tickets home); what Mirvish seemed to
be offering was a version of the classic immigrant tale—the American Dream—with Canadian trimmings.

His story played out, therefore, like an old-fashioned movie made
by some immigrant to Hollywood, and affirming the power of hard
work and dreaming and good old-fashioned chutzpah. The industri-
ous son of a failed encyclopedia salesman from Kiev, Ed Mirvish had
begun working in his father's tiny grocery store when he was nine (I
read in the clippings); at fifteen, he'd dropped out of school to take
the whole place over. He'd sold his wife's insurance policy to rent a

little space on Bloor Street in 1948—open only one afternoon a
week—and he'd worked for twenty hours a day, year after year, to
turn his little property into a kind of retail Lourdes of Toronto, where
he had been known to hand out dollar bills to the poor and to lease
out Lincoln Continentals to people who dreamed of following in his
footsteps (buying his first Oldsmobile for ten bucks).

When the Royal Alexandria Theatre had come close to going
bankrupt, Honest Ed had charged in to rescue it and restore it to its
former glory; buoyed by that success, he'd gone across the water and
bought the Old Vic in London, too, over the disapproving murmurs
of the Anglo Old Guard (all this was told on the walls of his store).
He'd opened six restaurants, big enough to seat 2,600 people and,
true to his newcomer's sense of propriety, had insisted on a dress
code in some of them, so that (the legend said) he'd turned away a
troupe of Boy Scouts, and denied entrance to some Chinese diplomats, for coming in without a tie. Even now, the septuagenarian millionaire—according to the paper's twice-told tales—was at his desk
every day by 8:00 a.m. and signed every check in his $55 million-a-
year empire.

A small Russian man bumped into me at that point, asking me
where the "Something Department" was, and, as I stood outside,
working out exactly what he'd said, any number of Korean and Mexican and Iranian shoppers shoved past me. Inside the store, just past
the picture of the eight-year-old triplets modeling camisoles for
Mirvish in the Eisenhower years (and the notices pointing out how
his name featured in the titles of even his Italian and Szechuan
restaurants), I was in a world of Indians and Guatemalans and Chinese families and Poles, sorting through $.99 salad bowls and trying
on $4.99 jackets (the store keeps its prices insanely low in part by
offering no credit, no service, and no parking—though, in a typically
Edian flourish, Mirvish does employ his own street cleaner to keep
the block half-immaculate). On pillars and walls and signs all around
the place were reassuringly bumptious one-liners and upbeat
slogans: OUR PRICES ARE BOTTOM!!! (DIAPERS UPSTAIRS) and

DEVELOPE A SMILE AT ED'S PRICES (the misspelling itself surely part of the reassurance). One whole wall of the store—unusual, I thought, for a shop owned by a Jewish man—consisted of crucifixes, and, amidst his black velvet representations of the Toronto skyline hung framed pictures of the Last Supper. Honest Ed certainly knew his market: though once he'd sold a swimming pool for $.88, Elvis figurines here went for $99.95 and "Tomato Machines" for $267.77.

The biggest surprise of all, though, past the framed photos of Jerry Springer and in front of the stairwells decorated with hymns to Ed written by eighth graders, was a sign near the steps, advertising an IMMIGRATION SERVICE (2ND FLOOR EAST BUILDING BY MENSWEAR). I went up and found what looked like a travel agency, with stirring posters of Canada and solemn treatises on Flag Day on its walls, and a team of "Certified Immigration Counsellors" offering advice on "Landed Status / Ministers' Permits / Live-in Caregiver / Refugee Claims / Detention Reviews."

There were signs for a dental clinic around me and posters advertising lunch with a ventriloquist; there were clippings noting that Honest Ed had entered the Guinness pantheon by erecting the largest neon sign on the planet. But the most essential accessory of all seemed to be the list, hand-scrawled on a wall, of all the paralegal services offered, from "Canadian Pardons" to "U.S. Waivers," from "Name Changes" to "Landlord Problems." Mirvish—an Officer of the Order of Canada and showpiece of the city (he'd once even led a walking tour of the neighborhood with Jane Jacobs, and reproved the Queen Mother for not visiting his store while in Toronto)—was doing everything he could to help the new immigrant find a future here.

In 1972 (one of the clippings recorded), while Mirvish was guest-editing a column in the *Toronto Sun,* a fifteen-year-old had asked "Mr. Toronto" (born in Virginia, as the papers did not so often stress) whether he preferred "Toronto the Old (Hogtown) or Toronto the New (Fun City)." With all the wisdom of a village elder, Ed had looked past either/or distinctions and written, "We are all of us in

Toronto a product not only of our aspirations, but also a product of
our past. . . . As important as what we become is what we were"—a
sentiment slightly different from the one I might have read if Mirvish
had stayed on in America.

When I walked out of Honest Ed's, I found myself in a whole area
now known as Mirvish Village, and largely given over to artists'
haunts (because, they say, Ed's wife likes to paint); in the trademark
Toronto style, brownstones sat next to open-air cafés, chic boutiques
were scattered among workingmens' residences along the leafy side
streets. Slipping into a store full of architecture books, I happened to
pick up Rem Koolhaas's *S, M, L, XL,* a treatise whose very title
impenitently announces its ideal of a new world made generic, with
cities constructed like shopping malls.

Architects are among the shrewdest readers of our globe, I often
think, not only because it is their job to gauge the future but also
because it is their task to make their most abstract ideas concrete.
Besides, in the modern, postnational globe, many of the leading
architects—Toronto-born Frank Gehry, Norman Foster, I. M. Pei,
and Koolhaas himself—are working in several continents at once,
literally fashioning the international monuments of a new transnational culture. It's not difficult to think of Koolhaas as a cross-
cultural Jane Jacobs of the new millennium, sharing her impatience
with pious orthodoxies and received notions of the quaint, yet translating that iconoclasm into a vision of a "Bastard Metropolis" of the
future, for "people on the move, poised to move on," a community
without neighborhoods or hierarchies or even much of a sense of
shape. "The 'Western,'" Koolhaas writes with typical (if sometimes
excessive) panache, "is no longer our exclusive domain. . . . It is a
self-administered process that we do not have the right to deny—in
the name of various sentimentalities—to those 'others' who have
long since made it their own."

This radical, unideological vision of a city as a kind of motel room writ large made sense to people like me, who'd grown up without a stable sense of base, and who never felt the need to ask whether I belonged to East or West—it seemed as irrelevant as whether I was wearing a white shirt or a blue shirt (and I hardly cared if someone chose to refer to me as an "Indian writer living in America" or an "American writer living in Japan" or whatever tag appealed to them). And as one who felt at home in impersonal spaces, I could not quarrel with the polemical quotes Koolhaas arranges, like the one from Douglas Coupland (another Canadian inspector of tomorrow): "I like hotels because in a hotel-room you have no history; you have only essence." I was even ready to accept that, as Philip Johnson claimed, Koolhaas, the designer of cities more than of buildings, might be to the twenty-first century Empire of Internationalism what Edwin Lutyens had been to the British.

Yet the effect of his wholesale elimination of the past, not in one life but in many, was that Koolhaas's ideal of a "Multi-Ethnic" city was a place like Singapore, a "city without qualities," as he puts it, created out of nothing but an abstract marriage of Confucius and Victoria; a "virtual city," as he writes, in which nothing is random and authenticity itself is a fraudulent notion. Singapore, for Koolhaas, was pure facsimile—almost an architectural blueprint, in fact—in which the red-light district was mowed down to make room for a theme-park re-creation of sin, and the famous old transvestite bars on Bugis Street were rehabilitated to serve as tourist traps featuring "*female* female impersonators."

This was all very well, except that cities, no less than people, rebel against being nothing, and Singapore—a British boarding school with Chinese prefects—had the disconcerting habit of boasting of its British legal system and then, when challenged, talking about its "Asian values." Toronto, by comparison, seemed to me a much more hopeful and witty vision of a world not conforming to the old categories without dwindling into a universal Nowhereland: layer joined upon layer here to form a kind of colorful palimpsest, as in Kensington Market, where what had begun as a Jewish area, and become a place for Ukrainians, Hungarians, and even Portuguese from the Azores, was now a pell-mell mix of Abyssinian, Middle Eastern, and West Indian stores, where a maple leaf flew above a *carnicería* and counterculture types pointed out that Emma Goldman had fought her last battle here, on behalf of Italian anarchists.

Sometimes, too, the multicolored present actually redeemed an unaccommodating past here, not by bureaucratically erasing it (as in Singapore), or by turning it into a food court, but by offering unorchestrated cacophony. I had heard of Christie Pits—a park on Bloor Street—that it was the place where the whole city had turned on its Jewish residents as they played games there (in the thirties, when areas like the Beaches posted signs saying NO JEWS AND DOGS ALLOWED); now, when I went there, it was to find Jamaicans playing soccer in what was largely a Korean and Hispanic area, while Willie Nelson sang "Home Again" above an all-white baseball game. The signs above the public rest rooms denominated UOMINI and DONNE (though people also reminded me that one of Hitler's most vocal supporters lived only a few minutes away, inside a padlocked castle).

The brightest expression of a counter-Koolhaasian vision, though—a lyrical way of rising above differences—came, again, in a novel, from Michael Ondaatje, the latest in Toronto's distinguished line of visionaries exploring a global future. The most radical thing about the people in his *The English Patient* is, quite simply, that they are not hybrid beings so much as postnational ones—the place where they were born or grew up is as irrelevant to who they are as the color of their socks. The "English patient," famously (and dangerously) isn't English (and is an agent), and the sapper defusing bombs for the British army is an Indian (and a Sikh, to boot, a sort of Kim in reverse, whose honorary fathers are not Muslim, Hindu, and Tibetan Buddhist, as Kipling's double agent's were, but Canadian, Hungarian, and English). Nearly all the main characters are actively involved in trying to escape their names, their pasts, their seeming nationalities—the very differences that can only be the death of them in war—and in seeking to achieve a new kind of order as in the desert, where tribes meet and join and fall apart, and "we are all communal histories, communal bodies."

Ondaatje is a poet—meticulous in his details—and the whole book is a vision of this new order, an "Oasis Society" that he calls the "International Bastard Club" (which got softened in the film to the "International Sand Club"). He sets the action amidst frescoes of Eden and pieces of Kipling cake, his characters recite Adam's words from Milton, and read from *Kim*, their names—Hana, Caravaggio, Kip—tell us almost nothing about where they're from, and the places where they live, as floating bodies, are mostly temporary: a monastery, a cave, a lover's heart. At the very time when the very notion of nation-states is tearing the world apart, Ondaatje concentrates on the private destiny of mapmakers (and double agents) who suggest a world in which the individual is sovereign: quite literally a world unto himself, as vast and hard to categorize as a solar system. "Erase the family name! Erase nations!" is their cry: "All I desired was to walk upon such an earth that had no maps."

One of the extraordinary things about reading *The English Patient*, which sets it apart from all the traditional works of English literature I read at school, is that it has no central figure, really, and certainly no point of orientation; it is impossible—and indecent, almost—to ask whether the author is an "Orientalist" or an "Occidentalist," and Ondaatje, with siblings on four continents and an American wife in the Toronto where he's lived for thirty-five years, is unlikely to tell you. Sitting above all provincialisms—and privatizing even the most famous conflict among empires—it dares to suggest a "New Age" in which people can live with a nomad's (or a monk's) freedom from attachments.

The other dizzying thing about the book was that it could feel a lot like contemporary Toronto, where there seems to be no ground zero from which everything is measured; unlike a Los Angeles or an Atlanta, it has a downtown, and one that enshrines the notion of a meeting place of wanderers, but the definition of that space will differ radically, depending on whether you address it from a Ukrainian, or a Serbian, or a Taiwanese perspective. In the end, it seemed no coincidence that the novel Ondaatje wrote immediately before *The English Patient* was about the immigrants who built a great "Prince Edward" bridge to link one side of Toronto to the other.

Because I was caught up in the revolvings of the new here—all the things I'd never seen before—it took me a long while to notice how much of the old remained, implacably, at the heart of Toronto (how much, in fact, of the very heritage I'd grown up among). Walking up Spadina Avenue, in an exhilaration of foreign faces, a Chinese cinema in the place where once there had been a burlesque house (and before that a Jewish theater), a Global Tele-Express stall standing next to Zen Travel and the Club Shanghai (and, on a sunny Sunday afternoon, a Chinese Buddhist monk sitting in the midst of the commotion, knocking clappers together slowly), I saw the Toronto that I'd met in many of the recent novels. Yet only one major block away, University Avenue, parallel to Spadina, defined the center of the city as if it were still a British battle station known as York (and the next main street along, Yonge Street, looked like a junior version of the Avenue of the Americas). Slice Toronto along one north-south artery, and you'd find a seething, spicy, uncategorizable something best described by the Little China restaurant, which advertised "Indian Pakistani-style Chinese food"; slice it a little farther along, and you'd find pure white Highland shortbread.

In all my twenty-one years in England, I slowly realized, in all the months I'd spent in Bombay and Hong Kong and Singapore, I'd never felt so close to the Queen as on the day I spent wandering around the center of Toronto, walking up University Avenue, past the city's grand financial towers, past the nineteen stories of the Princess Margaret Hospital (and, nearby, a slightly wistful statue of Mary Pickford—even "America's Sweetheart" had been born here), and then around Queen's Park Crescent, past the sandstone Provincial Parliament Building, up to the gray Gothic spires of the University of Toronto. The Queen was beaming down at me from every government office I passed, of course. But she was also represented by a letter adorning the walls of Osgoode Hall, the home of the Law Society of Upper Canada (QUEEN'S BENCH written on gold plates outside its courtroom doors, and COMMON PLEAS on others), and even at the top of a nearby department store (CANADA'S STORE / CANADA'S STYLE), where she was sitting with her consort in a photograph, shivering under a blanket in Edmonton in 1951.

Of course the Royal Family would feel more at home in High Toronto, with its English-speaking openness, than in cantankerous Australia or New Zealand, or tropical India or East Africa; the Dominion had not even claimed its own flag till 1965, and for many years the Anglican archbishop had been called Walter Scott (he was now named Aloysius Ambrozic). Surveying the maps at home, the Windsors must have felt warmed by the sight of Kitchener and Waterloo and Cambridge all more or less on top of one another in the suburbs, and when I read the names in the Deaths column of the Anglophile *Globe and Mail*, I could have been back in my school, in the shadow of Windsor Castle, listening to a roll call in 1972: "Beecroft, Bradley, Buckland, Campbell, Currie, Dimock, Dority, Finlay . . ."

Yet what I also came to notice, in and around the grand monuments of Empire, and what made the vision of *The English Patient* seem more plausible, was that something alien was going on here, much as you see African rites and voodoo performed in the old Spanish churches of Brazil. When I went to a department store to inspect a collection of Princess Diana's dresses (assembled in sacramental near-darkness and watched by thousands in a reverential hush), the girl who gave me my ticket was darker than I was, and called Shivani; next to the Arcadian Court nearby (TASTE OF BRITAIN), my tea and scones were brought to me by a man who, as my housemaster in school would have put it, was "born under sunnier skies." The signs under many display cases in the Royal Ontario Museum dutifully complained about the "overtly racist" attitudes of Empire (right under ads for an audio tour of a visiting exhibition from the Victoria and Albert Museum in London, narrated by Prince Edward), and in a book in which I found thanks given to "the Venerable the Archdeacon of Trafalgar," further thanks were given—six lines down—to the "Reverend Jane Watanabe." Outside the backward-looking buildings of the university, there hung a rainbow-colored banner for the Multicultural History Society of Ontario.

This same pattern, of course—Tropical Victorianism in reverse, as I sometimes thought of it—was evident in Britain, too, and in many of its white protectorates: nearly all the staff in the ultraimperial Windsor Hotel in Melbourne came from different corners of South Asia; and the Booker Prize, given to the best British novel to be published each year, had gone to Salman Rushdie in 1981, and, in the next dozen years, to two Australians, a part-Maori from New Zealand, a South African, a Nigerian, a woman of Polish descent, and an immigrant from Japan (the runners-up featuring such modern British names as Mo and Desai and Achebe) before being given to the mongrel Ondaatje. Empire was physically, as well as in other ways, in the hands of its most distant legatees.

But in Canada, again, there seemed a sweeter, more optimistic tilt to the takeover, as if it were being conducted more in a spirit of redemption than revenge: Toronto admitted the very Hong Kongers and Barbadians that Britain had rejected, and served up England to her former subjects in a more open, friendly form. The Continuing Education classes offered at Winston Churchill Collegiate, I noticed, were nearly all in Tamil, Farsi, Vietnamese, and Serbian. What had long been known as Lord Simcoe Day, in honor of a former governor, was now generally regarded as Caribana Weekend, the centerpiece of the city's most exuberant Saturnalia, in which more than a million people danced down University Avenue with no thoughts of boundaries or divisions. When a novel came out here about a British district officer tending to his colonies, it came from the hand of an Indian from Dar es Salaam, born in Nairobi.

I picked up in the Royal Ontario Museum a copy of the newsletter of the Multicultural History Society of Ontario, and was greeted by the following: "The Japanese Canadian experience is very much a Canadian story. It is the story of immigration and the difficulty of settlement, denial of rights and citizenship, expulsion from the West Coast and seizure of property during the Second World War, forced dispersal east of the Rockies and the resettlement of many to Ontario" (an unblinking self-condemnation of the kind I'd seen only in such institutions in Australia and New Zealand). The "Japanese Canadian Redress Settlement," I read at the bottom, was funded partly by the Association of Serbian Women, the Barbados Investment and Development Corporation, and the Toronto Nikkei Archive.

At the very least, I thought, the government was trying, in its earnest, sometimes too ponderous way, to do the right thing, and I felt that there was a public consciousness, a sense of relaxation and even trust between citizen and country that I hadn't seen so much elsewhere. The man sitting along the sidewalk on upper Yonge Street held up a sign that said, disarmingly, $ FOR POT and the "squeegee workers," as they were called, who cleaned my windshield were as often as not young girls with rings in their noses; a sidewalk artist in the new world order was a Chinese man smiling outside the Eaton Centre (CENTRE OF THE MEGACITY) long after midnight on a Saturday night, trying to interest passersby in his handmade signs—YOUR NAME WRITTEN ON A GRAIN OF RICE and PALM READING / ANCIENT METHOD (while a colleague performed the obligatory drawings of Madonna and Brad Pitt).

Toronto had for me a little of the savor of Paris in the twenties, a self-conscious place for people from other places to forge a lively culture based on internationalism ("Writers have to have two countries," Gertrude Stein had written there, "the one where they belong and the one in which they live really"); people here seemed amused at the world, while living at a small distance from it—able, that is, to play Iago as well as Hamlet (not far from the Planet Kensington jazz bar in Kensington Market, and Toronto's Spice Terminal, listing all the major stops on the backpacker's trade routes, a large sign announced GLOBAL CHEESE, followed by the boast "When it comes to cheese . . . we speak your language!"). The hustler working Bloor Street on a sunny summer morning was a man standing in front of two ABM machines (as they're locally known), saying, "I can do your financial services for you. Especially you contact me early in the morning. Accounts, taxes . . ."

I knew that Greeks had recently disrupted the hoisting of the Macedonian flag in Toronto (and the paper had described Sikhs burning an Indian flag at City Hall); in 1992, the city had been shaken by its first taste (since 1837) of what it rather overanxiously called "race riots." Yet there was a steadying quality, too, among the immigrants, and when I went to the Toronto Islands on a Sunday, I saw grandmothers wheeling strollers, and families enjoying picnics— couples courting as if they were still in Hanoi or San Salvador (the "old Canadians" going in the opposite direction, towards their "cottages" in the north).

An Indian on the Toronto map (though he turned out to be from Pakistan) was the young man who picked me up in his cab, one spring afternoon on University Avenue, and said, in the quiet, questioning inflections of his place of birth, "I have, like, lots of Indian and Sikh friends, and they're nice people? Like, I've heard the problems you have over there in India / Pakistan"—the two terms becoming more than ever one here—"they're made by the government? But here we've got a Canadian government, so we don't have those problems?"

We were driving down streets decorated with nine-pounder cannons of the kind used in Crimea and Waterloo, and statues of Scotsmen, past a memorial to a "gun park" and a monument to "those who went out to battle and died for freedom's cause" ("freedom" in this case a euphemism for "Britain"). We were driving towards King Street, past the statue of Winston Churchill that oversees a Speakers' Corner, which, in archetypal Canadian fashion, encourages all speech so long as it's nice ("the Canadian Criminal Code prohibits slanderous statements or statements promoting genocide or hatred against an identifiable group or race").

"In any case," said this new Canadian, "most of the people who've come here, they've come to get away from all that? Like, I'm not interested in those issues?"

It could have been New York, except the man was smiling.

One night, I went to have dinner with my friend David, whom I'd met on a plane down to Havana (he springing out at the first stop to play catch on the tarmac with a boyhood friend who turned out to be the editor of a Canadian magazine called—of course—*Borderlines*). David lived in an area that was now known as Portuguese (most of its signs Italian and Vietnamese and who knows what), and his girlfriend, Alicia, was a shining young Goan Christian who'd spent her earliest years in Pakistan. We sat around their kitchen table, eating tomatoes, munching on olives, the sounds and smells of Portugal wafting in through the garden window. I admired a framed print of Rabindranath Tagore ("Yes. David gave me that for my graduation!") and Alicia's sky blue *salwar kameez* ("I got it in Hyderabad, actually. Twelve dollars. Because it's bright: Toronto needs bright colors").

My eye fell on the box of "Global Frozen White Eggs" that sat by the door, on a program for a conference Alicia had just organized, called Competing Realities (eager to find a voice for her own heritage, she was studying South Asian writers, especially female; David, meanwhile, held Spinoza reading groups every Tuesday night to try to draw closer to his Jewish roots).

"Did you see the paper today?" he was saying now, picking up the *Globe and Mail*. "That piece on the back page about multiculturalism? I went to high school with that woman. Beth! I couldn't believe she was writing so beautifully about the blending of cultures.

"See, when I was growing up"—David, I recalled, was a born storyteller—"we had this really strong nationalism, this xenophobia, and it was directed against Americans! One time—I'll never forget this—I was sitting at my friend Beth's dinner table, and her father was there, too, this quintessential New York Jewish intellectual. He used to cook, and he had polio, but that didn't stop him from getting up between courses to play the violin. He lived as if he were still in New York!

"But to the nationalists, that meant a kind of ambivalence! And one time he was talking, and this other guy at the table, he just said, 'I can't take any more of you Americans!' and he threw his glass—this big heavy glass—over his shoulder. Went right through the window; I'll never forget it."

He smiled at the thought of how far the country had come. "Now, the new form of nationalism is *multinationalism.* This nationalistic impulse is toward all nations. And I love it! It makes me weepy. Ask Alicia—it's true. Two things, they can make me cry: one is the new multiculture we've got here. The other is the lakes and wilderness. Make me weepy every time."

"It's true," said Alicia, smiling fondly. "It does."

"It's a beautiful thing," David went on. "There's nothing else like it in the world. It can bring tears to my eyes, this multiculturalism: the glorious promise of it."

Suddenly, the phone rang—it was one of David's best friends from his "postcollege, choose an identity" days, a full-throated Italian who was playing hooky at the racetrack—and Alicia showed me the complete program of her conference, sponsored in part, I noticed, by the Multiculturalism Programme, Canadian Heritage Department.

"You should come here sometime for Desh Pardesh," she said as he talked with his friend. "You know, the South Asian arts festival they hold every year in the summer. It's really different from most of those things. it's gay and lesbian and bipositive: antiracist, antipatriarchal, anticommunal."

"Sexy, too," said David, returning to our conversation. "Really sexy: all these beautiful young things coming out to party."

"What does Desh Pardesh mean?" I asked, and they both looked startled: a Hindu who couldn't understand a common Hindi phrase.

"'Home Away from Home,'" said Alicia. "I'm amazed you didn't know that."

"The problem is," said David, picking up the strand of what he'd been saying before, "it's all theoretical. Everyone is told, 'Be who you are,' and so everybody is taught to resist. Multiculturalism here is about resisting; it's not about sharing. Like these Portuguese here"— he motioned out the window. "I talk of them, but not in a very friendly way. How many times have I been to their houses?"

"But you can taste Portugal. You can feel it and smell it and see it."

"Sure I can. But on the streets, in the restaurants. That's not the same as being in their homes."

"That's what I was saying," added Alicia. "On the level of food, everyone will get together. But not in a deeper way. Multiculturalism actually increases the distances between us."

This was the pattern I'd got used to hearing in Toronto: high hopes, followed by second thoughts—and I recalled what I'd read in a book earlier in the week. "Except for the odd visit to an 'ethnic' restaurant, we *do* stay with our own kind" was the verdict of an American exile here, who loved the city but found it more "clannish" than any major city he knew. "Perhaps this is a reason Americans, on holiday from their disintegrating cities, find Toronto such a peaceable and agreeable place. What they do not appear to realize is the extent to which this 'peace' is a result of extraordinary self-policing and self-segregation."

And yet, I also thought, here were two people from radically different countries, religions, cultures, and they had found much to join them. Canada was the place where they could put such categories aside.

"See, everyone would like to be closer," said David. "They would like to accommodate themselves more to what's going on. And so, although people are in their own niches, they're being changed, getting less homogeneous than they think they are. The glory of Toronto is that everybody accommodates to the new. The WASPs who rule here, they just handed over the keys to the city. The immigrants who come in don't have to adjust to the city; it adjusts to them. I think of my father, a poor immigrant from Russia, and he came here because it gave him a chance, and was a civil place. And it *is* a civil place."

We sat at the table and talked of Israel, India, Pakistan: all the many places where pieces of our past were scattered. I thought of my drive through the suburbs a little earlier, coming upon one grand monument after another, in the midst of empty fields—a huge oniondomed Ukrainian Catholic church, a mosque, a Salvation Army Korean church, a site for a Durga Mandir—each of them glowering, I'm sure, at the others. (Jan Morris's image would now have to be changed, to one of a hundred arriving immigrant women among a few pale, classically polite "Torontonians.")

"When I was growing up in Malton," Alicia said, matching David's reminiscence with her own, "there were only one or two South Asian families there (now, sometimes, I'm riding on a bus there, and, except for the fact it's comfortable, I look up and think I'm in India. Everyone's South Asian!). But when I was growing up, my best friend was called Julie English. Which was funny, because her family really was English. Our family and hers shared a driveway, and the driveway became this kind of special space.

"And I remember having to explain my skin color to her in terms of suntans and things like that, so that I would be acceptable to her. Because the Englishes were blond-haired, blue-eyed; they had a dog, they had a cottage—the kinds of things my family would never have dreamed of having. And in those days, suntans weren't even very common.

"So when she asked about why my skin was so dark, she was being innocent. But as we grew older, those layers of innocence fell away. When I hit dating age, all my closest friends became these Italian girls, because their families were superprotective of girls and had all these strict rules about dating, just like mine did. And strict rules about what clothes they could wear and where they could go."

"They were probably more Italian than they'd be at home," I said. "Foreignness can intensify the customs we've forgotten."

"Yes. But it was still strange, the way we grew apart."

"Maybe what you regard now as racist really was innocent," I said, thinking that the fact people here seemed so sensitive to even the shadow of intolerance might be the most hopeful, New World thing about them.

"I know. But racism became the convenient language to use whenever we did anything different. If I saved a seat on a bus for a friend and a white girl didn't like it, she'd call me a 'Paki.'" (And vice versa, too: a few days earlier, the paper had reported how a Sikh boy in Vancouver had faked a racial attack on himself so as to get the new haircut and nonethnic clothes his parents had forbidden.)

Alicia told us about the Christmas meals she'd had as a girl—turkey, but with rice "and all these fruits in it" (as in the novels again, the Christmas turkeys of Romesh Gunesekera stuffed with *ganja* and mandarins); she told us how she'd never even noticed that some of her relatives had accents until she'd got an answering machine. Both David and Alicia, I saw, pronounced *project* with a long Edwardian *o*, and *schedule* as if it were cognate with *shh*.

"You know, it's funny: I've noticed that my relatives can be much harder on other Indians than on other groups of immigrants. Almost as if they've learned to internalize the attitudes they hear around them. They'll say, 'Look at those Sikhs! How can they block the road like that for their festival?'"

"My own son," exclaimed David, "he'd never known what racism is till he went to India! Suddenly, everyone was staring at him, wanted to touch him, wanted a piece of him. He'd never had that over here."

For Alicia, however, that was a Western reading.

The heart of Canadian exceptionalism, as we conceive of it at least, lies, of course, in its sense that it's not exceptional; through an unhappy accident of geography, it's the only country in the world that sits right next to the planet's dominant superpower, which it resembles just enough to be reminded constantly of the differences. Sometimes this can strengthen identity, sometimes it can erode it, but the fact remains, as I once heard the director of the McLuhan Program in Culture and Technology say, that Canadians have to look for their own movies in the "Foreign" section of the video store. It's easy, therefore, for Canada to think of itself as one of the world's great afterthoughts, an overlooked Taipei to America's Middle Kingdom; and even as Canadians are routinely asked which part of America they come from, Canadians in America are taken to be full-fledged foreigners: one of the sharpest editors I've worked with in New York was, by virtue of being from Toronto, "technically 'without papers'—or, as my immigration lawyer has it (it's a wonderful phrase), 'out of status'"—and so, while polishing the prose of America's strongest authors, deluged with literature inviting him to learn "English as a second language."

Such a legacy of slights made me feel, often, in Toronto, that even as I was watching it become the Next American Nation, its own people were worrying about why it wasn't the last one. Whenever I would tell Torontonians how liberating I found their town—not stuck in its old image, as England or America might be, and yet not too precipitously clinging to a new one—they would look bewildered, express their pride with an apology or a shrug, define their city by telling me everything it wasn't. One curiosity of being a foreigner everywhere is that one finds oneself discerning Edens where the locals see only Purgatory.

This tradition of self-doubt seemed doubly ironic at a time when so many young Americans, traveling in Europe, painstakingly stitch maple leaves onto their backpacks so they'll be mistaken for Canadians, and when Toronto itself is the *beau idéal* of what the world conceives to be America: for years now, the Canadian city has been Hollywood's favored stunt double, and photogenic stand-in for New York (as Vancouver has been for San Francisco and Seattle)—the North American city that looks most like what an American city should look like (except cleaner, safer, more manageable, and less expensive). When the world dreams of America, it is dreaming of Toronto, though the imagination's trade imbalance continues as Canadians think constantly about America, while America the Beautiful hardly spares a thought for Toronto the Good ("Canada's a beautiful city," I heard a bus driver say at the Atlanta Olympics).

I went one evening to a typically chic, tribal, purple pool-table bar on College Street, and talked about the city with six bright Gen Xers who were making it in the media, music, photography. As the night grew more liquid, and blurred into the early hours, the area around us filling with smoke (all six were waving cigarettes), the conversation turned, as it might have done even had I not been there, to what Toronto really was.

"You know, everyone says that Toronto is the New York of Canada. But I think it's really the Boston."

"Paul says it's actually the Chicago of Canada."

"You know Torontonians are regarded as the Americans of Canada—more aggressive, bullying, always saying how everything's bigger and better at home?"

I asked why it was that Canada has produced such an astonishing line of female singers, especially folkies (from Joni Mitchell and Jane Siberry to Sarah McLachlan and Loreena McKennitt); in response,

someone told me pointedly that its main resource, in fact, was comedians—Rich Little, Rick Moranis, John Candy, Jim Carrey: not
earnest innocents, in short, but satirists. "Maybe because we've got
Americans to laugh at," he said (and, I'd have added, an un-American
sense of mischief to bring to its neighbor's broad spaces).

"You know why all the newscasters in America, all the game-show
hosts are Canadian?" someone else said. "Peter Jennings, Alex Tre-
bek, Robin MacNeil? Because they're all so bland, and speak without
an accent."

"But what about the Cowboy Junkies?" I said, as the local band
played "Sweet Jane" on the system. "Wholesome world-weariness:
isn't that you?"

"Maybe," somebody else said, and Canada's defaulted identity was
turned over and over like a pig on a spit, the same person who told
me the talismanic tale of how Morley Callaghan, the Canadian writer
who'd gone to Paris in the twenties, had challenged Hemingway to a
fight (and punched him out!), going on to conclude, "Toronto's just a
provincial Protestant town" (making me think that that was the country's misfortune in a nutshell, its provinces, instead of states, generating the most dreaded of adjectives).

To see how this uncertain sense of self would play out in what is
effectively Canada's unique (and uniquely un-American) religion, I
went one day to the International Hockey Hall of Fame, or Le Temple de la Renommée du Hockey, as it is even more aptly known in
French. The shrine is located, as it happens, within one of the city's
plushest buildings, constructed in 1855 to house what was then the
largest bank branch in the country (and the original Stanley Cup is
kept in a darkened steel-lined vault that could have been housing the
jewels of the Tower of London at least). Old Canadians and new
were ascending a grand staircase to the Great Hall, a chamber
topped by a forty-five-foot stained-glass dome, with twenty-four

fanned panels depicting allegorical dragons guarding gold from eagles. "For Canada, our national pride and composure hung on the eighth game of the series" said a board that took one through every palpitating moment of the Summit Series in 1972, in which the Canadians took on the Soviets they had originally taught to play the game. A silver coin put out by the Royal Canadian mint to commemorate the victory sat in the display case.

"Our team was made up of a cross-section of the Canadian ethnic mosaic," the explanation concluded, summarizing the triumph— "French Canadians, English Canadians, Ukrainian Canadians, Polish Canadians, German Canadians, Italian Canadians. The mixture of backgrounds was an important ingredient in the success of our team" (how, I couldn't begin to imagine, since the Soviet team must have drawn upon no less a degree of diversity).

Yet for all the national pride, the headquarters of the National Hockey League, administering Canada's religion, was in New York City. At Nagano, only three months before, I'd watched Canada fail somehow to win the gold medal in men's hockey, in women's hockey, even in curling (while the so-called Canadian curse meant, yet again, that a Canadian world-champion figure skater failed to claim Olympic gold). Canada did finally win a much-publicized gold in snowboarding, and then its new national hero was briefly stripped of the medal after testing positive for marijuana.

For me, spending time in Toronto had the same effect as slow adrenaline: here was all New York's intelligence, I felt, with none of the neurosis, and all of London's sophistication, without the sourness. There was a sense of tempered idealism here—an optimism made rigorous by irony—that both warmed my heart and inspired confidence: I found myself telling Torontonians that their city had all Manhattan's software without, so to speak, its hard drive.

Yet Canada's proverbial lack of confidence seemed as impossible to shake as America's sense of being Master of the Universe (however much both were contradicted by circumstance), and when I opened the city magazine, it was to find a whole article listing "the most inept teams in our city's history" (no easy task, it said, given Toronto's "long and storied tradition of abysmal franchises"). At the traveling British exhibition in the museum, someone had been so impressed that he'd written, "It's just too good for Canada," and when the local Blue Jays had finally made it to the World Series—the first non-American team to do so—the Marine Corps had famously unfurled the Canadian flag upside down. Everything seemed fodder for this sad sense of excludedness: while I was in Toronto, a small controversy broke out in the U.S. about the fact that its home-run champion Mark McGwire was using anabolic steroids (legal in Major League Baseball, as they are not in many arenas). Instantly, to my amazement, in Toronto, the discussion turned into an "Us against Them" lament in which people complained that McGwire was being lionized for using the same substance for which Ben Johnson had been stripped of his 1988 Olympic gold medal. Ten years on, the memory lingered of how Canada's world-champion gold medalist had been almost instantly exposed, and disqualified, as a cheat (with black Canadians adding that when Johnson stood on the podium, he'd been acclaimed as a Canadian; but as soon as he was disgraced, he'd been identified again as a "Jamaican").

A few hundred yards away from the International Hockey Hall of Fame, in a corner of the underground labyrinth that stretches for eleven square blocks in the center of Toronto—a shiny, well-ordered Everyworld underlining the clamor of cultures above—I happened into a small bookshop, and decided to see what I could find on Canada. There were two shelves of volumes in all, beginning with the expected picture books hymning the nation's mighty rivers and its untamed wilderness (at the time he was writing, Marshall McLuhan claimed, as many as 250,000 lakes in Ontario alone remained unnamed).

Apart from such *Glimpses of Our Great Canadian Heritage,* though, nearly all the books played out Canada's anguished debate with itself. *Misconceiving Canada* sat next to *Inventing Canada; Symptoms of Canada* was not far from *Scorned and Beloved. Who Are the People of Canada Anyway?* asked "Citizen X" (an "over edu-cated student of Canadian politics who wants to tell the truth"); the copy on his back cover asked, straight out, "Does Canada have a future?"

Marshall McLuhan, in sharing his loonie's worth on this inescapable theme—"The Case of the Missing Face," as Hugh Ken-ner called it—had put a positive spin on undefinedness. Canada's "low-profile identity," he suggested, its "multiple borderlines," and flexible sense of self—all prepared it ideally for our borderless, vir-tual world, and, he went so far as to say, "the Canadian North has replaced the American West." Besides, in the U.S., too, I might have seen books with subtitles the equivalent of *Canada at the End of the Twentieth Century* and *Canadian Social Values at the End of the Mil-lennium, How We Talk About Canada* and *An Essay on the Canadian Identity.*

Yet still it cast a somewhat miasmal aspect—*The Trouble with Canada* sitting next to *Fighting for Canada.* "Instead of asking 'What's wrong with Canada?' author Will Ferguson asks, 'What's wrong with Canadians?'" the flap copy of another volume offered. The title of that book was *Why I Hate Canadians.*

In the U.S., I'd long felt, immigrants had actually breathed new force and energy into the country's sense of itself; by acting as if the American Dream were true, they had helped to make it so. In Canada, I thought the latest immigrants would be performing their most invaluable task if they could remind their new neighbors that possibility could be strengthened, and not undermined, by skepti-cism, and that greatness did not stop at the forty-ninth parallel.

Writers, again, had the potential to be central to this task of self-definition, in part because so many of them, recently arrived in

Canada, were dealing with exactly the same issues, loosed from traditional categories and trying to find new meanings for citizenship and
belonging as they worked to make a peace between their different
selves. Traditionally, an exile is an outsider, worrying at private issues
of divided loyalty and homesickness that distance him even further
from the rooted people all around; but in Toronto, often, a mongrel,
many-headed exile was surrounded by a mongrel, many-headed
city—a community of exiles looking for itself as he was—and so
could find himself central to a city as floating as he was.

So even as the city was schooling me in new terms for foreignness,
its latest immigrant writers were teaching me new ways to talk about
the divisions among foreigners, and among the different kinds of foreignness within them; blessed, often, with identities "at once plural
and partial," in Salman Rushdie's phrase, they were seasoned at discussing how the Janus-headed man could be regarded as two-faced,
and the woman with dual nationality could suffer from double vision.
It is no coincidence that many of the characters in Toronto fiction
are spies, double agents playing one side off against another, or
changelings commuting between opposing sides of a hyphen—in
Chang-rae Lee's powerful phrase, "several anyones at once."

The destinies, the double crossings of these people who think, in
Derek Walcott's phrase, "in one language and move in another" have
become one of the essential themes of modern literature, especially
among those who live between many homes; and Toronto, of course,
has become the spiritual home of those who wish to thrash out the
issue. The two classic paths of exile have long been the ones defined
by James Joyce in Paris (re-creating the city he loved in inex-
haustible, obsessive detail—as it looked on June 16, 1904) and Samuel Beckett, nearby, flying beyond all particulars to some universal
abstract space. In Toronto, to an uncanny degree, the traditions had
been updated, for the international age, by Rohinton Mistry, re-
creating his lost Bombay, and Michael Ondaatje, envisioning a world
beyond nation-states.

It was no surprise, then, that one of the most visible students of
nationalism, Michael Ignatieff, though now based in London, was
born of a mother from Nova Scotia and a father whose own father
had been the minister of education in the last cabinet of Tsar
Nicholas II (his maternal grandparents living on Prince Arthur
Avenue in Toronto); or even that the most vivid accounts of modern
Iraq and Iran I'd read—the other side of the Rushdie debate—had
come from a Welshman who reimagined the Middle East on
Toronto's Balmoral Avenue. Again, as in the Paris of old fancy, there
was a sense that many people had come here specifically to dissolve
nationality, and to subscribe to Wole Soyinka's creed: "I am a writer
and therefore an explorer. My immediate tribe remains the tribe of
explorers."

One day in Toronto, I picked up a local first novel called *The Electrical Field* and found that the text was rich with Japanese words,
though none of them italicized (they were Canadian words now, it
was telling me). When I happened to talk to the book's young author,
Kerri Sakamoto, visiting Japan, she said that she probably felt more
at home in Los Angeles, in Little Tokyo, than in this foreign country
to which she was linked only by a last name and distant grandparents.

Another day in Toronto, I picked up a book called *Borderline*, by
an author who described herself as "divid[ing] each year between
Australia, North America and Europe" and one of whose earlier
works was called *Dislocations*. The author, Janette Turner Hospital,
seemed absolutely to belong to the Ontario where sometimes she
lived; her characters were people thrown across a moving globe
("She felt at ease in airports" is how Hospital introduces her protagonist, "and in the hearts of great cities. Because, she said, they are full
of other people who don't belong—my closest relations"). The action
begins, literally, on the border between Canada and the U.S., a kind
of phantasmal zone where we meet a white woman born in India, a
serial adulterer, and a truck that, opened for inspection, reveals, in
the midst of hanging carcasses, a group of "illegals" peering out,

"refugees from another time and place—the Ice Age, say, or the age of myth"; and as the book develops, its characters seem always to be calling in from foreign locations, sleeping with spouses not their own, living in borrowed places.

Such novels, of course, could be written anywhere—and, in fact, more and more are—but there was a particular aptness in their being set and conceived in a city that had always worried about how exactly it fit into things, and how best it could balance its English and French and American pasts. "A Canadian poet is an exile condemned to live in his own country," the Montreal poet Irving Layton had written, and his friend and running mate Leonard Cohen, in his novel *Beautiful Losers,* writes, "There are no Canadians. There are no Montrealers. Ask a man who he is and he names a race." Only one generation earlier, many of Canada's strongest writers—Mavis Gallant, Mordecai Richler, Cohen himself—had gone to Europe or America to find themselves; now, with the world turning on its axes, suddenly exiled writers were coming to Canada, and what had once been the periphery was becoming a center. In Ondaatje's anthology of "Canadian stories," *From Ink Lake,* the "Canadians" came from Malta, South Africa, India, and the West Indies, and one of the few "indigenous" stories, "The Man from Mars" by Margaret Atwood, tells of how an immigrant looks to the classic white Canadian (she doesn't know whether he's Chinese or Japanese—an interpreter, she thinks, though south or north of the DMZ?—and she doesn't have a clue about what to make of his attentions; he is an alien from another planet).

There is, to all this, a simple economic component: publishing has become as global as every other business nowadays, and writers, in any case, are speaking to—and for—readers as hybrid and many-souled as themselves. Successful novelists often become perpetual tourists, visiting all their markets on a never-ending tour, in many languages, so that airport departure lounges and hotel rooms are the settings in more and more novels, and publicists who used to talk of copies sold now boast of how many languages they've reached (Arundhati Roy's debut, *The God of Small Things*, went into thirty-six languages, from Estonian to Croatian, in its first year). Even the advance words of praise on a postcolonial novel—I'm thinking of Chitra Divakaruni's *Mistress of Spices*—come from a perfectly balanced group, including one Latino, one Chinese woman, one black man, one Japanese Hawaiian, one Japanese American, and, for fairness' sake, one white Southern male.

But beyond such details, there was a higher and more exacting sense that the new international writers—the writers of Harbourfront—were actually creating visions for the postnational future, inspirations, in a way, for Toronto. Rushdie, for example, invoked the ideal of Moorish Spain—a *convivencia* in which Christians wore Arab clothes, Jewish literature was translated into Castilian, and Moorish styles prevailed—as a model for his beloved, multicultural Bombay (being threatened by fundamentalists who would wish to shrink the Many into One), while Caryl Phillips, by setting some of his last novel in fifteenth-century Venice, was looking at the birthplace of the ghetto (where Jews were quarantined), which also, in Shakespeare's vision, looked for its defense to a Moor. In 1913, even before the Mexican writer José Vasconcelos dreamed up a whole new miscegenated race—*la Raza Cósmica*—the Canadian C. J. Cameron, noting how people were coming into Canada from all directions, was anointing it "a vast laboratory of grace in which God is fashioning the final man. The final race will not be any one nationality but will be composed of elements from all races."

While I was visiting the Harbourfront Writers' Festival, Carol Shields won the Pulitzer Prize for fiction, traditionally given to the best American novel of the year. Shields, an American who'd lived in Canada for thirty years, had also, however, won the Governor-General's Award for fiction, given to the best Canadian novel of the year, and been a finalist for the Booker Prize, for Britain's strongest novel. The best thing about contemporary writers—and Canadians in particular—was that no one seemed to know where they were from.

My last night in Toronto, I found myself in the Bar Italia (where, I was told, groups of Serbian kids sometimes got together with groups of Croatian ones, in a conscious effort to show their parents that they had entered a new country) on ever-more-mingled College Street. Ours was a typical Toronto gathering—five people, four of whom were from parts of South Asia as different as Jerusalem and Damascus. Our talk, as so often in the modern city, was of home and belonging; the simplest questions brought not-so-simple answers.

"You're from Lahore, I gather," I said to the tall Muslim man I'd just met—a video importer—and he said yes, while adding that he'd grown up here, and his parents lived in the suburbs; he'd been educated at Vassar, and his girlfriend was a Christian, from Hyderabad, in southern India.

"Once Indians start migrating," he smiled, "they never stop."

"But that's true of all diaspora people," offered our token white, a Jewish man with two non-Jewish sons. "Look at the Jews. The company I work for, they're all Latin American—that is, people who left Europe in the late thirties, settled in Uruguay, Peru. Now they're here. It could be the U.S., it could be anywhere. Once you leave home, you could be anywhere."

The man from Lahore was not convinced; his partner, after all, was born of parents who'd grown up in Mysore, then moved to England, and then to Kansas, and then to Nova Scotia, where (this was the New World) they settled down in a small village filled with other Christians from Mysore.

"They think I'm a traitor," the woman said in a husky drawl that was pure America. "They still have Indian passports; I've got two— British and Canadian."

"Why Canadian?"

"Because when I was in high school, I wanted to become a page in the House of Commons. And you have to be a Canadian to work in the House of Commons."

I looked at the two of them—Muslim and Christian, dark and fair, India and Pakistan: the man from Lahore was here because he wanted to recruit Indians for his company, and the ones in India were banned from visiting Pakistan: it said so on their passports. So he had to come all the way to Toronto to find South Asians who were technically Canadians.

"The two of you would probably not have gotten together if you'd been at home," I said.

"That's true," the man acknowledged.

"Also, here I could appreciate our commonness more," the woman added. "I mean, I felt more comfortable with a South Asian because I knew we shared certain assumptions."

"That's right! When I came to the U.S., as a seventeen-year-old from Karachi," her partner said, "all my friends were Jewish. It wasn't a conscious thing, but something in the way they interacted with their parents, and the values they had, their relation to their grandparents, I could relate to."

"I know what you're saying," said the Jewish man, motioning to his Indian partner. "As soon as I met her parents, I felt at home. The way they spoke, the way they acted with her, the smell of their house, the feel of it: I was in my aunt's house. I felt instantly at home, comfortable; I fell asleep!"

This was how conversations went in Toronto, all the old categories dissolved, none of us able to tell—or needing to tell—who was Canadian and who was not, which person was the Indian born in Pakistan, which the Pakistani who'd grown up here. There were Christians and Jews and Muslims and Hindus (and none of the above) in our group of five, yet what brought us together was precisely the fact that each of us was surrounded by four different religions.

"But don't you think the world is retribalizing?" the young man from Lahore asked me.

"Yes. But on nonnational grounds. It's forming into tribes based on Web sites, communities of interest, affiliations described in nontraditional ways. The beauty of the present is that we can find ourselves in the company of the cultures that we never expected to encounter otherwise. I mean, forty years ago, you would never have had the chance to find you had so much in common with someone from a different country and religion and group; they would have been the enemy."

"That's true," said the oldest at the table. "Take this place; it's so chichi now. Toronto the Diverse began right here, with the Italians; but now it's all changed. This place used to be pool tables and faded wallpaper and gangsters; now it's all international."

"Yes," said the video importer, going back to the earlier strand. "And maybe what I related to in her was the isolation she felt, as a Christian from Hyderabad. I'd felt the same as a boy from Karachi in Poughkeepsie. In those days, I used to read all the time: I read Salman Rushdie in Mississauga, and then I read Philip Roth in Lahore, *Portnoy's Complaint*. And that made perfect sense. To me, Philip Roth wrote the Great Pakistani Novel!"

These were the surprises that hardly took us back now; the private revolutions we spoke at dinner tables in open-air cafés, crossing cultures, abandoning boundaries without even noticing we were doing so. "At home," I'd often make no effort to extend myself to the people who looked and thought like me; abroad, I'd find myself drawn to the piece of home they represented. And for many of us, now, all the world was abroad.

As the evening drew on, the conversation turned, as it often had that week, to the recently completed World Cup, and how "the streets would fill up with cars and we wouldn't even know where the people were from. They'd be waving flags, and we'd have no idea what flags they were. Suddenly, there'd be a thousand black guys racing down the street!"

"One day England was playing Argentina," someone said, "and I had to work that day, and I really didn't want to know the result, so I could watch the game on TV when I got home. So I didn't log on to the World Cup Web site, and I made sure not to listen to the radio, and I pretty much screened myself off from the news all day. I did everything I could to keep myself in a state of ignorance. But then I went outside—on my way to see the game—and there were all these cars honking their horns, and people waving Argentinian flags. The streets were all Argentinian!

"In Toronto!"

THE GAMES

"Best thing about Brooklyn? All the countries of the world are here.

Worst thing about Brooklyn? None of us get along."

— An elderly black man in Wayne Wang's and Paul Auster's mock documentary, *Blue in the Face*

W henever I wish to get an update on the state of our One World order—how much it is coming together, how much it is falling apart—I try to take myself to an Olympic Games. The image of global harmony the Games consecrate is, of course, a little like a gossamer globe entangled in a crackly cellophane of bureaucracy and bickering, and all the world knows, more and more, how much our official caretakers of purity are tarnished by corruption, as much off the field as on; to attend an Olympiad these days is to sit amongst 100,000 security guards, with teams of Doping Control officers under the stands, while Olympians in the shadows collect illicit payoffs.

Yet for all these reminders of the world outside, the Games do provide as compact and protected a model of our dreams of unity as exists, with hopeful young champions from around the globe coming together in an Olympic Village that is a version of what our global village could be, to lay their talents on the altar of "friendly competition." At their best, the Olympics pay homage to the very sense of "world loyalty" that Whitehead called the essence of religion.

I've been to six Olympiads in the past fifteen years, and at five of them I've been responsible for every sport on offer, and so found myself racing from cycling to three-day eventing to badminton arenas every day from dawn till after midnight for sixteen days. Every city had its scandals, of course, and no one could soon forget the terrorists of Munich, the bankruptcy of Montreal, yet on every occasion I found myself stilled by the simple, piercing humanity of it all: the sight of Derek Redmond, the British hurdler, hobbling over the finish line with his arms around his father's shoulders, the older man having raced down from the stands as soon as he saw his son pull a hamstring; Iranians trading pins with Iraqis in the sanctified neutral zone of the Olympic Village Plaza; the people of Barcelona streaming out into their spotlit streets, for night after balmy night in 1992, so delighted were they to have their Catalan culture discovered by the world.

The Olympics pose a curious kind of conundrum for people such as me, of course, if only because they affirm affiliation to nation-states in an age that has largely left them behind, mass-producing images of nationalism and universalism without much troubling to distinguish between them. They ask us to applaud the patriotism of others while transcending the patriotism in ourselves, and they draw our attention to the very boundaries that are increasingly beside the point (I, surrounded by cheering fans waving flags, am often reminded how difficult it is for the rootless to root for anyone, and, reluctant to ally myself with a Britain, an India, or an America that I don't think of as home, generally end up cheering the majestically talented Cubans or the perennial good sportsmen from Japan).

Still, there's something almost primal—tribal, you could say— about the nationalistic sentiments the Games release, and, in spite of the fifty-foot Gumbies on the skyline, they touch a spark of sweetness that leaps inside us like a flame: forty thousand Japanese stand in thickly falling snow to cheer their ski jumpers to victory, and even Norwegians (or hardened journalists) who've come all the way around the world to pursue their own agendas can't help but smile and say, "Congratulations!" The Games begin with the forces of 197 nations marching out behind flags, strictly segregated and almost military in their color-coordinated uniforms; they conclude, just two weeks later, with all the competitors spilling out onto a central lawn, till you can't tell one team from another. The colors run.

. . .

Backstage, away from the scripted tableaux of the cameras, the Games unveil a more human and vulnerable side to international relations, which helps to correct, and sometimes to redeem, the grander shows of global unity. I remember once in Barcelona escaping the ranks of seven hundred TV cameras and the hundreds of thousands forever climbing up Montjuich, past Bob Costas's floodlit throne, to try to catch my breath in the relative calm of the strictly guarded Olympic Village, a utopian global campus complete with its own religious centers, hair salons, nightclubs, movie theaters, daily newspaper, and even mayor. Walking around the stylish new complex, built beside two private beaches, I found myself suddenly surrounded by three very small, very polite, slightly lost-seeming figures. They were archers, from Bhutan, as it transpired, who couldn't quite orient themselves amidst this crush of alienness.

They'd never seen a stadium before, one of the teenagers explained, and they'd never seen a subway. They'd never seen a high-rise building or a working television set, and they'd never seen a boat. I remembered how, in their landlocked home, I'd watched students practice archery between the willow trees behind the Druk Hotel, their arrows whistling through the silent air.

None of them had ever boarded a plane before, one of them went on (in careful English—the Raj having penetrated even those places that television could not reach), and none of them had ever competed before crowds (besides, Olympic rules are so different from Bhutanese that they were all but guaranteed of last place). "I thought Barcelona was going to be peaceful, like Thimbu," one of the young students said. "It's so busy!" The Olympic Village alone was almost the size of their capital.

At that point, the country's first (and only) defense minister interceded to give a more official account of his nation's meeting with the world (he doubled as the Dragon Kingdom's Olympic Committee), and to make the right diplomatic noises; yet what stays with me, many years later, is the image of those guileless, bewildered, excited souls, one day in a hidden kingdom where everyone has to wear medieval clothes and all the buildings are constructed in fourteenth-century style, and the next, in the midst of the greatest planetary show on earth. And then, after two weeks surrounded by exploding flashbulbs, to be back in their forgotten home, where the only concrete mementos they'd have of the surreal episode would be their photographs. Whenever she had a free moment, one of the archers told me, she hurried off to take pictures of the harbor. She'd never seen an ocean before.

The figures who oversee our official dreams of harmony—the 115 members of the International Olympic Committee—are often described as presiding over one of the last great empires on earth. Their doyen is the Grand Duke of Luxembourg, and the chief of drug enforcement for all its thirty-one years has been a Belgian prince. It was a count, famously, who assured the world that it was fine to hold the Olympics in Hitler's Berlin (provided a few embarrassing signs were covered up), and the current, increasingly embattled president, Juan Antonio Samaranch (once the sponsor of a Barcelona roller-hockey team), likes to be addressed as "Your Excellency."

Boutros Boutros-Ghali, while head of the United Nations, cited "Olympism" as a "school of democracy"; in fact, its self-elected rulers, officially appointed for life, administer a realm in which their word is final, and senior citizens trump athletes at every turn.

The Olympic Movement is a force that no one should underestimate. It has its own museum, near its headquarters in Lausanne, and it brings out its own glossy magazine; it boasts an honorary degree from the Sorbonne, and recently instituted a prize for Sports Science that, worth $500,000, is the most lucrative such award in the world, other than the Nobel Prize. At Cultural Olympiads, Nobel laureates in literature discuss the future of the soul and at International Youth Camps, children absorb the principles enunciated in a seventy-four-page Olympic Charter. The organization even, like every self-respecting government, now has its own front-page scandal, with six different investigations uncovering improprieties.

In recent years, this unofficial empire has expanded dramatically in part through alliances with the two great powers of our global order, multinationals and the media. Thus, eleven of the world's largest companies pay roughly $40 million each for the exclusive right to attach themselves to the Olympic Rings, the Mascot, and the Torch, and U.S. television networks alone sign contracts worth $3.55 billion. The Olympic Rings, its organizers boast, are "the most recognized symbol in the world," and 90 percent of all the people in the world with access to a television—3.5 billion at last count—watch such events as the Opening Ceremonies.

It's tempting to conclude, in fact, that the Olympic Movement is, in its way, more powerful than the UN, especially as it gets to show off its triumphs on the global screen (while the UN has to try to sort out real-world messes behind the scenes, with everyone criticizing it in what has become an ethical Babel). To this day, the IOC has more member states than the United Nations (whose founding it predates by forty-nine years), and all are pledged to an ideal Oversoul that rhymes with our highest, sweetest dreams.

Like anyone who attends the Games, I could never help squirming a bit at all the contradictions involved in the marketing of idealism, and a mischievous part of me rejoiced in the Jacobean notion of would-be Olympians trying to bribe the Princess Royal with a fur coat; when Samaranch reminded the world of the Olympic Truce in 1998 (an "ancient concept for the new millennium," as canny Olympic strategists dubbed it), he was conspicuously clad in a Mizuno coat, in a stadium equally conspicuously naked—by Olympic decree—of advertising. The IOC keeps dozens of lawyers on hand to protect the very terms *sacred torch* and *peace festival;* even the slogan "The World Is Welcome Here" is jealously copyrighted Olympic property. When Japanese fans were once seen to wave a banner saying, SEIKO, in support of their speed-skating star Seiko Hashimoto, they were told to desist, lest their cheers be interpreted as support for the watch manufacturer that is now an Olympic Gold Sponsor.

Yet always the hope persists that men will be wiser than their institutions, and, in a world where cultures are clashing by the hour, nobody objects to seeing the competition among nations turned into a game; when I was young, I remember largely scoffing at the self-serving claims of Olympic chieftains like Avery Brundage: "The Olympics is perhaps the greatest social force in the world today." Yet these days, even such uninvolved observers as the director of the Institute of American Studies in Beijing, while naming the dominant powers of our "multipole globe," cites not just the classic nation-states but also "such actors as the World Bank, CNN, International Olympic Committee and Exxon."

My own role in all of this, as a longtime member of the "Olympic Family," observes its own rituals, as pronounced as those of any church, and every time I prepare to attend an Olympic Games, I feel as if I'm entering a foreign country (albeit a migrant one founded on the principles of transnationalism).

Well over eighteen months before the Games begin, I apply for what is in effect a visa—a coded credential—and upon arrival in the host city, I am generally greeted by one of the fifty thousand smiling volunteers, who will take me to an Official Accreditation Center. There I am "processed" into a bar-coded entity whose ID will get me through the magnetometers that guard every venue, hotel, and subimage center. To thank me for my troubles, I am given a McDonald's pad, a Media Monster pin from Xerox, a Coca-Cola backpack, and a penguin wearing the IBM logo, so I can serve, in effect, as a walking advertisement for the Worldwide Olympic Partners (whose dream, their ad explains, is of "Creating a World With Principles").

There are often four times more journalists than athletes at the modern Games—fifteen thousand of us in all—and we are stationed in the Main Press Center (or MPC) and its high-tech cousin, the International Broadcasting Center (or IBC). These multistory buildings, constructed more and more according to an international plan, look like monitor-filled airline terminals from which not beings, but words and images, will be beamed around the world. Icons and logos and universally understood pictograms fill their long corridors, and vending machines serve up free drinks (so long as they're made by Coke), Global ATMs belch out banknotes (so long as they're accessed by a Visa card). The MPC has a post office and a travel agency and private offices for seventy different organizations, nearly all of which buzz with local middlemen—or, more often, middle-women—mediating between the host nation and thousands of foreign bodies (while six thousand "language agents" stand ready to turn Finnish into Korean).

For those without a large company at their back, there's a vast Common Work Room lined with rows of telephones and fax machines on which more than six hundred correspondents can send their copy back to Guinea-Bissau or Costa Rica. Around them, giant Panasonic screens broadcast all the action as it happens in twenty-six different venues.

The Olympics today are largely a made-for-TV production, based around the needs of crews from 160 different countries (to the point where South Korea, for example, in 1988, actually instituted daylight saving time just for the duration of the Games, so that its high-profile events, already scheduled for the morning, would chime even better with U.S. prime time). More even than the Academy Awards or a Miss Universe contest, the Games are a television producer's dream: every day for sixteen days, they can be relied upon to produce shocks, stirring heroism, and images that shake us to the core (and even villainy touches something universal—the showdown between Tonya Harding and the figure-skating rival she'd attacked, Nancy

Kerrigan, was one of the most-watched programs in U.S. television history). And so, as the largest Image Center in the world processes photographs for free (so long as they're Kodak), TV networks spend $7,500 for every dollar they spent in 1960.

And I, for three weeks every two years, move through a parallel universe that looks like a sleeker, on-screen version of our global future. Every day I travel from the MPC to the MTM (Media Transport Mall), by way, often, of IOC offices, on a special network of MTM shuttle buses. There are TVs on all thirty buses, broadcasting the events we're going to; there are TVs in the twenty-four-hour McDonald's outlets in the MPC; there are TVs next to every press seat at the larger venues, with closed-circuit programming of all the other events (Channel 101 plays a "scenic video" of the Olympic Torch burning for eighteen hours every day). Even in the small dormlike rooms in the Media Village (or, as it was nicely called in Nagano, the "Medea" Village), there are TVs in every room so that we can follow the action on BBC or CNN or the special Olympic network. We watch ourselves watching ourselves, with "videos-on-demand."

Perhaps the central event in my own Olympic preparation is a visit or two to the Olympic city a few months before the Games begin (and a few months before the local government tells its citizens to smile at foreigners, its taxi drivers to say "Have a nice day!" and its restaurateurs to stop serving dog: in 1998, in Nagano, even the local professional gangsters observed an official Olympic truce). The cities that compete for the honor of staging the universal road show are, nearly always, somewhat anxious and prideful and prickly places, with something they want to prove to the world. The Olympics provide an almost unique opportunity to address the whole of humanity at once, and to make over one's image at a single stroke: thus, Barcelona, in 1992, was determined to show the world that it belongs not to Spain but to Catalonia (maps appeared on its streets in which Spain did not even appear, and King Juan Carlos himself, while opening the Games, was obliged to speak in Catalan); Seoul, in 1988, aspired to muscle its way into the Executive Club of nations much as its hated rival—and unacknowledged role model—Tokyo had done in 1964; and Atlanta, in 1996, was keen to present itself as the "Next Great International City" (and one day after it won the bid, its paper ran the simple headline WORLD-CLASS!).

Yet what this means, in practice, is that small cities, which are often relatively provincial cities, become the focus for our grandest global expectations, and all our hopes of crossing boundaries converge on a place that is not always accustomed to looking past its own borders. As the cost of staging an Olympics mounts (to $7 billion or more), many of the people they're meant to help rise up against the costly gambles—even placid Stockholm was hit by a series of bombs recently, aimed at disrupting its Olympic bid (while in rival Rome, citizens brought out bilingual pamphlets entitled *Ten Good Reasons to Say No to the 2004 Games in Rome*). What it also means is that one of the fiercest competitions on display at every Games involves the representatives of second cities handing out favors in an attempt to prove themselves worthy of being a future Olympic host: Bishop Tutu appears to promote the cause of Cape Town, and Istanbul stages a Turkish Blues Night (complete with THE MEETING OF CONTINENTS tote bags), while Athens and Osaka spend $20 million or more on freebies and $1 million lunches and law-abiding Toronto complains about the necessity of bribing.

In its desperate attempt to prove itself a major global player (by winning the rights to the 2000 Games), Beijing closed down factories in anticipation of IOC visitations and released some of its famous dissidents (while placing other potential troublemakers in a lunatic asylum). According to the *New York Times* correspondents who won a Pulitzer Prize for their coverage of China, at least one mentally retarded man was beaten to death, lest his untelegenic presence

distract visiting Olympians from the banners saying A MORE OPEN
CHINA WELCOMES THE 2000 OLYMPICS.

In the case of Atlanta, which had won the right to host the "Centennial Games" over the sentimental favorite, Athens ("Coca-Cola won
over the Parthenon Temple," said Melina Mercouri bitterly), I flew
in exactly a year before the Opening Ceremonies to see how the city
of Reconstruction was preparing for its moment in the global sun. I
knew next to nothing about the place beforehand, other than that it
boasted the best growth rate of any city in America, and had become
a kind of shrine, worldwide, to black middle-class achievement:
its police chief, its congressman from the Eleventh District, the
editorial-page editor of its *Constitution,* and all its recent mayors
were African-American. Having pulled itself up from the ashes of the
Civil War, and having built its gleaming towers in a city where blacks,
fifty years before, had not even been allowed to vote, it called itself
now "the Phoenix of the South."

Almost as soon as I arrived, I could see that Atlanta was an
Olympic city in more ways than one. "In the beginning," said the
monitors in the arrivals lounge (broadcasting the CNN Airport Network), "the world was a big global market," and videos on every side
instructed one on how to set up a business in this "Competitors' Paradise." Walking through Hartsfield felt a little like walking through a
curriculum vitae: this was the "world's fastest-growing airport," I was
told, and home to what had once been the "world's largest passenger
terminal." It was the largest public employer in the city (Delta being
the largest private employer), and Atlanta itself was said to be the
"fastest-spreading human settlement in history," eating up five hundred acres of field and farmland every week. All this went a little
strangely with the fact that the door on the APM (or automated
people mover) was broken, and the robot reciting instructions in several languages was incomprehensible in all.

Just next to the mess of scaffolding that denoted the Baggage
Claim area, the city had set up a special Martin Luther King, Jr., display. THIS AREA TEMPORARILY CLOSED, a sign outside it said.

I lined up at the Hertz desk to collect a new Aspire—this seemed
the way to "do as the Romans do" in what I'd seen described as the
"new imperial Rome"—and, driving into town, I felt myself moving
into the Olympic Planet. Cars already had Olympic flames on their
license plates (my own had a CENTENNIAL OLYMPICS plate), and
buildings flashed numbers denoting how many days remained before
the Opening Ceremonies (366). On the AM radio, the "Official
Olympic News Source" was advertising the "Official Power Source of
the 1996 Games" and even the Electrical Workers Union downtown
had at the top of its red brick block the message COME CELEBRATE
OUR DREAM.

Atlanta had already been transformed by winning the Olympic bid
(through the curious system of balloting whereby a city that collects
many second-place votes can beat one that collects more first-place
ones); and one day after it was named an Olympic city, three corporations had named it their new national headquarters. By now, eighty
thousand new temporary jobs had come into being, and even in LAX,
where I boarded my plane, the terminal for Delta (the "Official Car-
rier of the Olympic Games") was a forest of Olympic shot glasses and
Olympic Gourmet Biscuits.

Yet Atlanta at first sight looked like nowhere on earth: suburb led
to interstate led to off-ramp led to suburb. I passed an Economy Inn,
a Quality Inn, a Comfort Inn, a Days Inn; I passed a Holiday Inn
Select, which gave way, soon enough, to a Holiday Inn Express. On
every side of me were look-alike office blocks and landscaped driveways, mirror-glass buildings and office parks: all the interchangeable
props of an International Style that could, in its latest incarnation, be
called Silicon Neo-Colonial.

I'd been told to look out for the Perimeter area (one of three
Perimeter areas in Atlanta), and so I got off the interstate onto

Perimeter Center West, and drove in the direction of Perimeter Pointe. I passed business parks and condo worlds, shopping centers and gated subdivisions—the urban equivalent of bottled water. Then at last, spotting another parking lot, a patch of grass, and some more concrete landscaping, I saw my "Hotel of Distinction."

"Hi there," said the woman at the desk. "If you want to look around, Perimeter Mall's across the street."

I walked out again and found myself in a web of stores almost parodically placeless—Home Depot, Home Place, Computer City, the Cosmetic Center. On every side were strip malls, minimalls, strip clubs, and shopping malls. And though this would have been no less the case in Los Angeles, where I'd woken up this morning, or some "Metro Lite" sprawl around Houston, Atlanta seemed curiously ready to define itself by its twenty-one malls—Cumberland Mall was advertising itself as "the first mall to sponsor a United States Olympic team"—and forty, by one count, airports. I felt myself in the "Phoenix of the South" in a less-than-mythic sense.

This was, in part perhaps, because Atlanta is a convention city, in the business of providing homes for people passing through; every year, 1.6 million souls walk through its streets with their companies' names next to their own above their hearts. Where other cities base their economy on natural resources or local industry, Atlanta had long been a center of emptiness and hospitality, a service-industry, Information Highway McSuburb before the terms had been invented: in 1930, though only the twenty-ninth-largest city in the country, it already was the second-largest in terms of office space, and a local had boasted, "Office buildings are to Atlanta what automobiles are to Detroit." Reading the literature in my room—"The complete conference center is a traditional meeting environment," it said, "focused to provide the ultimate small meeting experience"—I felt as if I had landed up in a city by Marriott, a place that was global by virtue of being featureless; as if a city had been replaced by a scenic functional base as picturesque and not quite real as the forests you see on the background of personal checks.

Picking up the tourist magazine by my bed, *This Week Atlanta,* I found a special boxed review of a strip club ("This architectural landmark serves as a shrine to adult entertainment"); in the Yellow Pages, there were 132 listings for the Babbitt Aachen Aaland Aalborg escort agency alone. One lap-dance palace boasted in the tourist magazine of its "corporate atmosphere"—its address was 1876 Corporate Boulevard—and, having cited its free valet parking, Internet address, and on-premises ATM, concluded, like some graduate of a middle-management workshop, "MORE THAN JUST ADULT ENTERTAINMENT . . . A CLUB WITH VISION."

The next day, when I woke up, the sky was still blue-black (parts of me, just off the plane, were still in Osaka, parts were in California), and when I turned on the TV, it was to see Andrew Young, the former mayor who had done so much to give the city an international profile, gathering with a host of other Olympic luminaries in the predawn dark to celebrate the one-year mark before the opening of the Games. Television crews from Savannah, from Chattanooga, even from New York, were assembled outside the still-unfinished stadium to join "Atlanta's Official Station for the Olympics" in broadcasting the pep rally, scheduled for 6:45 a.m. (before the heat became oppressive).

For me, the best commemoration of the city's global hopes seemed to be a visit to the birthplace of its greatest son, and so I got back into my Aspire and, pulling onto I-85, drove past any number of Host Inns and Dial Inns and corporate condos, past the sign GLOBAL BURGERS (Think Globally, Eat Locally), to the Freedom Parkway.

The area around Martin Luther King's birthplace is now a national park, visited by more people every year than go to Mount Rushmore or the Vietnam Veterans War Memorial. There were sightseers there when I arrived from Florida and the Carolinas and the Ivory Coast, mostly black, following a crisp young black woman, in a National Park Service uniform and Smokey the Bear hat, around the reverend's home, his church, and a museum in his honor. In the Martin Luther King, Jr., Center for Non-Violent Social Change, a huge portrait of Gandhi dominated the entrance, and in the broken little cafeteria, a sign was up for WOE (The Wretched of the Earth, Inc.), a group that helped the homeless.

I thought King would have been touched to see how much the world had moved towards a sense of global brotherhood since his death twenty-seven years before. Outside one of the houses associated with him, a white man was sitting with his black wife, on the porch, watching their two boys play, as the words rolled out of the speakers—"America is, essentially, a dream . . . a dream of a place where men of all races, all nationalities, can live together." Behind the King Center, an AMC van bore a motto of pride on its license plate—BLACK-OWNED—and in back of the Ebenezer Baptist Church (where King had preached, as his father and grandfather had done), a van was advertising something called Integrated Resources, Inc. There was a Martin Luther King Church in Atlanta now, and a Martin Luther King Chapel of Love; the state capitol itself, as in some fairy tale of freedom, stood at the intersection where Washington ran into Martin Luther King.

Yet just where the Historic Monument ended, only a block or two from King's house, Auburn Avenue was as desolate a hell as ever I have seen. Broken windows, boarded-up storefronts, abandoned houses with nothing but a Huey Newton poster here and there, an OPEN TO THE PUBLIC sign outside a dark and silent Elks Kitchen. Auburn Avenue called itself the "Street of Pride," and, in 1956, *Fortune* had deemed it "the richest Negro street in the world"; once, Bessie Smith and Cab Calloway had played there, and in King's time, it was a sign of all a black community could achieve. Now, though, five minutes' walk from the one-thousand-room hotels downtown, and within sight of the corporate blocks of up-and-coming Atlanta, there were few signs of the $25 million revitalization campaign the city had promised for it, or the local "Bourbon Street" Atlanta's director of planning had foretold: just kids hawking T-shirts of the black-power salute at the '68 Olympics, and people walking around looking lost.

At the very end of Auburn Avenue, where it bumps up against the glowing towers of modern Atlanta, a new African American Panoramic Experience was shown on all the maps: a 97,000-square-foot high-tech center that was "the planet's greatest show on African-American hope and heritage," according to the Peach State Black Tourist Association. It consisted, when at last I located it, of an empty parking lot, a temporary entrance, and a sign that said PLEASE EXCUSE THE INCONVENIENCE.

"I think," said a caretaker, with an apologetic smile, "they may get to work on it after the Olympics are done."

I walked back down towards the King Center, past the overgrown vacant lots and the listless men standing next to signs that said DOWNTOWN IMPROVEMENT DISTRICT. It was here, I'd just heard, that King had reminded his congregation that it was rich not just in spiritual terms but in actual ones: the collective wealth of black America, at the time, was greater than that of all but nine nations in the world. Now, I recalled, almost half Atlanta's children lived in poverty, and fourteen thousand homes were without telephones. By some counts, the "city too busy to hate" (as it called itself) had the highest violent crime rate of any city in America: King's own mother, our guide had explained, had been shot, six years after he was, while playing the Lord's Prayer on the organ in the Ebenezer Church, for no reason other than the whim of a "black deranged individual."

I sat down again on the porch outside his home, and as the sleepy summer morning drifted on, I looked out at the Ritz-Carlton down the street, the silhouette of the World Congress Center, and "the tallest hotel in the hemisphere." Men were sashaying blearily down the side streets, in and out of their shotgun houses, and my own car seemed precariously parked, a block beyond the sign that said FREE-DOM WALK ENDS.

"The world in which we live is geographically one"—the words, beautiful and wrenching, boomed out into the street. "Now we are challenged to make it spiritually one. We've made of the world a neighborhood. Now we must make it a brotherhood."

I could see another reason why the Olympics, and their mass-market globalism, are not universally popular—the opposite reason, in a sense—when I went to inspect Nagano, the rural counter-Atlanta that was the site of the next Olympiad. By the time I arrived, the old train station, which had long presided over the city as a two-story traditional temple of sorts, to usher pilgrims to the great Buddhist center of Zenkoji down the street, had been pulled down to make way for a space-age, video-filled terminal with a McDonald's at its south entrance, a McDonald's at its north entrance. Nagano had long prided itself on being the prefectural capital farthest in time from Tokyo (because there is no airport there); now a superexpress bullet train put it within seventy-nine minutes of city holidaymakers. Futuristic new stadia had been erected all around the unpretentious country city in the shape of a "fresh breeze," in one case, and in others "a drop of water" and a "range of mountains." In Zenkoji itself, amidst its forty dark-roofed temples, CBS had erected a tall glass tower, where members of its two-thousand-person crew (as numerous as all the athletes in attendance combined) could look down on a 1928 UPS mail truck now set up to commemorate another Worldwide Olympic Partner.

The temple's monks, it should be said, had been eager for the exposure and increased revenue, and Japan is more than capable of effecting such transitions without an Olympic juggernaut. Yet still it was strange to see this apple-cheeked, down-home city famous for its noodles now togged out with two official Olympic songs, four official Olympic "support songs" and four other promotional ditties that had received the official Olympic imprimatur—as well as five official posters, seven "official sports posters," and one fifteenth-century landscape poster just for the Opening Ceremonies. Nagano had won the bid for 1998, it was later claimed, because it had given IOC delegates video cameras, where its rival had handed out disposables.

"Every household in Nagano has to pay thirty thousand dollars for the Olympics," a local professor complained to me at a Christmas party in a tiny dark village in the Japanese Alps, its streets narrower than those of the Main Press Center corridor. "And for what? Now we have four ice arenas. Maybe we need one—but four? And now we have a one-hundred-million-dollar bobsled and luge course. Do you know how many people in Japan practice bobsled and luge? Fewer than two hundred. They've changed Nagano, and they can't change it back."

When the new train station put up a sign that said WELCOME TO NAGANO, with a painted torch on it, its bosses were told to take it down, because the torch was protected Olympic property; when *oyaki* dumplings were suggested for the Olympic Village menu, caterers had to decline because "Yamazaki Baking Co. hold the rights to sweet bean-jam buns."

Nationalism, in the Olympic context, took the form of a director of catering urging his troops, "We should regard even a slice of meat and a piece of tomato as representatives of Japan."

Yet for all such absurdities, the chance to be the center of the globe, if only for two weeks, remains as unstoppable as a runway scandal, especially as the world tends to focus its attention more and more narrowly upon a few single points, and the mergers we see in business find their counterpart in consciousness. The Olympics are designed to encourage a commonality of vision, in Emerson's sense (all of us focused on the same ideals), yet just as often they create a kind of community of television, all of us looking at the same images being instantly replayed. The upshot of this universal exposure is that more and more people descend on the hyperevent—not just the 2 million fans eager to enjoy sports and exoticism amidst the excitement of a nonstop carnival but also that whole shadow realm of people who make up our Greek gods in the celebrity culture: O. J. Simpson and David Hasselhoff and Kathy Ireland and George Foreman, here to partake of the greatest photo op on earth.

The Olympic song is written by Andrew Lloyd Webber (in three languages), and Celine Dion and José Carreras show up to belt it out. Carlos Saura directs the movie (in Barcelona, at least) and Annie Leibovitz does the photo shoot for *Time*. Hiro Yamagata designs the official poster, and the producers of *Jurassic Park* join the author of *Schindler's List* to make an IMAX epic of the Games.

In the ancient competition in Olympia, Plato and Herodotus and Pindar and even Diogenes used to fill the stands; now we have their equivalents in a motley assembly of athletes who want to become personalities, and ex-athletes who are working as commentators, and commentators who have become stars in their own right, and ex-stars who are developing talk-show "projects."

"What's the Olympics about?" I once heard Arnold Schwarzenegger shouting at me, above the din of a private upstairs reception in Planet Hollywood, celebrating something called the Inner City Games, sponsored (noisily) by Speedo. "It's all about fighting off setbacks and getting over hurdles. I learned about friendship through sport, I learned about overcoming obstacles; I learned about setting a goal." Around us, a whole assortment of semi-demi names—Evander Holyfield and Edwin Moses, Dexter King and Mayor Bill Campbell—mingled and photogenically mixed. "Where would I be without sports?" Arnold concluded his highly quotable sermon. "On a farm in Austria."

Outside, *Frankenstein* was being enacted in puppet form and an American Indian Pow Wow was offering "Alligator Demonstrations" and "Living Villages" in an "inter-tribal festival," not far from where Ladysmith Black Mambazo was doing its thing. Itzhak Perlman was giving a concert the same day as the Blues Brothers, and when I went to a women's basketball game, I saw Chelsea Clinton in the same general area as George Steinbrenner ("Women are becoming more marketable," said the U.S. center, Lisa Leslie, before slinking away to her next gig as a fashion model).

Outside the stadia, where tens of thousands gathered, Jews for Jesus were handing out pamphlets saying, "It's not too late to shot put your sins and triple jump to Jesus," while Islamic missionaries were distributing "A Welcome to the Olympics" brochure (which, when pressed, they admitted consisted of verses from the Koran). It was strange to think that Baron de Coubertin had revived the Olympics almost as a tribute to Empire (traveling around British boarding-schools to pay reverence to the "superior powers of the Anglo-Saxon world"); now they seemed a monument to the International Empire.

The entire Games, in fact, can sometimes seem to be little more than a full-blooded embodiment of Daniel Boorstin's classic argument in *The Image*, with more "human pseudo-events" (in his unforgettable phrase) piling up than at a political convention or a Vegas prizefight. One moves, at times, through crowds of "image directors" and "atmosphere managers," promotional flunkies from Reebok and professional optimists, with Saddam Hussein's eldest son over there (he's the head of the Iraqi Olympic Committee), and some flustered spokesperson over here, calling you by the name she's trying to read from your security tag.

In a universe in which names are more and more a floating currency—the only kind of value known around the world—the Olympics become a global stock exchange. Tipper Gore is writing a column for *USA Today*, Mary Lou Retton is doing color commentary for whichever network will have her, and Albert Grimaldi ("Occupation:" says his official biography, "Heir to the throne of Monaco") is riding on the Monegasque bobsled team for the fourth straight Winter Games.

And just below this grand assembly of all the temporary deities of our bold-face universe exists, unnoticed, its shadow side, in the people who appear all around the tunnels and corners of the stadia,

selling inflated tickets they've bought in bulk. They come from everywhere—Germany, Istanbul, Canada—flying from special event to
superevent (often on Business Class), and making a killing off the
discrepancies between supply and demand. While the official sub-
culture of "pinheads" swaps collectibles near the Ethnic Import
Plaza and the Society for the Buckwheat Noodles stand (no mere
hobby—Saks Fifth Avenue, to take but one example, has issued an
Olympic pin that's worth $340,000), the unofficial side of globalism
gathers round the edges: a Turk whispers to a Japanese, "*Speed-o
ticket-o?*" and then mutters something in German to a Swede so his
customer won't understand.

"Our life is like the great and crowded assembly at the Olympic
Games," Montaigne quotes Pythagoras as saying. Which is a backwards way of saying that the Olympics are less an interlude from life
than the thing itself in condensed and homogenized form.

My own response to all this, at every Olympics I attend, is to try to
escape the swarm of microphones, and to seek out the nonevents,
the regular, daily commotions that belong less to soap opera than to
situation comedy. This is never very hard, especially when so many
cultures are collecting all at once, and the Olympics, for me, are
often a happy carousel of moments that belong more to Virginia
Woolf than the TelePrompTer, with something resolutely human
breaking through the rehearsed affirmations of "tolerance and competition." Seoul was a hockey game in distant Songnam Stadium,
where rent-a-crowd matrons in billowing blue-and-yellow *hamboks*
sang mournful threnodies and dutifully donned and doffed their caps
in time to a scratchy melody crackling out of a handheld cassette
player (for the Dutch team, they waved tulips; for the Indians,
merely flags); Barcelona was a deserted country baseball field where
black-and-yellow butterflies landed on my knuckles as I sat cross-
legged on the ground and watched volunteers hand-operating a

scoreboard featuring Roman numerals. Nagano was a curling rink where women from the suburbs of Saskatchewan, in windbreakers that said MIKE'S MOM, cried, "Come on, button boy. Stop, baby, stop!" next to sleeping babies and bewildered Japanese grandmas waving KAMIKAZE banners. (The city had erected, next door to the gym, a Museum of Curling, which consisted of two half-bare display cases containing a signed brush, a nineteenth-century crampit, and all ten issues of the now-defunct Japanese magazine *Happy Curling*).

The International Olympic Committee stages a group shot of the Family of Man, and an uninvited miscreant appears in the upper-right-hand corner, making an inverted peace sign. English athletes at the Opening Ceremonies, gathering under the stadium, sport I SPEAK ENGLISH buttons (thus showing, in fact, how English they are) and the Iranians (forty men and no women, all arriving in dull beige POW sackcloth) refuse to walk behind a woman in the Parade of Nations. South Koreans cheer on North Korean skaters (an act for which they could be imprisoned at home), and in the disco in the Olympic Village, teenagers cross every language barrier just by giggling.

In Albertville, I watched the Byronic heartthrob Alberto Tomba ("This is Alberto-ville," he announced, even before winning two dramatic golds) through the eyes of the Philippine team, a sweet and slightly confused twenty-one-year-old from Cornell who didn't know much about the Philippines and had come largely to impress an unimpressionable girl back home. He felt a little weird, he said, representing a country whose language he hardly spoke, especially since, as a rich doctor's son born in Buffalo, he was standing for so many who live in bushes and under money-changing agencies on the streets. "If I had grown up in the Philippines," he confessed, "I probably wouldn't be here."

Yet the psychology major with braces on his teeth, asking three Moroccan skiers to pose with him before his tiny Sure Shot, was precisely the kind of person the Olympic Ideal was meant to encourage,

and not only because he was talking about dreams while more successful Olympians were discussing their $121 million contracts in
private Reebok press conferences. When he finished seventy-first—
the most successful Philippine result in Winter Olympic history (and
well ahead of many other downhillers from India, Costa Rica, Brazil,
and Taiwan)—he was greeted not by cheering crowds (they had left),
but by the Philippine Olympic Committee ("my mom and dad"),
bringing him two bags of M & M's.

A surprisingly large number of Olympic moments are just like that,
and often, surrounded by émigré linguists and other Global Souls, I
wandered around the Olympic Village in the evenings, watching the
fresh-faced kids of every continent trickle into the private cinema
that was showing *Toxic Event* and *Altered States,* or crowd into the
cybershack where they could E-mail the homes and friends they
missed. A tall Jamaican, in thick jacket and bobble hat, was using his
free telephone card to shout endearments to a girlfriend in the tropics; frightened-looking North Korean skaters, who missed such
resources at home, were banging away at the Blast City games in the
jam-packed video-game room.

"Excuse me. Are you from India?" I heard on the streets of
Nagano one day, and turned around, to see a young man, cool in sun-
glasses, and fluent in American English, who, when I asked, turned
out to be from New York, Tokyo, Bangkok, K.L., the UAE, and
Kyushu (a "diplobrat," in short, who'd grown up everywhere).

"Are you Japanese-American?" an American nearby asked him.

"Japanese-Americanized," he responded with what I found to be
characteristic silkiness.

Yet at the Olympics, more than anywhere, there is a parallel world
on-screen, and one of the most disconcerting things about the modern Games is seeing the new biculturalists move back and forth
between planes of reality, the fourteen-year-old putting aside her

stuffed bear and picking up her best-selling "autobiography" as the TV invites her to turn herself into a "human-interest story." Even some of the youngest today—perhaps especially the youngest— seem to have intuited the heart of Boorstin's thesis, that the hero has been replaced by the celebrity, and the most winning "real person" on TV is the one who can best play at being a TV character. Once, Boorstin writes, we looked in our heroes for traces of the handi- work of God; now we search in them for the thumbprints of their publicists.

I remember once watching a backstroker, not very well known, make the most of his brief moment in the global spotlight, after win- ning a gold medal. "Those experiences made me what I am today," he said, effortlessly going through deaths in his family, injuries that had almost crippled him, losses that had left him waiting for four years. "I asked myself a lot of whys. Really what matters is not what we do in the pool, and what medals we win. What I've learned is that I'm not just a swimmer, and that I'm probably a better man than a swimmer."

To be honest, I knew that I, in the same position, would have reached for sound bites just as energetically, though no doubt less successfully —indeed, I did so every time I went on book tour—and the nature of public discourse is to give the public what it wants: locker-room interviews are the Homeric recitations of our time. Yet still, as I heard this young champion, on the greatest evening of his life, say cheerfully of his bitterest rival, who'd deprived him of a gold before, "I thanked him for beating me," I realized that what was sobering was not so much that he didn't mean it, but that he did; even his most heartfelt sentiments came out as if rehearsed for "plau sibly live" transmission.

In all these ways, again, Atlanta seemed the spiritual center of Olympic dreams, with its bottom-line internationalism, its corporate optimism, and its go-getter's sense of the profits that could be made from ideals. "Atlanta is a pom-pom city," a friend of mine who'd been born here said. "Miami, where I used to live, has great vitality but no PR; Atlanta has no vitality but great PR. Everybody here's got their cheerleading outfit on." Once, famously, Mayor Maynard Jackson had hired an adman to find ways to market the city better: the pundit had suggested billboards in outer space and streets named after corporations.

As I began to drive around the Golflands and Girls-R-Fun outlets (sometimes wandering for long spells around parking lots where every other car was identical to mine), I was startled to see how unsure of itself the twin city of Olympia seemed. As a typical visitor, I was introduced to the "largest cable-supported dome in the world," and then to the "second-largest convention center in the U.S."; I was told that I was surveying the "world's largest granite outcropping," conveniently close to "America's First Regional Visitor's Center." Going through Atlanta was like going through the bulleted highlights of a company's annual report: I saw "the largest institution in the U.S. devoted to puppetry as an art form," "the largest black-powder cannon ball still found in the United States," "the largest urban park built since the war." It was hard to imagine Milan or even Jogjakarta boasting of "the largest toll-free calling area in the nation."

Atlanta's problem, I surmised, was that it had plenty of global reach and almost no global clout. Everyone relied on it, but no one spared a thought for it. For seen in a certain light, Atlanta was a central player in making the global economy go round. It was home to Coca-Cola, "the world's most famous trademark," and the center for CNN, "the largest news-gathering organization in the world." It was the headquarters of Holiday Inn, "the largest hotel chain both in name and reality in the world," and the home base of United Parcel Service. Delta, with its "Magazine of International Culture" and "World's In-Flight Shopping Mall" placed in every seat pocket, had its hub in Atlanta—had, in fact, pioneered the very notion of a hub in the city once known as Terminus.

Yet none of these features had brought Atlanta the status it felt it deserved. A tenth of the world got its news from Atlanta, 195 countries got their soft drinks from Atlanta, Hartsfield was soon to claim to be the busiest airport in the world ("Even when you die," I often heard, "you change planes in Atlanta"); yet the city seemed to hold less fascination for the globe than a Dallas or even a Santa Barbara. As in some shadowed fairy tale, all the superlatives in the world could not turn bigness into greatness. Being global and being central were very different things.

I went to pay homage to the CNN Center one of my first days in town, and found myself in a giant food court, with a Turner Store on one side, a Medalist store on another, and four fellow sightseers standing around nearby. (CNN asserts its global interest by offering tours in Turkish, Farsi, and Korean, as well as Serbian, Croatian and Norwegian.)

"Where are you all from?" the friendly man from Ohio asked the other three, who were clad in Hard Rock Atlanta T-shirts.

There was a long, long pause. "Iraq," the father finally said.

The Ohioan was clearly taken aback. "Iraq?" he said, nervously, backing away just a little. "Well—well, that's fine. If you're from Iraq, you're from Iraq."

A guide took us up the "largest freestanding elevator in the world," and, when we got to the top, he asked us to introduce ourselves.

"What kind of name is that?" he asked of the man in the Hard Rock Atlanta T-shirt.

"It's Arabic," the man confessed, and again there was a long silence. CNN might broadcast to Iraq, but it certainly didn't seem to know what to do with it.

Insofar as Atlanta did have glamour for the world, moreover, a large part of it seemed to reside precisely in the part it had worked so hard

to erase. Soon after leaving the CNN Center, and its continuous-loop
playing of *Gone With the Wind*, I found myself in the Road to Tara
Museum, a place that had been recently opened in the basement of
the once-famous Georgian Terrace Hotel to peddle the Burning of
Atlanta to the world. Inside were crinoline dresses and musket balls,
Hotchkiss shells and details of old plantation life—all the artifacts of
a slave culture, in fact, that David Selznick had turned into a central
part of the world's imagination. A high percentage of the visitors,
according to the guest book, came from far away—Brazil, Romania,
Ecuador, Germany, and, especially, Japan, young Japanese women
coming here, often on their birthdays, as to a holy site (the story of
Rhett and Scarlett is so popular in Japan that it was once turned into
a nine-hour musical with an all-woman cast). "I'm so happy to be
here," one exclaimed in the visitors' book. "I remembered old days,"
another exulted.

Margaret Mitchell had decreed that her home be destroyed upon
her death, so that she could enjoy at least the privacy in death that
she had been denied in life. But the prospect of Olympic visitors
from around the globe had moved the city to set about restoring her
house, and talking of a $50 million Gone With the Wind theme park,
and a renaming of a central square, Margaret Mitchell Square. Even
the video-distribution system for the Olympics was due to be named
Scarlett. Yet restoring the past in a city that had pledged itself to the
future made for contradictions that no one in Atlanta had quite
sorted out: the Loew's Grand, where *Gone With the Wind*'s gala pre-
miere had been held, had survived a massive fire in 1978, only (as the
Road to Tara Museum related) to be "torn down for the property
value"; the historic Hotel York next door was now another Days Inn.

That evening, I went to Fulton County Stadium (another landmark
due to be torn down after the Olympics, but, for years now, one of
the inescapable backdrops of cable TV, Ted Turner having taken to

broadcasting his Atlanta Braves games around the nation daily, thus turning them into "America's Team" on-screen). Tucked away in the middle of some beat-up neighborhoods known as Mechanicsville and Peoplestown, the place was as Atlantan as McDonald's apple pie. An ad for Office Depot graced the left-field fence, and in many of the stadium's rampways, Info-Vision screens projected the business news of the day; even the rest rooms were plastered over, as I'd never seen before, with ads for army supplies, for divorce agencies, for golf.

Every single vendor in the stadium—even the ones in the upper deck, somewhere behind the ATM machines—wore a button proclaiming THIS BADGE CERTIFIES THAT I HAVE COMPLETED TRAINING IN ALCOHOL AWARENESS.

Yet within the outlines of this right-thinking, business-minded, slightly puritanical new city were the faces of an older one, peeping in from another century. They were wearing EX-WIFE FOR SALE baseball caps and T-shirts that said JESUS EXPRESS: DON'T LEAVE HOME WITHOUT HIM. They were yee-hahing, and shouting injunctions at the black players on the field (amazingly, the only black faces in the place were playing ball or selling snacks). "I never saw peanuts in a bag before," someone cried behind me, waving a five-dollar tomahawk in the face of a startled blonde; someone else (the person who had written OLYMPUKES GO HOME downtown, or helped sponsor the billboard quoting George Washington's "A free people . . . must be armed"?) was saying, "You're so dumb, you tried to change the channel on a TV dinner."

I'd brought along the autobiography of Atlanta's greatest star, Henry Aaron, to read between the innings, and as the game went on, I read how Aaron, while closing in on Babe Ruth's record for the most home runs hit in the major leagues, had received 930,000 letters in a single year, or thirty-five times as many as any American outside the realm of politics. Nearly all of them had come from fellow Atlantans, he wrote—supporters of his Braves—and as he drew closer to claiming baseball's most prized record for Atlanta, he'd received more and more letters, addressed "Dear Jungle Bunny" or wishing death upon his loved ones. "I hope lightning strikes you, old-man four-flusher," one not very extreme correspondent had written; others had promised to shoot him or "take care" of his family if he came within twenty homers of the Babe.

By the time he finally secured the record, Aaron concluded that "all that Atlanta had to offer was hatred and resentment."

The fact of racial division, of course, was not unusual; but what made Atlanta singular, in my experience, was its hope that growth rates and slogans alone could make inequities go away. Be good for business, the "Atlanta Spirit" kept telling its citizens, and business will be good for you: "more people want to relocate to Atlanta than to any other major city," it reassured people in no position to move at all, and *Fortune* magazine has declared ours the fourth-best city on the planet for doing business, it reminded desperate souls hardly inclined to savor the Dow-Jones listings.

After a short while in Atlanta, I began to feel that the city's greatest energies went into covering up the wounds it could not heal (as it had done with myths of racial brotherhood from Brer Rabbit to *Driving Miss Daisy*). As I drove around the city of megamalls and superstations, I found locals telling me, over and over, how Alonzo Herndon, the founder-president of the Atlanta Life Insurance Company, had started life as a half-black slave—the owner of a barbershop. I got reminded, again and again, that Herman Cain, the head of Godfather Pizza, had been born to a black chauffeur, who drove Coca-Cola chairman Robert Woodruff around. I heard how Atlanta was the site of the National Black Arts Festival and home to the alternative black spring break, Freaknic. Why, not only did it house "the largest concentration of black colleges in America" but in one of them—Morehouse—there was even an Institute for Managing Diversity.

It began to seem, in fact, as if the deepest division here was not so much between black and white as between those who were willing to buy into the belief that profit curves could be the answer to suffering and those who were not. In the *Atlanta Daily World* ("the oldest black newspaper in America," its offices on Auburn Avenue), I read vivid accounts of black debutante balls, and in the *Atlanta Tribune,* a magazine devoted to the needs of go-go young black executives, I read, "In a business sense, Dexter [King] could succeed in managing, marketing and advertising 'The King Legacy' to heights possibly equaling the heirs and business associates of Robert Woodruff [the Coca-Cola Co.] and Walt Disney [the Disney Co.]" For those who endorsed the Atlanta vision, it seemed, equality could be packaged like Mickey Mouse.

For those who did not, though, it must have seemed as if the Civil War had never ended (and one reason why so many civil rights victories were won in Atlanta, of course, was that so many civil rights battles had been fought here). In the local paper, letters every day raged against "occupied Atlanta" and staunchly opposed the removal of the Confederate Stars and Bars from the Georgia flag (while want ads nearby solicited "old Ku Klux Klan outfits, burnt Klan crosses and other civil rights memorabilia"); meanwhile, in the main mall in town, Underground Atlanta, stores were selling signs that said PARK-ING FOR AFRICAN-AMERICANS ONLY and mementos from the National Negro Baseball League, where the Black Crackers had been the answer to the local minor-league power (run by Coke), the Crackers.

Atlanta had, in fact, been thrashing out the Olympics' central theme—"Can we all get along?"—since the time when Charles Maurras, visiting the first modern Olympiad, had said, "When differ-ent races are thrown together and made to interact, they repel one another, estranging themselves, even as they believe they are mix-ing." Yet the debate that had begun here exactly a hundred years before, at the grand Cotton States and International Exposition—

Booker T. Washington suggesting black and white work together but
apart, like the fingers of a hand, W. E. B. Du Bois denouncing that as
the "Atlanta Compromise"—was still going strong after the murders
of Martin Luther King and Malcolm X. Atlanta regularly reminded
us that it was the "Capital of the New South"; less often did it recall
that the term the *New South* had been coined in 1886.

On my first few days in town, I simply couldn't get over how small the
new Olympic host was. I knew it was sometimes referred to as a "forest in search of a city," and that part of its charm lay in its proximity to
nature, its roads following the zigzags of ancient Indian tracks; but
still I was amazed to find that downtown itself scarcely stretched for
five blocks in any direction: it felt to me as if San Jose were preparing
to host the world. Yet there seemed no point in seeing Atlanta only in
its worst light, and so, after a few days, I moved out of Perimeter
Center and into Buckhead. Buckhead is the center of gold-fixture
Atlanta (an "extremely competitive hospitality atmosphere," as the
locals have it), and the center of Buckhead is the flagship hotel of the
Ritz-Carlton chain, built next to the company's global headquarters.
The Ritz issues a full-page treatise on "Guest Attire," which it places
in every room, noting that "ladies may wear dresses or evening suits"
in the Dining Room and that jackets are "preferred" for gentlemen
even at the breakfast table. It serves afternoon tea every day in its
white marble and mahogany lounge, and guests are reminded that
"sterling silver strainers" are deployed, and "fine English bone china
and tea cups." To pick up his sugar cubes, a visitor is offered "silver
tongs."

Just five minutes away from the Ritz, as I drove down the leafy,
gracious lanes that house Atlanta's most established powers, edging
past Tuxedo Road and the other areas sometimes known as "Coca-
Cola Row," I saw real estate notices pointing to EUROPEAN VILLAS
and advertising ENGLISH TUDOR AND CARRIAGE HOUSES. I went

inside the Governor's Mansion and was shown, by gracious docents, its English fireguards and Italian marble, noble paintings of Confederate heroes looking down on us. In Swan House, nearby, I was introduced to faux marble in the bathroom and, instead of electric lights, fake candles; copies of the English magazine *Country Life* were scattered, as if carelessly, around the tables, and in the place where ancestral portraits would be hung in the English country house it was designed to resemble, the 1928 confection had put up generic pictures of old people.

Back in the Ritz, I found that one magazine in my room ("The Guide to the Civilized South") was devoted almost entirely to costume parties and charity balls, with a special pull-out section on "The Women of Polo"; another, *The Season*, consisted of picture after picture of lily-white women in their coming-out dresses (in between ads for cosmetic dentistry), one of the girls actually graced with the name of Memory.

Yet Buckhead's grandest claim to international status seemed to reside in the two large shopping malls that guard the Ritz like tutelary lions. One of them placed itself in a list of the world's most important squares ("St. Peter's Square, Union Square, Red Square, Trafalgar Square, Times Square, Lenox Square"); the other simply announced, "World Class City. World Class Facilities."

The malls were certainly spectacular—the equal of anything I'd seen in Bangkok or Cape Town—and in one of them I came upon a Snooty Hooty and Co. outlet, in the other a Successories franchise. Phipps Plaza seemed to stand for the very notion of mass-market exclusiveness, with its sweeping staircases and polished brass, a concierge standing amidst the white columns of Monarch Court to direct me to the Nail Elite outlet and a Hair Artisans salon, the Civilized Traveler shop and the Silver Spoon Café.

A DIVISION OF A 150-YEAR-OLD FRENCH COMPANY said the signs all around. JEWELRY IN THE SOUTH SINCE 1887; A TRADITION SINCE 1985.

It would be silly to make too much of this—silly, even, to make as much of it as Atlanta does—but the fact remains that it was at the Ritz (where "shirts must be worn at all times" even in the Fitness Center, and "name-badges must be removed in the public areas of the hotel") that my sixteen-dollar Payless Shoe Source loafers were filched within seconds of my placing them in the corridor to be cleaned.

Such petty mishaps can happen anywhere, of course, but they strike a less happy note in a city that is constantly reminding you of how civilized it is (and, in a lifetime of traveling, I had experienced such thefts only in South Africa). When I checked out the next morning, hopping shoeless to the reception desk (in violation of every tenet of the "Guest Attire" credo) and being ushered, in my socks, into a stretch limo to be taken to a Benny's outlet in a nearby mall to repair my loss, I noticed that the friendly young bellboy deputed to accompany me was the first black person I'd seen around the Ritz.

I remembered then, thinking back, how, going into a fish restaurant downtown for an expensive business lunch, I'd seen homeless bodies huddled on the spiral staircase, seeking shelter from the winter cold; and I thought back to the ragged men who'd come up to my car at red lights, as they do in Addis Ababa and Calcutta, to clean the windshield.

The impression I was beginning to form of Atlanta was perilously close to the first impression I'd had of it, coming down into Hartsfield: of a futuristic, globally linked web of terminals surrounded for as far as the eye could see by untamed wilderness.

One night, as I was driving back towards Buckhead, the bright neon towers of downtown behind me (and the sign for EQUITABLE, as always, saying only ABLE), I passed a sign informing me that the interstate was closed. Instantly, I took the next exit off the expressway, and felt myself falling through a crack in the Chamber of Commerce's brochures, into some unlit no-man's-land. Girls were walking along the unpaved highway in cutoff shorts. Men were huddled in the empty parking lot of a fast-food joint, gathered above some figure crouching in the dark. A policeman's red light was turning, turning, turning outside a run-down motel (COUPLES: $14), and, in the middle of the street, for no reason I could discern, small fires were burning.

The liquor stores with bars across their windows, the ribs shacks that looked as if they'd been looted long ago—none of the places here looked eager to welcome visitors. Rough music was pumping out of Harem Lingerie (ALL-GIRL STAFF) and another such place called Lady Relax, and, as in some night-town inversion of Buckhead, every face I saw was black. I needed to get directions, though, so I pulled into a vacant lot, and walked into a bar. Girls were sitting on stools in the near darkness, their nipples bare for customers' inspection.

In terms of exposure and global influence, the Olympics probably enjoyed their heyday, ironically, during the darkest days of the Cold War, when many of the world's most bellicose powers realized that the Games were a perfect forum for showing off the strengths of their systems and conducting war in peacetime clothes ("Military Patrol," after all, had once been an Olympic sport). Thus, twenty-one nations staged a noisy boycott in 1976, because a New Zealand rugby team had visited South Africa, and the U.S. led sixty-five other nations in a boycott of Moscow in the next Summer Games; in 1984, the Soviet Union returned the favor by leading its friends in a boycott of Los Angeles. At that time, many nations became more or less full-time Olympic factories, to the point where East Germany, with twelve thousand professional trainers and scientists generating brilliant new methods of cheating, won more gold medals than the U.S.

in 1976 (thanks, in part, to a cunning Machiavellian rereading of the Olympic spirit, whereby they concentrated on individual sports instead of team events so as to get the most bang for their buck). The East Bloc supported its stars with state-sponsored salaries and sinecures; the Western nations did the same with advertising contracts and television gigs.

These days, in the Games as everywhere, power politics have been translated into hard cash—the Games have been seen as highly lucrative ever since Los Angeles made a profit of over $200 million in 1984—and the IOC has added MTV-friendly sports like snowboarding and mountain biking, while hushing up (its critics claim) potentially damaging violations of its doping policy (because asthma-medication stimulants are allowed in the Olympics, 60 percent of the U.S. team in 1994 claimed to be suffering from asthma).

And as loyalty has been privatized and affiliation has begun to be conceived in virtual ways, the Games have had to adapt to a new world, in which markets cut through all national distinctions. This was evident in Barcelona, where a group of not very like-minded athletes marched out behind a straggle of twelve flags, as part of the so-called Unified Team of the Former Soviet Republics. It was even clearer a few days later when Michael Jordan, the most celebrated Olympian on the planet, threatened not to stand before the American flag if he was forbidden to wear his Nikes. The corporation had become the defining nation-state.

It is dangerous to make too much of all this—in ancient Greece, too, the best athletes routinely hopped between cities, going where the money was, and no ideals of "amateurism" ever prevented them from being rewarded for victory with jobs for life and statues in their honor. Yet what quickens our sense of modern athletes selling themselves to the highest bidder—classic commodities in a very free market—is that sports has become as great a force as Hollywood, almost, in working the global market (to the point where few of us think twice nowadays about seeing the Miami Heat take on the Detroit

Pistons in Tokyo, or hearing that Washington's team is led by a seven-foot-seven Romanian movie star who can dunk over a seven-foot-six Dinka tribesman). In 1998, the National Hockey League actually interrupted its season to send its stars to participate in the Olympics (having seen the National Basketball Association gain huge world-wide exposure in the Summer Games); the only trouble was that the North American league now contains so many Russian and Swedish and Slavic players that neither the Americans nor the Canadians reached the finals in a sport they professionally control.

The Olympians, meanwhile, find themselves not always knowing whether they're coming or going in a world where the flag is being eclipsed by the logo and the strongest Kenyan runner is not in evidence because he's in the process of becoming a Dane. Many an Olympic city these days is dominated by the latest Nike Town (though Nike is not an Official Partner), and in Nagano, for example, the whole world was warmed by the sight of two Kenyan skiers, complete with colorful Olympic stories (neither had ever seen snow till two years before), until it was revealed that both were, in fact, Nike constructs, having been discovered and sponsored by the giant shoe company as the hottest novelty item this side of the Jamaican bobsledders. "An Olympic athlete running in a Hertz uniform is a generation away," Mark McCormack, one of the strongest agents in sports, has said, and a festival that depends for its very existence upon the rivalry between nation-states (and the contradictory wish to show that we're all one under the skin) is being forced to push its square pegs into the round holes of a world drawn by Jackson Pollock, in which, people say, there will soon be "no Japan, only Japanese."

In 1996, the entire Canadian 4 x 100 relay team came from the West Indies (and was competing, of course, against other teams from Britain, France, and Trinidad, full of West Indians); Mark McKoy, a Guyana-born, English-bred product of Canada (living in Monaco with his German wife), was somehow running for Austria. And China's age-old supremacy in table tennis was being challenged only because the U.S., Canada, Great Britain, Japan, and Austria (again) were all being led by Chinese players.

"An athlete is always competing for himself," I heard Bart Veldkamp say unapologetically after becoming the only athlete to break a Dutch monopoly in five-thousand-meter speed skating. Veldkamp, too, was Dutch, as it happened (and passionately cheered on by ranks of orange-clad fans with a nine-piece brass band), but he had figured out that his best hope for success lay in becoming a Belgian—in fact, the entire Belgian Olympic team.

"I was born in Holland," he told the world's press, while flanked by Dutchmen. "I skate for Belgium. But if you start looking at the moon and ask, 'Where do you come from?' I come from earth."

As I got ready to leave Atlanta at the end of my reconnaissance trips, driving past the "Complete Apartment Communities" for the final time, and taking my leave of the faux antique villas, I began to wonder how it would ever get on with the world, given that its sense of internationalism seemed such a local one (a true cosmopolitan, after all, is not someone who's traveled a lot so much as someone who can appreciate what it feels like to be Other). The most global thing about it, in fact, seemed to be its divided nature: Atlanta did not know what it was exactly—even what it wanted to be—and so had ended up as a model of the aspiring city at the end of the millennium, high-rising office blocks coming up at its center, and wasteland all around. Half generic office park and half slow-moving backwater, it seemed too northern for most southern tastes, and too southern for most northerners (a mix of "Northern charm and Southern efficiency," in JFK's unforgiving put-down). To me, it looked mostly like a small-town innocent done up in a three-piece suit.

For postmodern theorists like Rem Koolhaas (who first called Atlanta "a new imperial Rome"), the city was a model of "the real city at the end of the 20th century" precisely because of its absence of character and weight. It was a posturban place, he wrote, "post-inspirational" and to all intents and purposes posthuman, a "ghost of a city" built around the corporate "void space" of the atrium (invented by Atlanta's own John Portman as a modern version of the ancient Roman courtyard). Its great beauty for him lay in the fact it had no traditional beauty, no center or community. For those condemned to live with this emptiness, however—especially for those in the black "hole of the doughnut"—such rococo notions probably offered less solace, and, as I looked back on what I'd seen, all I could think of, beneath the cosmetic pretensions, was the "Satellite City" of the Evelyn Waugh story, to which "Mr. Plastic the Citizen" gets sent, with a "Certificate of Human Personality." Its impersonal blocks covered up an empty, broken heart.

With its curious gift for advertising its least attractive qualities, the city had managed to sum up that image perfectly in the Olympic mascot it unveiled at the end of the Closing Ceremonies in Barcelona in 1992. For more than a quarter of a century now, Olympic cities have generated a noble line of bears and tigers and raccoons, "symbolizing the vision of the Games," which, in the great Olympic way, manage to be profitable by being adorable, and appear on millions of tiepins and camping knives for years before and after the actual competition. But when Atlanta's contribution to the heritage was revealed, the whole world caught its breath: was it a bird, a plane, or an astronaut? Whatizit, as the figure was uncompanionably called, seemed an indeterminate blob—or virus—without race or sex or even species.

Almost immediately, the PC Play-Doh man began drawing the world together in horror: even *Atlanta* magazine referred to it as an "animated airbrush," while Atlanta's local paper declared that any local symbol would have been preferable—a peach, a phoenix, even a goddamn peanut. The first Olympic mascot to be "specifically designed for children" looked uncannily like the first one to be designed by them (some of the names suggested for it had been I.M.

There, Gofer D. Gold, and Jimmy Nastics), and faced with the uproar, the city quickly moved to give its state-of-the-art morph a makeover. His body was filled out, his eyes were made brighter, lightning bolts were attached to his sneakers, and he was given the marginally less corporate name of Izzy. Izzy, we were suddenly told, was a teenager whose mission was to collect five rings in order to achieve his Olympic dream.

Yet to me at least, Izzy did from the beginning seem an-all-too apt embodiment of an undefined company town whose private sector was more prominent than its public face, and whose baseball team played one year in the National League West, and one year in the National League East. At a deeper level, Izzy confirmed my suspicion that Atlanta had fatally little sense of what the world expected; it was a small town's idea of what a big city should be. Atlanta was international, I was coming to feel, as CNN and Coke were—in other words, as an internationally known symbol of all-American pop. The city boasted an International Boulevard downtown, but its claim to fame was that, at a single intersection, it offered a Hard Rock Café, a Planet Hollywood, a McDonald's outlet, and a seventy-three-story Westin hotel (with four-by-six "corporate profiles" on the sundeck). The Chamber of Commerce boasted of thirty-two Aleuts and forty-one Guamanians in the city's makeup, but the same organization spelled the critical word "foriegn."

Even the way in which the city looked upon the future seemed to be curiously old-fashioned, as if harking back to a time when internationalism meant men in gray flannel suits gathering in space-age auditoriums (and imports represented less than 4 percent of America's gross national product). More than any American city I knew, Atlanta seemed to belong squarely to the 1950s, that can-do time of organization men and Dale Carnegie precepts, of atomic-age worries and suburbs meant to accommodate the car of tomorrow; the time when America promised to show the world how to achieve peace and democracy in ten easy steps. Even the most famous eating place in town (President Clinton dined there while I was staying in Atlanta) was a sock hop–era burger joint that took up a whole city block (though, in the trademark Atlantan style, it came with ATM machines, long-distance telephone cards, and fourteen kinds of souvenirs on sale among the onion rings).

Every Olympic host is asked to play its role in the Games' favored drama by showing off all the adversities it's weathered: Seoul, in 1988, was demonstrating just how far it had come since being a mass of rubble at the end of the Korean War, only thirty-five years before; Barcelona, in 1992, was airing a Catalan heritage that had been banned, in recent memory, at Franco's decree. Atlanta's mandate was to exemplify a highly American tale of reinvention: this, after all, was the city that had had just $1.64 in its treasury after General Sherman burned it to the ground, and had hardly recovered from that blow when, in 1917, a huge fire destroyed nearly two thousand buildings downtown.

Atlanta's very identity, in fact, seemed caught up in the outlines of the rags-to-riches story. It defined itself largely through a series of local heroes who had conquered impossible odds to make an impact on the world: Jimmy Carter, the country boy who had walked all the way from a peanut farm to the White House; Ted Turner, starting an all-news station in the basement of a country club that within a few years was being hailed by the secretary-general of the UN as the "sixteenth member of the Security Council"; most recently, Newt Gingrich, the congressman for Buckhead County, suddenly becoming Speaker of the House and bringing his earnest, somewhat loopy Successories ideas to a nation not quite sure what to make of him (the one time I heard Gingrich speak, he was affirming McDonalds's Hamburger University as a model of higher education).

In some ways, it seemed too good to be true (and perfectly Atlantan) that, thanks to Ted Turner again, the city was now the home of many of Hollywood's old movies—the very storehouse of American mythmaking—and was hard at work "colorizing" them.

Yet none of the city's transformations had really come about through interaction with the globe: unlike New York or Toronto or San Francisco, say, Atlanta had remade itself not so much with fresh immigrant energy as with new mottoes and corporate headquarters, and where, in 1990, nearly 40 percent of all the people in Greater Los Angeles spoke a language other than English at home, the figure at the same time for metropolitan Atlanta was 6 percent. For me, coming to Atlanta from Seattle and Miami, it seemed a strikingly unmulticultural place, whose destiny was played out in the old, half-forgotten shades of black and white (a binary culture, in a sense). True, there were more foreign companies headquartered in Atlanta than in any other American city, but for all the more than three hundred Japanese companies based here, there were scarcely five thousand actual Japanese in residence.

As I drove around Atlanta for week after week, I felt I was negotiating precisely that empty space that lies between globalism and true universalism (TIPPING IS NOT A CITY IN CHINA said the sign by the cash register in the tiny counterculture district). Yes, you could find a B and B here by calling RSVP Grits, Inc., and if you really scanned the customized Yellow Pages, you could come upon "Afrocentric psychics" and bilingual therapists, gay cruise operators and an outfit called Southern Bears, Inc. ("club for hirsute men and their admirers"). Out on the tattered edges of the Buford Highway, among pawnshops and tattoo parlors, I even located, my last day in town, copies of the *Atlanta Chinese News* and some Vietnamese bakeries selling "grass jelly drink."

But the overall tenor of the place—and the way it saw itself— seemed to be pulling in the opposite direction. As the Games approached, Cobb County, in suburban Atlanta, decided against being part of the Olympics because it would mean repealing a 1993 resolution condemning the "gay lifestyle" (that Atlanta had the largest gay population in the U.S., outside of New York and San Francisco, was another of the facts it chose not to publicize). And the

Chamber of Commerce in the county of Barrow voted 13–2 against letting Somali athletes train in the neighborhood, a move justified in the name of economics, but looking suspiciously like good old Southern xenophobia.

Those Atlantans conversant with the outside world seemed to understand that Atlanta might not travel well: Andrew Young told a colleague of mine, on the record, "The world really is here in Atlanta, but most people still live in their own cocoon. They are not ready for prime time." (And Jane Fonda, Atlanta's favorite adopted daughter, would later get into trouble for likening her new home to the Third World.) But the distinguishing characteristic of provincialism is not to know how provincial it is. Billy Payne, the self-styled "ordinary guy" who had dreamed of bringing the world to his hometown—the latest rags-to-riches candidate—had assured the world that his Olympics would be "the greatest peacetime gathering in the history of mankind."

Given that Payne himself had never been abroad, except on holiday, when he issued his invitation to the world, the promise mostly raised the question of how much he really knew of history or mankind.

When the Centennial Games finally got under way, I watched the would-be global city and the global village bump into each other, and back away a little, rubbing their foreheads. Suddenly, the center of downtown turned into a labyrinth of theme parks—Bud World, the World Sports Jam, the World Party—and gleaming new pavilions telling us we were all one: Reebok Center, Nike Park, a $20 million new Coca-Cola Olympic City. Gaggles of chirping kids in corporate uniforms invited us to enjoy Visa's "Olympics of the Imagination" and a fifty-six-dollar virtual reality ride, not far from the Olympic Experience store. Local banks boasted of "Bringing the World Together Through Barter" and, at the very heart of the new

Centennial Olympic Park sat a stunning $30 million spaceship of sorts—AT&T's Global Olympic Village ("Imagine a world without limits") in which "athletic ambassadors" and their families were invited to enjoy a "safe haven" from the commotion where they could follow events through holographic walls and "the largest video show in the world."

I happened to be staying in a Comfort Inn right across from Centennial Park—together with the Olympic teams of *Time* and *Newsweek*—and every time I descended into the street to make my way to the Main Press Center next door, I found myself in an all but impassable confusion of panpipers, Christian puppet shows and huge, inflatable Elvises somewhere around the "Celebration of the Century." Jostling past men with snakes around their shoulders and pamphleteers handing out reminders that "You are born in SIN. HEADED FOR HELL," I found myself yearning, with a palpable ache, for the silent hermitage above the sea where I would be going as soon as the Games were over.

The modern Olympic Games were developed, more or less, as sideshows to international expositions—even in 1908 they were including Anthropological Days shows featuring "savage tribes." But Atlanta took the hustle-bustle to a new cosmic level, RENT-A-LOT signs appearing above every patch of free grass and sidewalk hucksters peddling bottles of "great American water" for four dollars a shot. In Nagano, the Olympic Spirit would take the form of tiny hardware stores posting signs that said, GO JAMAICA and shopkeepers writing up their hobbies at their entrances ("Kite-flying. Joking and singing"). In Atlanta, as soon as you left the central web of the Atlanta Gift Mart, the Atlanta Apparel Mart, and the Atlanta Merchandising Mart (the sound of "Taking Care of Business" ringing in your ears from an Olympic basketball game), you found yourself in an international jumble sale, and stores selling "designer T-shirts with military equipment and insignia."

Brave the Olympian now who cited Avery Brundage's famous claim, "The Olympics is a revolt against 20th century materialism."

. . .

To many, I think, the Atlanta Games served to show, in seventy-foot-block capitals, how the global market hovers above the global village and sometimes threatens to swallow it up altogether. Atlanta has always been a Coca-Cola City (the company is responsible for its art centers, its parks, its concert series, and even, to some extent, the presence of the Centers for Disease Control—what the de' Medicis were to Florence, it's been said, Coca-Cola's Robert Woodruff was to Atlanta), but during the Games it began to seem as if the soft-drink company owned not just the city but the whole event.

Coke had attached itself to the Olympics as early as 1928, and in that year—it already reached seventy-eight countries around the world—it shipped one thousand cases of its "Wonderful Nerve and Brain Tonic" to Amsterdam, in the company of the U.S. team. By 1952, it was commandeering a World War II landing craft to run Operation Muscle, whereby thirty thousand cases of Coke went to Helsinki, and by 1972, it had simply taken over the catering operations of the entire Olympic Village. Coke was the first sponsor of the Olympic Museum, and the force behind the U. S. Olympic Hall of Fame.

You can take in much of this information in what is in some respects the central monument in Atlanta, the three-story World of Coke "promotainment" that sits on Martin Luther King, just two blocks from the state capitol. There, visitors are invited to spend $4.50 apiece to enjoy a spectacular advertisement for what is called "the most successful product in the history of commerce," and peppy multilingual salesgirls from Yokahama and São Paulo will direct you towards the Coke-shaped phone booths, the video theaters playing nothing but Coke ads, the free tasting parlor where you can enjoy Coke products from twenty-one countries. From display cases you can learn how Coke was already advertising on the back of school report cards in 1893, and by 1896 was bringing out a *Coca-Cola*

News, to inform readers that "Coca-Cola is a beverage, a restorative, a blessing to humanity."

But the Olympics are the centerpiece of Coke's efforts to make itself synonymous with youth and global harmony: the company has its own Olympic radio broadcasts and runs its own Salute to Folk Art (wherein "folk and crafts traditions" from around the world are brought to bear on the theme of the Coke bottle). The Coke Pin Trading Center is one of the central meeting places in most Olympic towns, and the company releases new pins every day of the competition; when collected and put together, they form the shape of a contoured Coke bottle (in Nagano, not untypically, every other lantern along the main street wore the insignia of Coke). Coke even runs the Olympic Torch Relay, which means that it selects more than half the dignitaries deemed worthy of carrying the "sacred flame" and presents the "ancient rite" in flags and documents and uniforms stamped with the name Coca-Cola.

It's often hard, in fact, to know where the Coke jingle ends and the Olympic song begins, as the stars singing *"Amigos para siempre"* at Barcelona all but intoned the new Coke motto of *"Sabor para siempre."* And sometimes, when I found myself watching bright young dreamers from around the globe gather to sing, "I'd like to build the world a home / And furnish it with love," I lost track of whether I was watching a Coke ad or an Olympic Moment.

As it happened, I took in the Opening Ceremonies in Atlanta in a Coca-Cola seat, surrounded by strapping blond regional managers and their ex–beauty queen wives, many of them high-fiving the ex-Olympians who'd been brought onto the team for visibility. Around us, the city gleamed with the new billboards of a $200 million "Olympic-themed" Coke campaign, and Olympic lawyers on every side sat ready to fight back if Pepsi attempted "ambush" or "parasite" marketing (in other words, capitalizing on the cachet of the Olympics without paying the $40 million that Official Sponsors pay to "rent" Olympic values).

The city didn't seem quite sure of how it should project itself to the world ("How are we supposed to make a number about economic opportunity?" the director of the Opening Ceremonies had asked. "Have five thousand dancing guys with briefcases?"), but as the Games got under way, I could see Atlanta revealing its true colors to every visitor: when they visited the central mall downtown, Underground Atlanta, they would pass ten "Rules of Etiquette" before coming upon the flagship property of Hooter's, the restaurant chain that serves up large-breasted waitresses in hot pants. When they wanted to take a trip out of town, they could visit the site voted "Best Outing" by *Atlanta* magazine two years before—a park "commemorating one of the Civil War's bloodiest battles." And when they turned on the radio, they would, as likely as not, catch "step-by-step" counsel for Christian businessmen from "someone who by the grace of God went from being broke to being a millionaire."

Everywhere we went, moreover, we were reminded that we were now in "the safest city in the world," home to "the largest security effort ever held for any event in the free world." As Carl Lewis himself would say—and he was more or less the Tiresias of the modern Olympic Movement—"These days there are only two things that can draw Americans together—the Olympic Games and war."

For my own part, I tried, in my usual way, to reduce the event to a human scale by going in the opposite direction from the crowds, and so, one afternoon, I found myself watching kids spraying one another with high-tech fluorescent water pistols as France took on Estonia in beach volleyball, at Atlanta Beach (230 miles from the nearest ocean), Bob Marley singing "Jamming" on the sound system and the smell of strawberry margaritas mingling with the coconut tang of suntan oil. I took a long bus ride to Athens (in its Georgian form), and met a kid in a deserted parking lot who said, "This is the laziest job I ever got paid for. I signed up for the Olympics, and I got parking attendant! For rhythmic gymnastics! But that's okay: it's the Olympics."

Inside the somewhat rickety arena, a sign on the pressroom door said PLEASE PUSH SLOWLY BEFORE ENTERING, and when I did as instructed, it was to find sixteen volunteers dancing attention on two journalists, the vast majority of them peering into a Xerox machine with a pencil flashlight.

My sense that Atlanta had abdicated from its own tradition somehow, leaving the South without quite arriving anywhere else, was only confirmed when I went down to Savannah to watch the sailing competition. Here, I felt, was a Southern town in all its unapologetic ease, with no pressing designs upon the world and no great concern about its image. The first day of Olympic competition in Savannah's history, most of the signs around town said, simply, BOILED PEANUTS, and the only emblems of Olympic fervor were a few hand-written banners, appropriate for a high school game, out amongst the Piggly Wiggly stores and Hot-Dig-A-Dee Dog outlets. Savannah was not without its controversies, of course, and some people complained that a city where 30 percent of all children lived in poverty should not be spending $37.8 million on sailing; but at least the place seemed sure enough of itself to leave the visitor in peace.

In Savannah, the volunteers for the Olympics were sometimes homeless men drawn to the city by the prospect of being paid to drive BMWs; and the Media Transport Center, when finally I tracked it down, turned out to be a man in a deck chair, his face covered by a newspaper. The transport itself consisted of an enormous bus peopled by three rather small-seeming souls, and when we disembarked at the other end, a volunteer told us that, prior to our arrival, he'd seen exactly two people in seven hours.

The Danish team had had to borrow a boat from its Spanish rivals when its own failed to meet measurement, and another crew had lost its compass. The Italians alone had three pairs of brothers in their boats, and the Special Opening Ceremony in Savannah had featured shamrocks running down Irish faces as torrential rains and a thunderstorm broke out over the eight thousand people gathered on River Street. At the local cash registers, where I expected to find Izzy key rings on sale, merchants were selling copies of the memoirs of a Savannah transvestite.

The Olympics invariably feature so many heart-stopping athletic moments that it's never hard to fill the three-hour documentary that Bud Greenspan generally films, and in Atlanta I know there was no way I could resist the eighty-two-kilogram freestyle wrestling event, in which an athlete from Kazakhstan took on another from Moldavia, who happened to be his brother, and, having beaten his sibling and coach, went out with him for dinner. I watched Cuban baseball players say, *"Domo arigato!"* to their Japanese opponents, and the Japanese replying gamely, *"Muchas gracias."* Nigeria somehow got the better of almighty Brazil in soccer, and in the hammer throw, a man called Kiss beat a man called Deal.

Though the Iranian president celebrated a wrestling victory (over a Russian, no less) by talking of "rubbing the nose of America in the dirt" and raising the Islamic flag in "the House of Satan," and though every other Chinese medal was followed by questions about doping tests and Mandarin curses about "hegemonists," the stadia themselves filled with happy men saying, "That's real Olympic of you," and Gigi Fernandez, for one, explaining how proud she was to be American, in Spanish. More than thirty thousand people showed up for a baseball game (between Australia and the Netherlands), at ten o'clock on a Monday morning, and in the Olympic Village one could see Monica Seles, one of the best-known millionaires in town, clearly relishing being just another kid again as she went bowling (barefoot) with other young athletes and headed out to cheer on the water polo squad. The Olympics often seem to have most meaning, ironically, for seasoned professionals like Seles, who get the chance to live like amateurs again for two weeks, playing for the fun of it and, in Seles's case, working off the memory of a near-fatal stabbing by a rival's fan three years before.

So the Centennial Games were a success, as Games, and provided the world with a new set of sellable heroes. But for the city that had waited six years (or, really, eighty) for its global coming-out, the debut was a catastrophe. Bus drivers hastily brought in from Baltimore and Chicago took athletes to their events by way, it seemed, of Maryland and Illinois, and, in one celebrated case, collapsed in tears on an off-ramp, confessing that they'd never driven on a freeway before. IBM's next-generation information network—INFO '96—listed the ages of young boxers as ninety-five, while Coca-Cola's pavilion happily announced crowds of 20 billion (or three times more people than exist on the planet). The first morning of competition, the world's defending judo heavyweight champion lost four years of his life when a bomb alert prevented him from showing up for his bout on time; on the first evening, at the gala prime-time unveiling of America's latest "Dream Team," the electricity in the Georgia Dome went dead for ten full minutes.

The great challenge and invention of the twentieth century, Bertrand Russell once asserted, was "suspended judgment." Yet globalism has made such a suspension more and more precarious, as more and more of us feel qualified to pronounce on more and more places (if only because we've glimpsed them on-screen), and every world event becomes as cacophonous as a neighborhood association meeting. In Atlanta's case, the whole world banded together in a rare show of unity to call the Games a "horror trip" (as the German press said) and a "big mess" (as the Israelis pronounced), a "shambles" (in the words of the British), and "a disgrace" (as even the polite Canadians confessed). For every foreigner who felt that America was an upstart power that confused bigger with better and money with power, Atlanta was a gift-wrapped joy, and *France-Soir* was only one of the many papers around the globe that pronounced, "After Atlanta, any country in the world can apply to host the Games." The poorest nation in the world, ran the consensus, could have staged the event with as much sophistication, and certainly more charm.

Some of this may have been a little unfair, and it's never easy to host millions of visitors from everywhere, some of whom will complain that there are too few Beer Express joints on hand, and some of whom will complain that there are too many. It wasn't Atlanta's fault that TWA 800 plunged into the Atlantic three days before the Opening Ceremonies, or that the weather was sullen and gray. Yet insofar as I shared the world's distaste for the city, it was because it had asked to be judged by the highest international standards, and, like any insecure being, kept on demanding that everyone around support it in the lies it told about itself.

More than once during the Games, I handed a waitress a credit card, only for her to look at it as if it were some kind of unintelligible foreign object. And as I took the subway out to Buckhead one day, surrounded by slogans for global brotherhood, I happened to ask a Nigerian how he found the city, and turned around, to find a local (not a redneck, but a prosperous-looking businessman, as it happened) referring to us as "animals."

Every time I stepped into a cab during the Games, moreover, I felt as if I were stepping into a tribal fury. Nearly always, the cars were driven by recent immigrants from Ethiopia, and nearly always these men were as gracious and dignified as is their wont. But as soon as I'd say how much I'd been impressed by their country, they would tear—almost every one of them—into a violent tirade against the Tigreans, who had taken over the government, they said, and reorganized it along tribal lines (others might say, along different tribal lines than before). Around us, as they cursed, the billboards spoke eagerly of "solutions for a small planet."

And every time I attended an event in the new showpiece Olympic Stadium, I found myself dropped off in one of the most desperately poor areas in the whole impoverished city. A "Great Atlanta

Clean-Up" had been set up to move fifteen thousand of the city's less sightly residents out of the "Olympic Ring," and bright signs all around urged us to keep our eyes firmly on the gleaming Sponsors' Village and the $209 million new stadium in the distance. But the road to complementary champagne ran past broken shacks and kids offering "pop" for two quarters, untended vacant lots and signs that sometimes said $10 PARKING. FREE SECUREITY.

We could see black men on the porches of these houses, sipping beer in rocking chairs and listening to the action coming out of tiny jerry-rigged speakers; inside their old homes, we could see Zenith TVs with rabbit-ear antennae shuddering images into the dark. From down the street, you could hear roars greeting the millionaire athletes (and, some keen-eared visitors from South Africa and Yugoslavia would say, the sound of automatic gunfire).

For me, the crowning hero of the Games—and the ideal embodiment of all the contradictions that lie at the heart of the Olympic Movement—came in the perfect, almost unassimilable form of Carl Lewis, "the greatest athlete in history," as he's often called, and one with a keen sense of how much greatness is worth in our inflated universe of the image.

I'll never forget the first time I saw Lewis, at a special Mizuno press conference in a private room high in the hills above Barcelona: I'd never seen a human form so sleek, so pantherine, so beautifully smooth all the way to the tips of its ebony limbs. He sat on his dais, facing the cameras and questions of a hundred countries, and looked to me like a king, perfectly at ease, flashing his flawless smile and answering with a soft-voiced articulacy I hadn't expected. I couldn't imagine why so many sponsors and sportswriters had no time for him, unless it was just because he was too good to be true.

In Atlanta, though, I saw him burnish that impression with an act of self-transcendence that took my breath away. Nobody had really expected Lewis to be competing at all—he'd only made the U.S.

team by an inch (in the long-jump event), and, in the qualifying round at Atlanta, again, he seemed certain to fall out: going into his final jump, he was placed fifteenth in a competition in which only twelve people make it to the finals. Yet somehow, out of nowhere, he soared beyond himself, and beyond everyone else in sight, to sail into first place and the finals.

On the day of the long-jump final, I went along to the Stadium to see the old man take his curtain call. Again, he seemed to be showing up mostly as a formality—he'd planned to retire five years before, after all—and everyone knew he hadn't jumped twenty-seven feet ten inches at sea level in four years. Yet somehow, again, on his third jump, when everyone was looking the other way, he stretched and he strained and he stretched, and he pulled off a jump of twenty-seven feet ten and three-quarter inches, eight inches farther than anyone else.

Then, with the air of godly entitlement that had not always endeared him to his rivals, he simply sat back and watched them try, one after another, to beat him (and fail). Imperial to the end, he even declined to take his final jump, as if it were not worth his time to try to improve on his lead. And so, as the dying sun turned faces to gold and the last long shadows fell across the field, just as everyone turned to the expected Olympic hero, Michael Johnson, about to run the four hundred meters, there, somehow, was Lewis, carrying an American flag around the stadium on a last great tumultuous victory lap.

I didn't know what exactly I felt as I watched him on that run, but I knew I'd been stirred beyond words: like very few performers I'd ever seen, other than Michael Jordan, Lewis seemed to have some magical quality beyond his natural genius that allowed him to rise to the occasion when nobody could expect it, and to reinvent astonishment just as we were getting used to him. When he came into the press conference room a few minutes after his triumph, he looked at all the cameras and broke into a smile—"What are you guys all doing in my dream?"—as if to say that he'd been as taken aback by his feat as we were.

Then, for forty-five minutes, blending show business with seeming sincerity in the style he'd made his trademark, Lewis proceeded to deliver a "clinic," as the sportswriters say, in the art of public relations. "Don't give up because everyone says you're too old," he said, turning himself into a parable (and addressing himself already to the young of the world); "I don't want to dig up dandelions, I just want to smell the roses," he countered smoothly when someone asked him about his archrival, Johnson.

He even showed himself willing to be the master of the case against him. "I don't think track wants another Carl Lewis," he said brightly. "They'll take the athlete, but they don't want the whole package." And then the package contrived to turn even his apparent vanity to advantage. He couldn't recall his first gold, he confessed wryly, because "that was twelve years ago: almost sixteen hairstyles ago, hundreds of gray hairs ago, almost fifteen pounds ago."

I came away exhilarated at seeing such a display of professionalism, both on and off the field ("You've got to present yourself," Lewis had said. "You've got to look good; you've got to speak well"), and knowing that Atlanta would present no more memorable moment. Then, just as I was beginning to ponder the depths of what I'd experienced, I got word that Lewis was mounting a campaign—he'd appeared on fifteen TV stations more or less overnight, he'd conducted a special press conference at Nike, he was expressly soliciting messages of support from the public—to be admitted to the 4 x 100 relay team in place of some more qualified runner. He wanted to break his own Olympic record of nine gold medals with a tenth.

As dramatically as he'd built a monument to himself, he set about tearing it down.

When I left Atlanta for the last time, and the global road show directed itself towards its next stop, in Sydney (with its restaurants from 271 different countries, and a new "solar-powered suburb" to house the Games), and then in Salt Lake City (home now to the next great World Religion, and, thanks to its missionary needs, one of the world's great language centers), I realized that there were two indelible images that I'd take away with me.

The first had begun on a chill winter's afternoon, on blighted Auburn Avenue, where a small but enthusiastic group of girls in saris and volunteers in RACISM (JUST UNDO IT) T-shirts, and a few interested spectators such as me, had piled into the Freedom Hall of the King Center for a Multicultural and World Prayer Program.

A middle-aged Japanese woman had stood at a microphone, and, as children came forward from the wings, one after another, each bearing the flag of one of the 197 countries that would be participating in the Games, she solemnly intoned an "individual pledge of peace" and an affirmation of the "interconnectedness of our human family." The rite went on for a long, long time—the pledges intoned 197 times—and then the Atlanta Baha'i Workshop staged a Dance of Racial Harmony—three white dancers, dressed all in white, coming together with three black dancers, dressed all in black. "There is no other hope," one of the Baha'is said, "than to acknowledge and recognize the oneness of the human race."

Finally, a little girl who couldn't have been more than ten years old, standing on a chair so she could reach the microphone, her high voice trilling on without stumble or hesitation, proceeded to deliver an eloquent speech, urging us to recall "how connected we are." We treat siblings in one way, she said, and strangers in another: but could we not see that strangers were just the siblings we never knew?

It was impossible not to be stirred by such a display of innocence and hopefulness; and it was impossible not to wonder how it could really apply to a world in which right is usually set against right.

The next day, however, on an unseasonably warm January afternoon, all the people in Atlanta who mattered—black preachers and civil rights veterans, movie stars and politicians and folks who'd just paid their dues—came to the Ebenezer Baptist Church and shook the

rafters of the little place with their fire and conviction. It was a soar-
ing, exultant afternoon, one person after another coming forward in
Martin Luther King's memory, and, speaking from the heart, and
without notes, urging us to honor King's legacy to the world, while
others in the congregation got up and cried, "Do it, Lord!" and
"Thank you, Jesus!"

A twelve-year-old boy came forward and led the assembly in a kind
of litany, pointing his finger and shaking his cadences like King himself, and a black minister in front of me got up and waved his hands
all about, crying, "Say it, son!" and "Listen, listen!"

Then Bill Clinton, just returned from Bosnia, and thoroughly in
his element, took the microphone and, smiling down at the boy (now
returned to his seat and looking like any shy and bespectacled seventh grader), delivered a radiant speech of his own, eyes glistening as
he joined hands with King's widow and son and sang out, by heart,
every word of the National Negro Hymn ("Lift Every Voice and
Sing").

It did not matter, I thought, that the black bigwigs around me had
copies not of the Bible but of *Kiplinger's Personal Finance Magazine*
in their hands, and Casio cell phones on which they were muttering
plans for the highly exclusive Salute to Greatness dinner and All
People's Gala. It didn't matter that there was something a little too
tidy about the appearance of a speaker from the AFL-CIO, another
from the Bureau of Indian Affairs, a Hispanic representative, and an
emissary from Nelson Mandela and the "New South Africa." It didn't
even matter that the accommodation of so many special interests
meant that the service went on for three and a half hours, throwing
everyone's schedule (and especially the city's, cordoned off as it was
to cater to the president's motorcade) way, way off.

What did matter to me, as I looked around, was that there was a
man in a yarmulke and a Chinese couple and a white general in uniform, and an Indian with a ponytail (leaning back to say something in
Hebrew to a rabbi)—all in my own row—and nobody seemed to

notice. Everybody was joined together by something beyond his circumstances—pop star and nonentity and politician and volunteer—and, after a grizzled black sheriff, who'd marched with King, gave his badge to the reverend's family, everyone got up and linked hands for a final singing of "Kumbaya" and "We Shall Overcome."

The Japanese consul had put it best when he'd said, "America's great and lasting significance is its existence in the mind."

My final memory of Atlanta and its Games came a few months later, in the dead of night. The competition was half over now, and finally beginning to find its rhythm: buses were more or less running on schedule, and computers were almost up to speed, and on the perfect first Friday evening of the Centennial Games, Kerri Strug, the forgotten member of the American women's gymnastic team, had somehow, while hardly able to walk, pulled off her last vault to ensure the team's gold medal. Here was the stuff of which Olympic dreams are made, the tiny teenager with the hobbled leg ascending the podium in the arms of her coach, and, while colleagues of mine prepared an image of the new American heroine to place on the cover of *Time*, I, in our Main Press Center office, put the final touches on an ode to the Olympic spirit.

Just then, there came a terrible thud, as if a filing cabinet had crashed to the ground on the floor above us, and the whole building shook, as in the kind of minor earthquake that I had come to know too well from living in Japan and California. People began running every which way, and we could hear sirens in the street, and see the television screens fill with pictures of mayhem and flashing lights and bodies sprawled out at Centennial Park, just a block away. Some of us tried to leave the building, to see what was going on, but police blocked our way, and the whole place was plunged into the full-blown anarchy that breaks out when a city's lights (actual or moral) go out and nobody really knows what's going on.

A press conference was scheduled for 3:30 a.m., in the building in which we were now captive, but then it was delayed—and delayed again—so that all the world's media could be present. Tom Brokaw jumped out of his pajamas to steady the nation on NBC, and rumors began to circulate about a security guard. The whole night was one of jumpiness and jitters—every time a beeper went off, people screamed; and every package on the floor looked newly sinister. There was a new sense in the air of how one tremor in Atlanta could set a whole world shivering.

Finally, at dawn, the press conference was completed, and I was allowed to go back to my room next door. I looked out of my window, in the early morning drizzle, to the park below, which for weeks had been so crowded that one could hardly move, and where concerts had continued till 2:00 a.m. each night (forcing me to write in the toilet).

Now, though, there was no one in sight save for a few men in gray jackets, FBI in yellow on their backs, and a handful of others, in dark blue and green uniforms, poking through paper clips in the early rain. Everywhere, a sad abandoned mess of green benches overturned and strewn garbage.

An electric flame still burned outside the Coca-Cola Olympic City, and a sign kept flashing in front of the empty square: YOU ARE HERE. But nobody was there in the postdawn quiet outside the AT&T Global Olympic Village ("Imagine a world without limits"), and the World Party area was just a jungle of folded chairs. The whole city, from where I looked, resembled a party of silent ghosts arrested in midbreath, and the only signs of life in sight were a Department of ATF van (EXPLOSIVES INVESTIGATION, it said on the side), and, in the middle of the cordoned-off street, in the rain, a single Good Humor ice-cream truck.

I remembered how, the previous night, when I'd raced out into the street in the chaos after the bomb exploded—sirens whirling around me and people crashing through police barricades—I'd seen a man grabbing someone else as people flew all around. He'd been a white man, and the man he'd grabbed looked like a visitor from the Middle East (here, no doubt, to enjoy the festival of nations). "You see," the local had all but spat in the bewildered foreigner's face, "you see what happens when we let you people in?"

THE EMPIRE

I have been a queer mixture of the East and West, out of place everywhere, at home nowhere. . . . I cannot be of the [West]. But in my own country, also, sometimes, I have an exile's feeling.

—Jawaharlal Nehru

I can still remember, just, as a boy, growing up on stories of passage, nearly always of bright young boys from the colonies—tropical Dick Whittingtons—coming over to England to make their fortunes (the same England where I was reading of them): of Mohandas Gandhi, dreaming of becoming an upstanding English barrister, and schooling himself in French and dancing lessons and dandyish fashions long after he left the Victoria Hotel in London; of Lee Kuan Yew, later to say he'd always felt indebted to his British principal at the Raffles Institution for caning him, and coming over on the Cunard ship *Britannia* (shocked at the people copulating freely on the lifeboat deck) before returning to Singapore as Harry Lee, with the only starred First in Law at Cambridge; of Nelson Mandela, named after Admiral Nelson no less, combining in his person, those close to him had told me, "the perfect English gentleman and the tribal chieftain." In the stories, the pattern was always the same: the young foreigner mastered the ways of Britain so fully that he was perfectly equipped to undo them, armed, as Michael Manley, the prime minister of Jamaica, and a Marxist anti-imperialist, would say, with "nothing more than the finest tradition of self-criticism taught in British schools."

Now, though, as I sat overlooking the backs of the Cambridge colleges on an outstretched English summer evening—the light as lingering and golden as in any tropical boy's imaginings—I was hearing a different second act. "The thing is, I admire the idea of England, but I can't stand the reality." My old Indian friend had a voice as plummy and rich as a major general's, the kind they don't seem to make any more. "I don't know—call me sentimental, if you like; I suppose it's the weak, Indian, wishy-washy part of me—but I always thought that England meant fairness and free choice and all that kind of thing, that this was the center of decency. And now, of course, I find I'm much more English than the English.

"I mean, at least before, there used to be some sense of compassion. I know a colonial master-slave relationship isn't ideal, but if you're a slave, it's the best thing you've got. I suppose some people would say those were all myths, of decency or whatever, but it's still better to have those positive myths than what we have now."

I look at him in his New and Lingwood sweater, with the Coutts checkbook he's made sure that I notice: he lives in a thatched Elizabethan cottage in the country, of the kind he must have dreamed of once, its address all bushes and thorns, "nr. Newmarket," and I feel as if I'm watching someone play Othello after the theater has emptied and the lights are all turned off.

"I mean, if you're an Indian, they're happy to accept you so long as you speak like Peter Sellers and smell of curry and all that, because then you know your place. But if you don't, you might as well forget it. Because the typical Englishman doesn't understand that there is such a thing as class anywhere outside England, and that you or I are different from the Bangladeshi waiter at the local. The right wing want you to be nice smiling colonials, and the left wing want you to assert your solidarity and oppressedness by being 'ethnic,' and they refuse to allow you to be what you want to be. In many ways, the extreme right almost enjoy the extreme left—the Vanessa Redgraves—because they can see them as a good enemy. But if you're sort of middle-of-the-road, you get run over by both sides."

I look at him and don't know what to think. The punts are drifting past the shortbread-colored towers, and the late-summer light is

gilding the fields and distant spires as in the kind of watercolors the
Empire sent around the globe. My friend has a big heart, I know, and
a quick mind, but both are so lost inside the character he's chosen to
play that all I can hear, sometimes, is the sound of a lover disappointed, a boy who's left everything he knows to pursue some ideal,
unattainable woman, and arrives at her doorstep, only to find that
she's given herself over to some mobster from Las Vegas.

As our new world order spins, ever more intensely, so, too, do our
dreams, and almost any immigrant who arrives today at the place
he's hoped for will find it's become somewhere else. The day my
friend and I meet in Cambridge, the paper announces that, when
the twentieth century began, two-thirds of the map was colored
pink, for Empire; now the only places left in that shade are places
like Tristan da Cunha, Ascension, the South Sandwich Islands, and
Pitcairn. When my friend ran away from home as a teenager, to
come to England, it must have seemed the center of the world, in
India; by the time he arrived, though, it was already a colony itself,
looking across the waters at a half-distrusted master it secretly
longed to emulate.

"None of this was in the English literature I grew up on," he says
as he bundles me into his car to drive through country lanes, past
hedgerows and oaks, to a little country pub that serves the most
delectable curries. "The only true English people you'll find now are
born abroad—maybe because they share our romance of England,
and don't know what the reality is. They're much closer to the good
qualities of England, at least as I imagine them, than anyone in England is."

"It's only we who live away from England," says the character in
Maugham, "who really love it."

. . .

The story of migration I must have heard most deeply, growing up—piecing it together, only slowly, over the years—was the one of my own parents, coming to England just before the forces of globalism turned everything on its head. I can see my mother, neat in her English blouse and skirt, reciting the lyrics of Brooke and Shelley at the Cathedral and John Connon School in Bombay, and being rewarded by Mount Carmel sisters with playing cards of the Virgin Mary, which the girls swapped (she told me) as eagerly as I and my friends did Soccer Stars; even now, any Jehovah's Witness who comes to her doorstep, eager to convert the dark heathen within, will be greeted by a knowledge of the Bible more formidable than his own.

I can see my father, too, graduated from the Doctor Antonio da Silva High School in Bombay and coming over to England two years before she did, and three years after India won her independence, to the "dreaming spires" that both of them had read of in Arnold's "Scholar Gypsy," sent there by the beneficence of the South African industrialist Cecil Rhodes, who believed that to be born an Englishman was to be awarded first prize in the lottery of life.

Arriving at Oxford, my father had asked to be moved from his warm modern rooms to ones in the ancient cloisters, near Addison's Walk, and near where the Prince of Wales had recently stayed; and had shivered all year in a historic place chilling to a boy from the tropics who'd never known autumn or winter before.

The one common link between my parents, as was not uncommon then, was the English history and literature in which they had been schooled, the one shared inheritance in a country as divided as Jerusalem, which gave the rest of us words like *communalism;* though both of them grew up in the same city and went to the same college, regional differences would have kept them apart in a world cut up into Hindu and Muslim and North Indian and South and caste and subcaste (one reason why Indians have always thrived in all corners of the world, and become among the great chroniclers of internationalism, I suspect, is that they were multiculturalists centuries before the term existed). The *Rubaiyat of Omar Khayyam* (in the Fitzgerald translation) brought together what Hinduism and Brahminism tore apart.

When she was in her teens, my mother told me much later, she impressed my father (also in his teens, though already a professor) by reciting some lines of Tennyson to him; and on the last day of every school term, tears would run down the cheeks of the girls at Cathedral as they sang of England's "green and pleasant land" and were ushered forth into the world.

The setting of Blake's Jerusalem could never have been quite what the girls expected, if ever they took the boat to England, but the shock must have been many times greater when Britain became a suburb of the International Empire. The one thing "convent-educated" Indians were not prepared for, surely, was an England made up of Islamic fundamentalists (and of settlements like Glastonbury, where flaxen-haired kids sport names like Sita and Krishna and Ganesh); according to the British Tourist Association, the national dish of Britain now is curry (having triumphed, I assume, over doner kebab and pizza), and the most popular flavor ordered from the Domino's pizza chain in the UK in 1994 was tandoori chicken. What seemed most to upset people like my Indian friend was that so many of the people in England now looked a lot like him.

To an English-born outsider like myself, the spicing of England was all to the good—the island has grown stronger and darker, like a mug of lukewarm water left to steep in 2 million Indian (and West Indian) tea bags; the Earls you meet these days in London are from Trinidad, and *The Times* will inform you, without apparent rancor, that there are more Indian restaurants in Greater London than in Bombay and Delhi combined. Insofar as Princess Diana was taken to be an avatar of the "New England," it was not just because she brought "American" values—health clubs and Prozac and McDonald's and talk-show therapeutics—into the mainstream; and not just because she upended the traditional order by allying herself increasingly with the rival, new aristocracy of the celebrity culture; but also because she was linked, romantically, to a Pakistani doctor and an Egyptian film producer, while visiting a debutante friend, Jemima Goldsmith, who'd married the captain of the Pakistani cricket team.

Yet those who'd always looked up to a certain England (brought to them, often, by homesick Oxford men abroad) were left not knowing where to turn. Recently, a friend told me, the readers of Sri Lanka, always eager to keep up with the latest in English letters, had asked the British Council to send them some voices of "Young England." Ever sensitive to the niceties of racial diplomacy, the British had sent Hanif Kureishi (half-Pakistani), and then Caryl Phillips (born in the Caribbean). No, the Sri Lankans said, clearly disappointed: send us a *real* British writer (in other words, someone who looks like the people who held us down).

I went, one summer's day in England, to watch an international cricket match at Headingley, in Leeds, on the fifth and final day of the First Test between England and the West Indies. Only six other people got off as I did at the tiny country station near the grounds, and all of them, I noticed, were of my parents' age, or older. Perhaps this was because England had lost to Australia, to India, and to Pakistan in recent years and hadn't, in fact, beaten the West Indies on British soil in twenty-two years (of the last forty-one matches between the two, the West Indies had won twenty-five and England two). It's the unemployment in the Caribbean, the old people were saying as we walked towards the grounds, and besides, all the competitive fire's gone out of England; there's a special value placed on success if you grow up in one of those poor countries.

Around me in the stands, most of the plastic seats were unoccupied for this climactic day (because of the recession, said the men with rolled-up brollies); so few had shown up the previous day that everyone in attendance had been given free tickets to return today. Now I saw a few men in ties, scattered here and there, following the action on Walkmen, and two others dressed from head to toe as Ninja Turtles (or Hero Turtles, as they are ineffably known in Britain).

The man next to me wore a Bart Simpson baseball cap and delivered a passionate encomium to *The Silence of the Lambs* ("Fucking brilliant—amazing!")

The players on the pitch, as I'd never seen before, had chalk on their faces, so they looked like Burmese village girls, and the ads around the grounds advertised Daewoo; one of the spectators nearby muttered about one of England's players being "very patrician," and was quickly told, "Actually, not so patrician: he grew up in the East End, and his father used to stand on the street selling birds. The trouble was, they were homing pigeons."

On the radio, the famously articulate Old Etonian announcer, who had just dined with the Queen, was murmuring like a tributary of the Thames about "handsome strokes" and "cultivated cricketers" and shots pulled out "like a silk handkerchief being removed from a top pocket."

So much of it was like the England I'd grown up with, watching the regal West Indians effortlessly thrash the combined Oxford-and-Cambridge team in the Oxford Parks: the redbrick buildings grouped together under chill gray skies, the hand-operated scoreboard and the puddle on the pitch, the intermittent clapping as batsmen returned to the pavilion after "ducks" or bowlers completed "maiden overs" with their "googlies" and their "Chinamen." In one part of the stands, a small band of merry West Indians was playing barbershop ditties, and, as the match began to go against them, started to sing "Please, God, Please" ("I think," said one of the fans around me, "it's a West Indian rain dance or something"); before the match had begun, I gathered, the Yorkshire Club president, Sir Lawrence Byford (once Her Majesty's chief inspector of constabulary), had reminded the assembled throng that the West Indian lads should be treated "with the respect they are entitled to deserve" and had issued a stern headmasterly caution that "bad behavior and abusive language have no place in a cricket ground." That hadn't stopped one woman from stripping off her top in the "Arctic cold" to show off her independent spirit.

Now, though, as England began to close in on an unexpected victory, its fans struck up a beery, cheery chant of "God Save Our Pring" (as if to amend the "Queen Save the God" that West Indian steel bands play during Carnival), and the "man of the match" was given a jeroboam of champagne. In the national jubilation that followed, a member of Parliament suggested to the House of Commons that the prime minister and the sports minister be publicly thanked for the miracle (to which the Speaker replied that the government had played no part in the victory, so no such thanks were in order). The one thing that was not so often mentioned—and more obvious to a visitor, perhaps—was that the main reason England had prevailed was that nine of its thirteen players came from the colonies—from Australia, South Africa, the subcontinent, and, in fact, the Caribbean (and "much the most orthodox and secure of the England batsmen," according to the *Daily Telegraph,* had the newly typical English name of Mark Ramprakash); the one time in recent years England had fielded a team without any colored players—their style was a little languorous, the gentlemanly arbiters of cricket had suggested—it lost a five-day match before the third day was over.

This was not so much to say that the Empire had reversed direction as that the very sense of what direction it pointed in was somewhat by the by; the same day that a "pitifully small" crowd showed up at Headingley, 61,108 had packed into the high church of British sports, Wembley, to watch the London Monarchs take on Barcelona in the World Bowl championship of the newly popular American football league in Europe. There were cheerleaders and marching bands and cartoon characters performing somersaults, and the

crowd, said the *The Times*, was full of "youth and keenness" as well as
"almost universally wearing some form of Monarchs' merchandise."
When the Monarchs held up their trophy—a forty-pound illuminated glass globe—in the stands, much as the English footballers had
done in 1966 after winning the World Cup, the entire stadium had
turned into a field of Union Jacks, and the players (all but four of
whom were American) had gamely run around the stadium collecting and waving the English flag. It was "as fine a celebration," a
British sportswriter said, "as ever seen in Wembley" and for a while,
England was back on top of the world. Not the dangerous plaything
of hooligans (as soccer could be), not the polite diversion of gentlemen (as cricket occasionally was), American football had seemed to
save the English from themselves.

Cricket, of course, was for decades the compressed form in which
children in the distant colonies absorbed imperial ideals—"playing
with a straight bat," applauding a good sport, never doing what isn't
"cricket." In his classic book, *Beyond a Boundary* (referring to the
"boundaries" that cricket enshrines as well as to the ones he crossed),
C. L. R. James describes how it was cricket that gave him a taste of
Burke, even in Trinidad, and cricket (together with Thackeray—he
knew *Vanity Fair* almost by heart, he says) that colored his dreams
(of England, and of an arena in which the West Indies could get the
better of England, and prove themselves more elegant). Even as a
founder of African nationalism and a strict Trotskyite, he could
recall, with fondness, how cricket had taught him the white-flannel
proprieties of the "public-school code" (and could write, with undisguised admiration, of a captain of the English team who was a "Char-
terhouse and Cambridge" man).

As a schoolboy, in the Queen's Royal College in Port of Spain,
James wrote accounts of Oxford-Cambridge matches of fifty years
before (and later won two volumes of Kipling with his essay on

Empire); and when finally he sailed for Portsmouth, in 1932, "the British intellectual was going to Britain," as he wrote (with an irony probably encouraged by his reading). Upon arrival, of course, he learned—as the tales of passage decree—that most of his colonial masters had never heard of Becky Sharp, and had little time for black upstarts raised on old issues of *Young England*. Yet what is most striking about his account is his description of how the imported code of stoicism and sportsmanship—"Well played!" "Hard luck!"—had been perhaps the one unifying factor among the scattered islands of the Caribbean, and, as his fellow West Indian George Lamming would point out, at the end of the fifties, Indian cricket teams were Indian, Australian were Australian, English were English, and West Indian were "Indian, Negro, Chinese, white, Portuguese mixed with Syrian" (the Caribbean, he wrote, "though provincial, is perhaps the most cosmopolitan race in the world"). Now, of course, it's almost impossible to tell the English team from the West Indian (or, indeed, from the Indian, or even the Dutch, or the eleven representing the United Arab Emirates, since all of them mix players called Smith with Patels and Chanderpauls). A modern-day James might not know where to place his dreams.

I thought of James, and especially his judgment (delivered with a characteristically heroic lucidity)—"I was an actor on a stage. . . . I not only took it to an extreme, I seemed to have been made by nature for nothing else"—the next time I saw my Indian friend, in Los Angeles, as it happened, at one of the Bombay Palace restaurants now reproduced around the globe. He had come to America in search of a new life, I inferred, and I was reminded, sadly, of how the unhappiest people I know these days are often the ones in motion, encouraged to search for a utopia outside themselves, as if the expulsion from Eden had been Eden's fault. Globalism made the world the playground of those with no one to play with.

As my friend began talking, I felt I was hearing exactly the same lines as before, in Cambridge ("Who is Kim-Kim-Kim?" asks Kipling's hero); it was as if he were perpetually conducting a discussion (an argument, really) with himself, or someone who said nothing in return. "I see so much hatred in England now," he said, as if to explain his presence here. "Maybe it's just because I'm more aware of it than I used to be, but I know bloody well I speak better English than they do, and the English won't accept that. The English hate me for being more English than they are; they want you all to conform to some image they can patronize. But because I know more about English literature than they do, and because I believe in the good old notions of fair play and decency"—there they were again, the same qualities Salman Rushdie had claimed to expect of England—"they can't stand me. I should have won an Oscar for the role I played."

The sentences went in circles, much as he did; he'd lost track of where he was, I felt, playing an Englishman while he cursed the English, fleeing an India that was surely his great calling card in England.

"You see, I grew up with all these notions when I was young," he continued, tucking into the hottest food the waiter could find, his voice as sonorous as Gielgud's. "I remember, I used to open a page of Shakespeare's, and read a line, and my great-uncle could always give me the next line. I think it was from there that I got my love of English literature, and the buildings, the history, all that. The men who raised me believed in all the Victorian values."

But Victoria, I wanted to say, had died almost a century ago, and I wondered how many of these memories had actually grown up in his nostalgic accounts to Englishmen. "When I was a boy," he went on, "my aunt used to bring me a cable-knit sweater every year, handmade from Dehra Dun; now I'd do anything to get a cable-knit sweater. It's funny: I suppose the only people who believe in the old values any more are a few old fogies writing for the *Daily Telegraph*, and talking about the loss of the country they love. So I find myself agreeing with the people I want to hate."

Just as I was beginning to despair, a shaft of self-knowledge, and I thought how deeply Indian he sounded even in his affirmation of Englishness (so assertive, so earnest, so passionate even; besides, few Englishmen would have been caught dead talking so warmly about the Beeb or *The Times* or the Marylebone Cricket Club).

"Whenever things fall apart," he said, and I was touched again, unexpectedly, "I turn to India. Indian restaurants, Indian faces, Indian news." But he couldn't go back, of course, until he'd made it as an Englishman, and I couldn't imagine many Englishmen wanting to be told by him what "Englishness" really was. America was a desperate last resort.

"The Indians living in England seem to me to embody all the worst qualities of England, to do with greed and undereducation," he said, "and none of the best. Maybe it was never really like that, but I always felt that this country stood for something, that there were ideals here." In the made-for-export version, I thought, perhaps cruelly; in the never-never England "before the war" that both of us could idealize because we'd never seen it.

"I left England," I said, maybe only to provoke him, "because I felt that, having gone to the 'right' school and college, I had no incentive to do anything; I could have been a homicidal maniac, and still, I felt, I could always get a good job."

"Then why didn't you stay?" he responded to this unkindness, and I realized that what I should have said was that anything can be a source of resentment in England: the details are neither here nor there. What colonialism had given me was the chance to grow up so close to the heart of Empire that I could never be enthralled by it.

But that wasn't what he wanted to hear, and, in fact, I felt he didn't want to hear very much at all.

"I can't help thinking they've changed the rules on me," he said, and again I felt as if he were talking to himself. "They taught me to believe in one set of values, and I do; and now it's a completely different England."

. . .

Indeed it is, and the old, simple relation of dreamer to dream had been shaken about in the Global Age, as if by a hyperactive child in the heavens. When I got off the plane at Heathrow, on a recent trip, it was to find the London cabs swathed in ads for Fujitsu and Burger King, and the billboards in the tube stations advertising Afro-Caribbean hair treatments and an all-black production of *Antony and Cleopatra* (on my next trip, they were advertising a production in which Cleopatra was played by a man). The laundry list in my little hotel had a special box for "Arab Gown" (and spelled *college* with a *d*); in the Yellow Pages, a place still known as St. Bede's Church now advertised itself, impenitently, as a "Temple of Fitness" where you could "work off thy last Supper" with "our 100 American state-of-the-art machines."

Every myth (as the great fashioner of them, Wilde, explains in his parable of Dorian Gray) has a power to hang on long after the reality has shifted, and Little England would surely uphold old notions of "Englishness" long after Great Britain had reached out to the larger world; the country I'd grown up in greeted me in the tabloid's gleeful cry, HE'S FOUND THE CHINK IN CHANG'S ARMOUR, or in the fire notice in my room—not far from a laminated card offering direct-dial service to Häagen-Dazs—warning, "Do not prejudice your safety by stopping to collect your personal belongings" (in the event of a conflagration). Cities face the same choice that celebrities do when measuring their shadows—they can either play to the cameras or turn their back on them (do a Norman Mailer, you could say, or a J. D. Salinger). England had unapologetically chosen the first course, marketing the Royal Family for all it was worth, and encouraging bagpipers to play outside the Dunkin' Donuts parlor in Theatreland. In Keats's house, you can buy a teddy bear wearing a sash that says I AM A R♥MANTIC.

To me, again, much of this was welcome. No one but an American is likely to deny the appeal of American culture, and I can still remember, as a child in Oxford, sitting transfixed before Hanna-Barbera cartoons, or Lucille Ball in all her incarnations, not because they were American but because they were better and more vivid than anything else on TV (and later, in adolescence, finding images of possibility and hopefulness in Henry Miller or the Grateful Dead that simply weren't available in England); anyone who's grown up on Wimpy Bars and greasy "transport caffs" can appreciate how life in Oxford was made unimaginably more pleasant by the advent of first Baskin-Robbins and then McDonald's in the late seventies, offering clean and dependable places in which to eat that were neither cheap nor expensive. Again, in fact, like America, England seemed to have been invigorated by its visitors from abroad, and it never seemed a coincidence to me that many of Britain's proudest new traditions—the Globe Theatre, *Granta*, British Airways, and the modernized Oxford colleges—had been rescued by energetic "Yanks."

England now looked to me, as most places do, more American, more European, more Asian—more everything but its old self—and that meant that the food was better, the culture was livelier, and the grudges were buried under a new glossy sheen; everything, including the colors, was richer than before (to the point where London had even managed to "rebrand" itself as a city of young lovers whose "Cool Britannia" styles were drawing kids from around the Continent). To some extent, the island was being forced to grow less insular, more tolerant to a whole world streaming into it (the Empire in reverse), and anyone who wanted to say, as Nancy Mitford had not untypically done, "Abroad is unutterably bloody and foreigners are fiends" had to do so now sotto voce.

But what this convulsion was doing to desire was something stranger: I stepped into a phone booth my first day back—somewhere between Foodland and Chinatown in the heart of central London—and noticed that the little slips of paper plastered all over its windows said HOT AS A VINDALOO (advertising a nineteen-year-

old "Busty Indian Beauty") and TURKISH PRINCESS, CARIBBEAN
BARBARA and STUNNING MEXICAN MODEL. Foreignness was being
presented not just as a fact of life but as something tempting, to be
desired as much as the traditional English pleasures (while I was
making my call, a polite kid popped into the booth and slapped up
two more stickers: FULLY EQUIPPED DUNGEON and NAUGHTY
FRENCH MAID).

That same trip, I happened to meet two old friends from India,
both of whom (several years younger than I) had graduated from one
of the subcontinent's most up-to-the-minute business schools. Nothing in England was very new to them, I suspected, because they
already had Thai restaurants and McDonald's, cell phones and
Swatch watches in Bombay. Land prices in their city were higher
than in Tokyo, they told me, and forty cable channels were about to
become eighty; their own two-year-old daughter, who sat quietly at
our table, was already familiar with the streets of Hong Kong and
Singapore and Bangkok and Dubai.

We walked along Coptic Street after lunch, passing cycle rickshas
moving in the opposite direction, and on the Tottenham Court Road,
we passed shops advertising "Ansaphones" in their windows. TUBE
STATION WORST CHAOS YET said the tabloid sandwich boards outside the Underground station, where some boys were shouting and
spitting at an old homeless man.

We walked into a park so their little girl could use a slide, but the
place was filled with fourteen-year olds, mostly of Indian origin,
cadging cigarettes, and a man was urinating in the bushes. The hotel
nearby, with its chambers called Le Bar, Le Terrace, and Le Restaurant, seemed a better option.

The story of this transaction, of foreign romantic and stubborn
Albion, has, of course, been written many times over, not least
because one of the great bequests of Empire was the English

language, which its colonial subjects, with their un-English energy
and quickness—their outsiders' willingness to try anything and haz-
ard all—had turned into an anarchic new confection. Indians still
recall how Macaulay, in his 1835 "Minute on Education," proposed
the creation of a class of interpreters "Indian in blood and colour, but
English in taste, in opinions, in morals and in intellect"; yet by the
time that Emerson visited England, scarcely a generation later, it
already looked, to his outsider's eye, as if the country, at the height of
its Victorian confidence, was "an old and exhausted island [that] must
one day be contented, like other parents, to be strong only in her
children."

The children came in many forms, of course, but their complaints
formed a multipart harmony. "You see, in America, a black is an
African-American," a young "Jamaican" lawyer (born in England)
said to me one day, as if to a fellow conspirator. "In Germany, they're
Afro-Germans. But here, they are always Afro-Caribbeans. Never
Afro-English. You and I, we could never belong; we were born here,
we're as English as Jack and Jill, but we're never allowed to be English. You know what I mean?"

I didn't entirely agree with her—and I knew that Indians were less
sympathetic to West Indians than many Englishmen were—but I
couldn't contest the strength of her feelings. "Not that I care, mind
you," she went on, sounding very English. "I mean, look at them—
who'd want to be English?"

Yet the same words had an even greater resonance, often, coming
from India, if only because the largest and one of the oldest of the
British colonies had been so much a part of the national consciousness that, as Jan Morris puts it, it seemed "the second focus of a dual
power," and its relations with the motherland had always been as
vexed and poignant as those of two people with too much in common
sharing a crowded room. If my Indian friend had been reading
Tagore instead of Shakespeare, he'd have found the Bengali poet
striking the note of colonial warning as early as 1878, when he wrote,

"Before I came to England, I supposed it was such a small island and its inhabitants were so devoted to higher culture that from one end to the other it would resound with the strains of Tennyson's lyre." And my friend was already in school when Nirad Chaudhuri, in his *Autobiography of an Unknown Indian*—the title itself bespeaks a crowded genre—dedicated to "the memory of the British Empire in India," had noted, "Our ideas of the Englishman in the flesh were very different from our ideas of his civilization."

Chaudhuri had moved to a house in North Oxford, a few minutes from where I was born, to berate the English for not being English enough, and to assert the force of an England that mostly existed, if it existed at all, in Indian memory, and in the copies of Wodehouse you still find in country railway stations across the subcontinent, the iambic pentameters of Derek Walcott hymning his native St. Lucia, the stern Arnoldian rules that Lee Kuan Yew took back to Singapore (a fine of ten thousand Singapore dollars for importing chewing gum, a fine of ten thousand Singapore dollars for feeding birds, a fine of . . .). In all these backhand tributes, there was a strain of wistfulness and fondness that you will seldom find in, say, slaves' accounts of their masters, and even a nostalgic warmth that reminds one that it's always easier for godchildren to respond to the virtues of an older authority figure (even if it's a nation)—reminding him of the reasons he once had to be proud—than it is for his own children.

The classic modern account of such mixed feelings, written for the last generation to grow up under Empire's rule, is, no doubt, V. S. Naipaul's *Enigma of Arrival*, which recounts, with a clarity (and loneliness) that transfixes, all his exertions to come to a country that gave him his sense of vocation, and offered him the possibility of self-respect. Yet when he landed in England, inevitably, it was to find that to arrive, in practice, is to find you're not wanted, and the place isn't what you expected it to be; and that to arrive, in the long run, is to look past all the archetypes and illusions and explanations that fascinated at first, and to realize that it is a place in which to die.

The book takes in, with its eerie intensity, all the sorrows of my Indian friend, and others like him, as Naipaul reports, with a humbling candor, how he landed up in a shabby Victorian boardinghouse full of migrants like himself, and tried, in vain, to match the landscape around him to the passages of *King Lear* and Hardy he loved (the one thing that was changeless in England was his expectations of it); he found himself, he suggests, an exile in his dream, like the haunted figure in the empty colonnades of the de Chirico painting after which the book is named. Even the "idea of winter and snow [that] had excited me" was denied by England's hazy grayness and in-betweens.

Yet the strength of Naipaul's book—a register of its honesty and rigor—is to move beyond such age-old laments and circular complaints, to acknowledge that the ground under the author's feet is shaking. The area where he landed up would become "an Australian, a South African, a white colonial enclave," he writes, and the great metropolitan city he had dreamed of was becoming a haven for tropical refugees like himself; he's made exactly the same mistake—in reverse—that the Europeans had made when arriving in the New World, and, heavy with expectations, claiming to see "Indians" there. Naipaul replaces "the idea of decay," he writes, "the idea of the ideal which can be the cause of so much grief, by the idea of flux."

Thus ends the story of my friend's generation, or my parents' (Naipaul arrived in England in 1950, the same year as my father, who lived just a few hundred yards away from him in Oxford), and as the British Empire has given way to the American and then the International one, as the classic colonial refugee has given way to the Global Soul, what was once a binary relationship is now many-pronged, spraying out into every direction at once. The latest Indians raised in convent schools are likely to find themselves in Harvard Business School or San Jose or Sydney or Toronto; while V. S. Naipaul and his brother went to England, and became writers rooted in tweeds and *The Spectator*, their nephew and niece both went to Canada to write in the Empire of the future (where London is just a suburb, and

Graham Greene a "First Nation" actor who starred in *Dances with Wolves*).

Naipaul's direct contemporary, from the West Indies, Derek Walcott, dodged disappointment by going to America instead (and keeping one foot in the islands—his principal figure being Odysseus, the wanderer who never loses a keen sense of home, and whose journey is always back to his family's harbor); his successor, from India, Salman Rushdie, could afford to turn his back on England because he'd grown up there, and had written a whole half-Moorish book of sighs as a celebration of Indian pluralismo, an act of proprietary nostalgia that could have been called *The Enigma of Departure*. The lyrical reminiscences of the precious stone set in the silver sea, which used to be the province of Indians, could now be written by people like Kazuo Ishiguro, who, even as the Britain around him was exploding to the sound of Johnny Rotten or Irvine Welsh, was writing of a soft, prewar England of stiff upper lip that was close enough to him for him to see through.

Nowadays, the latest Indian kids, in Birmingham and Vancouver and Brampton, Ontario, find their voices in movies with *masala* in the title, or in Hanif Kureishi's bad-boy tales of Indian boys on ecstasy sticking out their tongues at old fogies from both continents; yet still a residue of melancholy remains. In the elegiac, poetic novels of Romesh Gunesekera, a Sri Lankan exile based in London, all his fellow Sri Lankans are caught between a beloved homeland that is being torn apart—when it's not being turned into a Shangri-la hotel—and the Victorian houses and "flat, newly built motorways" of England, where "crumbled glass sparkled like a Shangri-La night under our feet." His characters can go everywhere now—they stay on the twenty-fifth floor of "smart-card" hotels—and have access to everyone, but the return addresses on the faxes they receive are blurred, and their messages get cut off because the answering-machine tape's used up. "I know how to live with only a modem and a strip of plastic," says his deeply lonely and displaced narrator, just before a matriarch (who seems to be the soul of old Sri Lanka) dies and is buried at a London funeral without mourners, "but with each jolt I find I yearn for a story without an end."

And as in any love story that divorce does not really terminate, complications never seemed to end: I happened to be in London on Poetry Day in 1995, when the BBC asked its listeners to vote for their favorite poet. The winner (after the responses of 7,500 people were tabulated) was, to many people's surprise, Rudyard Kipling, Margaret Thatcher's favorite poet, as well as one of Gandhi's. "It must be an awful thing," I remembered his writing, "to live in a country where you have to explain that you really belong there."

My Indian friend, though it sounds too perfect to be true, had always hoped to make it in England as an actor, and I went along one evening to see him in a play in the West End, on the Strand, just across from India House and the Bush House the play mentioned. It was a piece written by one of Britain's most distinguished playwrights, drawn from his boyhood years in India, and yet it followed the pattern of almost every English account of India, as a story of a young Englishwoman haunted by some doglike, "Englished-up" Indians who keep her in a constant state of sexual agitation. One of the actors on stage had actually played a judge in *Passage to India*, a magistrate in *The Jewel in the Crown*.

"Chelsea," says an Indian who loves Tennyson and Macaulay, is "my favorite part of London" (his next sentence is "I hope to visit London one of these days"), and the play turns on a series of witticisms along the lines of "I cannot be less Indian than I am" or "Oh, I thought you'd be more Indian." Next to me, an Irishman was lecturing his pretty young Indian girlfriend on the hazards of multiculturalism as they played out in her native Malaysia.

After the curtain came down, I went to the Opera pub nearby, to meet my friend, his makeup rubbed off and his fancy dress (if not his accent) put away for the night. "I know you're not going to like me saying this," he began (casting me, perhaps, in his private drama as a hypocritical Englishman), "but this is a very, very racist place, and it's getting worse with all this political correctness. You get ahead by playing the exotic Indian, and this political correctness stuff is just another kind of fascism; another way of putting you in a turban."

He'd had difficulty finding parts, I assumed (and it could not be easy finding parts for Indians with a RADA voice); the result was that he'd sometimes gotten gigs reading Kipling's works for books on tape, and once had "swallowed my pride, and played a racist magistrate telling a black to go homo." Even in this play, he said, they'd wanted him to wear a turban—till he'd pointed out that, postpolo, an Indian was far likelier to be wearing jodhpurs.

"It's getting to the point where they only let you play the parts you know," he complained. "It's like South Africa: we're all getting ghettoized." He blamed some of it on the Jews, "and I feel really angry after we fought to save them in the last war, and now they're turning on the Indians." What made it worse, though, were the other minorities. "The notion of a colored minority is a myth, because the Jamaicans hate the Trinidadians, and they both hate the Indians. But no one's letting on."

He would have been bitter anywhere, perhaps, but mobility had given him more people to blame, and the chance to turn every decision into one of race.

"The one good thing about England," I said, to try to change the subject, "which almost redeems it, is the sense of humor."

"English humor is so cruel," he said, and he sounded so deeply shipwrecked, I didn't know how to answer. "You know, I really miss that Indian thing of just giving a hug."

But soon the curtain came up again, the vulnerability was covered in makeup, and he was telling me how he'd just gotten a call from the Nehru Centre, from one of Gandhi's grandsons, as it happened, asking him to participate in a special reading. "Here it is, the bloody centenary of Tennyson, and the only ones celebrating it

are the Indians! The only ones who care: don't you think that says
something?"

I said very little, maybe because I felt he wanted only a confirma-
tion that would compound his various agonies, and he turned on me,
bitterly, with "You're so English!" ("English" now meaning formal,
cold, reserved.) "If there's one thing I don't like about this country—
and there are many things I love; otherwise, I wouldn't be living
here—it's that they don't admit to their feelings. They keep them all
inside."

He paused to take a breath, a sip of his beer, and to give me a gen-
uinely warm and forgiving look.

"I mean, I love things here—like village cricket and going to the
pub." (The very two elements a lonely English expat in Paris had just
singled out for me as the idealized England he missed.) "But the
place is racist. It all depends on who you know, who you went to
school with, all that kind of thing. And, of course, the other Indians
here I really don't have very much in common with. They're from
East Africa; they don't know anything: they're all Bangladeshi restaurateurs. They don't even know how to say *Ramayana.*"

I didn't know how to say *Ramayana,* either, so I kept quiet:
there was nothing I could say if the place where he belonged was,
almost by definition, the one where he didn't want to be, and the
place where he wanted to be was, almost by definition, the one that
wouldn't have him.

"I should let you go," I said finally, since I knew where the conversation would go, and I had nothing to contribute to it.

"How terribly English of you. Saying you want to let me go
because you want to go yourself."

When I was five years old and (as it seemed to me at least) the only
little Indian boy in Oxford, I had my first role ever, onstage, as the
changeling in Shakespeare's *Midsummer Night's Dream,* passed back
and forth between fairy king and queen amidst the dreamy lakes and

illuminated, spirit-haunted trees of Worcester College in Oxford. The Oxford University Drama Society must have been delighted to find a "real" Indian boy to play the half-real, motherless child, "stol'n from an Indian king," in the play, and so, richly bribed with Rowntree's Fruit Pastilles and Corgi cars every day for two weeks, I got up each evening in turban and jeweled brooch and allowed myself to be fought over by rival worlds.

I knew far less about the "spicèd Indian air" than many of the English students around me, I'm sure, and probably had less interest in a place that was neither home to me nor exotic; many years would pass before I could see the aptness of the part (going to school in England, to learn that it was rumored, incredibly, that I was the son of a maharajah, and hearing for years kindly Englishwomen say to me, "You speak such good English, dear"). Certainly, I could never see how people like my Indian friend, and those of my parents' generation, could have such a fondness for Oxford, the grimy, everyday industrial town in which I'd been born. England for them was Fabians and Romantic poets and high- and public-minded civil servants; it was Mountbatten, perhaps, and Jowett and Plato; for me, it was union strikes and fish and chips and the sound of broken glass when the pubs closed down at 11:00 p.m. I couldn't really share their admiration for an England I knew too well, I felt, or their partisanship for an India I didn't know at all. England—where they were fifty times as likely to be beaten up on the streets as a white (even in 1990)—was familiar as yesterday's breakfast.

That part, of course, is the standard pattern of how a generation gap plays out across different continents in an immigrant household, and nobody is entirely smitten with the place where he was born. Through pure coincidence, my family had ended up following the very course of Empires, from India in the last days of the British, to England as it was falling under the spell of America, to America itself, in the mid-sixties, when the American Century was at its zenith and the psychedelic California in which we found ourselves was suddenly on every screen. Later, again by chance, I would go to Japan just as it was buying up Rockefeller Center and Columbia Pictures, in the late eighties, and becoming what looked to be a new center of gravity.

But what I also came to see, more slowly, was that some of the distance I felt might be the product of being a Global Soul, for whom all notions of affiliation are hazy; it wasn't so much that my parents were born in India and I in England as that they knew they came from India (albeit a British India), where I always felt I came from nowhere. Our worldviews didn't clash so much as they didn't overlap; my parents knew where they belonged, what they believed, and where their allegiances lay, and remained unchanged in this for all their lives (in thinking that India was a home, and Pakistan was an enemy, and Macaulay and Churchill had been enemies to India); after fifty years of living in the West, they still, quite rightly, kept their Indian passports.

I, by contrast, lacked their furies and felt I'd inherited none of their enmities. I had no tradition to protect, I felt, and I reveled in those like Adorno saying, "It is part of morality not to be at home in one's home." Instead of their passions, I (like many a Global Soul, I think) was more prone to floating dispassion; and instead of their fierce sense of right and wrong, I had a more unanchored, relativistic sense. "Perhaps there is an advantage in being born in a city like Monte Carlo, without roots," says Brown, the suitably anonymous character in Greene's *Comedians* (having seen his "unknown brother" Jones die along the international road), "for one accepts more easily what comes."

The biggest difference between me and those of my parents' generation, I felt, was that I'd never had a strong sense of departures (or arrivals); I'd grown up without a sense of a place to come to or from which to leave—and where someone like my Indian friend was caught in the space between two worlds, as between mother and father in a custody battle, someone like me, I figured, could (for worse as much as better) fit in everywhere. My friend had a map made up of clear divisions; mine was a shifting thing, in which every-where could be home to some extent, and not home to some degree. My sense of severances was less absolute, and though I could visu-alize the partings in the old stories—the boy at dockside, carrying his family's hopes across the seas, perhaps not to see them again for years—I knew I could get anywhere very soon, and nothing was final.

It was many years, then, before I could understand the spells that distance could create, in an age when people really might not know whether they would ever return and separation had a different meaning. It was many years before I could see pictures of my father, proud in his Indian formal wear, president of the Oxford Union, and realize that he was flanked on every side by the kind of Englishmen that an Indian might have dreamed of in Bombay (one would go on to become editor of *The Times*, one deputy prime minister; one would become head of the Liberal party, one the steady sage of the BBC). I imagined his family gathered round the crackly transistor radio in the small flat in the Bombay suburbs, listening to their dis-tant hero on the World Service broadcast opposing such notions as "This House refuses to take itself seriously," and I realized that by going halfway through the open door, he had allowed me to walk out of it on the other side.

One day, when I met my Indian friend, it was to find that, somehow, and unexpectedly, he'd set up house within his dreams: he'd met a highly eligible young Englishwoman—well-born, beautiful, intelli-gent, sincere, and highly successful—and this very picture of the blushing English rose had consented to be his wife. Now, as he spoke, in his Old World cadences, of the "human sufferings" and pri-vations of an India he'd scarcely seen, she sat, quite literally, at his feet, eyes filling with tears at the thought of all he'd been through. Her father, I was not surprised to hear, was a domineering imperial type, still administering his own corner of Empire in the East; she was guilty, anxious to atone, a vegetarian.

Her eyes came to life as she spoke of the possibility of visiting her new in-laws, in the place her husband had worked so hard to flee; he said Hawaii sounded preferable.

A little later, when the romance was over, she would say that he was a hypnotist, another dark sorcerer from the East come to ensnare this young Englishwoman out of Forster; he had tried to turn her into an Indian woman, she complained, walking six paces behind him, and doing up his shoelaces. "Come now, my dear," he had said, "what is this, *Othello*? In Thatcher's England?"

But he had made one mistake that no shrewd Englishman would make, and that no Englishman of the old order would forgive: he had faked a ruling-class pedigree.

"I said I'd gone to Winchester," he told me, a little defiantly, when I saw him next (down on his luck again, and sad), "because I *felt* I'd been there. I remember, when I was fifteen, a man in Singapore telling me, 'You're my little Wykehamist. You talk like a Wykehamist, you act like a Wykehamist, you believe, like a Wykehamist, that manners maketh man.'

"I thought of myself as an Oxonian," he said, a little plaintively, "because Oxford is the home of lost causes."

The last time I was in England, just for a week, to visit friends, I found myself walking towards Trafalgar Square, on a sweltering Sunday afternoon in August, to go to the National Portrait Gallery. Around me, policemen were leading cocky young boys with slicked-back dark hair, and women in veils, and black men in skullcaps through the streets, stopping the traffic as they passed. In the square itself, ringed by the century-old buildings that said CANADA and UGANDA and CANADIAN PACIFIC, and near the statue of George IV, a man was standing on a platform, his voice rough with rage, and he

was shouting, "There is no security in a state where there is no freedom. There are four million Muslims here in England. We are here
as ambassadors of Islam." Around him, massed under banners that
said BIRMINGHAM, NOTTINGHAM, BLACKBURN, stood thousands
of believers, gathered as one and looking towards the stage as if at a
rally in Tehran or Damascus. Dark-bearded boys in militant T-shirts
were telling passersby that they were here to bring peace; angry non-
believers were telling them they were importers of war.

Certainly, the speech makers were not talking of equivocation:
they had come to attack liberalism, they said, to challenge democracy
and the secularism of the state; they were here to wield the sword of
faith. Hundreds in the square were there as if to resist them, handing
out leaflets, hastily spelled, about the treatment of women in Iran, or
reading, in one case, from the Gospel according to John.

On the far side of the street, held back by police cordons, was a
mob of other people, waving signs that said JEWISH SOCIALISTS
GROUP and SHAME, STOP THE VICTIMIZATION OF WOMEN IN
IRAN or, simply, HATE. The cacophony all round was loud enough
almost to block out the public address.

"These people come from countries where you criticize the government, you are dead," said a little old English woman seated on a
bench. "But they want to come here and supplant democracy. These
people are refugees from countries of oppression. And now they're
coming here and bringing their oppression with them. It doesn't
make sense, does it? Even if you think it's wrong, what's happening to
democracy?"

The woman, I was coming to see, was not just a bystander caught
in the cross fire; she had come here to join in the debate. British
ardor comes in the form of resisting outsiders, and British patriotism
arises mostly in response to attack; certainly, on this occasion, the
British were giving as good as they got.

Onstage, a young Englishman had come forward to relate his con-
version experience. "Eleven years ago," he was saying, "I became a

Muslim. Before, I was a Christian; I was confused; I got drunk. Now my name is an Arabic name. It means 'forever.'"

"See," said the woman, stopping her harangue to assess the crowd. "They've moved the homosexuals from round there to over there." I followed her gaze, and sure enough, there was a whole crush of people waving signs that said LESBIAN AVENGERS and VIGILANTE LESBIANS, some of them engaged in long, passionate kisses for the TV cameras. The Islamic Labour party Hizb-ut-Tahrir, I gathered, had denounced gays as "filth" and "scum"; now the signs on the far side of the street said SCREW HIZB-UT! and OUTRAGE!

The chanting all around me continued steady, unabating, as one figure after another came up to bear witness. Tourists drove past in open-topped double-decker buses, staring at the English conflagration in action; women in veils sipped shyly from cartons of Ribena and Muslims from Malaysia sat nervously around the edges. Teenage boys went around collecting money for the mujahedin in Bosnia, their jihad; a fresh-faced, sandy-haired American, carrying a bag from Barnes & Noble, wearing a money belt that said MAGELLAN, stopped off to put forward a missionary response.

"It's a pity the bomb wasn't perfected earlier," an Englishwoman grumped, apropos of nothing I could see. "Because where they should have dropped it is Germany."

"My name used to be Robin," came the voice onstage. "I used to be a born-again Christian. . . ."

Around the square, men were seated at tables, selling pamphlets entitled *Islam and the Space Age* and *Fundamentalism and the New World Order;* others were waving banners in Turkish under a statue of Major-General Henry Havelock, KCB, the soldier who had fought in Lucknow during the Mutiny ("Saved by the valour of Havelock," in Tennyson's words, "Saved by the blessing of Heaven!").

Suddenly there was a distinctive blast, and, as so often happens in central London, for as long as I can remember, a team of jangling Hare Krishnas came past, banging drums and cymbals and chanting, their faces daubed in paint, their shirts and pantaloons pink, delighted, no doubt, to have found such a large crowd today for their exertions.

It was the England I remembered, though the colors and contours had changed a little; a country where the hunger for opinions was exceeded only by the eagerness to vent them. Many of the people around me, I now realized, were here because they loved the chance to fight, and their outrage was working to inflame the Muslim anger, while the Muslim anger was working to fuel their own rage. This was Speakers' Corner—a few minutes away—with real flames.

"This man Sarid Kassim," said a woman who had clearly done her homework and come prepared, "I hate to use the word *fanatic,* but if I could use it, I would use it for him." Her audience—a man in shorts and heavy brown-laced boots who looked as if he were here for a Sunday hike—nodded dumbly. "You see, this is monitored," she went on cunningly. "Nothing escapes the gimlet eye of the service."

A young English boy onstage was shouting, "I used to believe in freedom; I believed in democracy; I believed in secularism. Now I believe in only one thing: Islam."

Irish Catholic girls in veils walked by; football hooligan types and black guys with their blondes. Around me someone was saying, "So you think it's okay for women to go around naked? In this society, there is incest; people are doing it with animals," and someone else was saying, "Jesus was a Muslim, believe me."

"They won't help the Bosnians. Why? Because they are Muslim."

"What is this? No education; self-educated. I don't want to hear this on a Sunday afternoon."

The antinukes were here, and the feminists—on the far side of the road, under the building that said SUID AFRICA on it, around the sculpted nymphs and Latin inscriptions. The cranks were shouting about "nuclear war" and the "Third World War" that would come in 1999. It was easy to write the whole thing off as just the way the English (and newcomers to England with a missionary bent) liked to spend their summer Sunday afternoons—in simulation of war and furious debate.

But thinking of my Indian friend, and of what had drawn those of his generation here (British India preparing them not at all for Indian Britain), I couldn't dismiss the tumult so quickly. The grand statue around the corner had DEVOTION written on one side and HUMANITY on another; at the very top, it said FOR KING AND COUNTRY, and at its base, PATRIOTISM IS NOT ENOUGH. I MUST HAVE NO HATRED OR BITTERNESS FOR ANYONE (from Edith Cavell). The angry Muslims, as ever, had chosen their site and their timing well.

"This Nelson's Column," an African was crying. "You think it just appeared here? Well, it's the same with your own body? Look at Nelson's Column. Look at your own body."

"Listen," a man said. "Jesus was a fanatic of his time. He was a terrorist of his time, an extremist of his time. Why? Because he challenged the law of his time!"

A thin-haired Christian looked around at the ring of debaters that had formed around him. "I don't even see a crowd like this in my church," he said.

Perhaps the last time I had contact with my Indian friend came after a long absence. I had happened to call him to tell him of a death in the family, and he, fumbling for words on the international phone lines, had left a message on my answering machine in which he reached for a quote from Christina Rossetti, then lamented that he couldn't quite summon the right words from Eliot, and then concluded, in his antique voice, "Look after yourself, dear boy," with a resonance that sounded theatrical and emotional both, India and its version of Great Britain.

When I saw him a couple of months later, though, he was playing the same tape as before, over and over, as if some mechanism had gotten stuck somehow and, in the process of emigration, he'd gotten caught in a revolving door, unable quite to come through to the place he'd set out for.

"Of course, if you talk with a thick Indian accent, they'll love you. But if you're middle-class and have some sense of decency, they feel threatened. The working-class white hates a middle-class Indian much more than a working-class Indian with a thick accent and Cockney slang.

"Oh, I don't know," he finally said, turning the tape off at last. "I suppose I just miss an England that is built on elegance and love of language and love of literature, instead of money. Maybe I'm kidding myself; maybe it never existed. Perhaps Bernard Shaw was right in saying 'Patriotism is the last refuge of a scoundrel.'" (I didn't have the heart to tell him it was Samuel Johnson.)

"But I just grew up believing that if you played with a straight bat, things would turn out all right. And somehow it's as if everything's changed. I don't believe in England anymore, and I don't know what I do believe in. And that's a sad and lonely place to be."

THE ALIEN HOME

Daily the world grows smaller, leaving understanding the only place where peace can find a home.

— HUSTON SMITH

And so our dreams of distant places change as fast as images on MTV, and the immigrant arrives at the land that means freedom to him, only to find that it's already been recast by other hands. Some of the places around us look as anonymous as airport lounges, some as strange as our living room suddenly flooded with foreign objects. The only home that any Global Soul can find these days is, it seems, in the midst of the alien and the indecipherable.

And so, a wanderer from birth, like more and more around me, I choose to live a long way from the place where I was born, the country in which I work, and the land to which my face and blood assign me—on a distant island where I can't read any of the signs and will never be accepted as even a partial native. Specifically, I live in a two-room apartment in the middle of rural Japan, in a modern mock-Californian suburb, none of whose buildings are older than I am, with a longtime love whose English is as limited as my Japanese, and her two children, who have even fewer words in common with me. Once every few months, I see a foreign face in the neighborhood, and occasionally my secondhand laptop greets me with, "Good morning, Dick. . . . The time is 6:03 p.m. [in Houston]," but otherwise, long weeks go by without my speaking my native tongue.

You could say that much in the area is familiar—my apartment building is called the Memphis (as in the city of the hero of a thousand karaoke bars), and my girlfriend worked for years at a boutique

called Gere (as in Hollywood's most famous Tibetan Buddhist). The
Gere store is to be found inside the Paradis department store, which
houses the Kumar Indian restaurant on its fourth floor and sits just
across from a Kentucky Fried Chicken parlor, a Mister Donut shop,
and a McDonald's eatery. But the very seeming familiarity of these
all-American props serves only to underline my growing sense of a
world that's singing the same song in a hundred accents all at once.
The Kentucky Fried Chicken parlor is generally rich in young girls
with black silk scarves around their throats, waiting, in thick black
furs and fedoras, for the lucrative (elderly) dates they've just
arranged to meet on their miniature cell phones. Mothers with silent
kids beside them sip demurely at blueberry flans and pear sorbets,
rice taco salads and tomato gratin, while a country-and-western
singer on the sound system croons about the sorrow of lost truckers.
Colonel Sanders is dressed, often, in a flowing blue *yukata,* though
the recipients of his old-fashioned Southern hospitality are largely
carrot-haired boys and girls in black leather microskirts slumped, in
untraditional fashion, across the spotless tables.

On rainy days, the unfailingly perky cash-register girls (with TEAM
MEMBER and ALL-STAR written across their chests) race out to place
umbrella stands in front of the entrance, and hand out "Gourmet
Cards." The scented autoflush toilet plays a tape of running water as
soon as you go in (just past the elegant sink for washing your chicken-
stained hands). And every time a cashier presents me with my
change, she cups my palm tenderly to receive the coins.

I go for walks, twice a day, in and around the neighborhood—the
"Southern Slope of Deer," as its name translates—and pass through
silent, tidy streets that look like stage sets in some unrecorded *Star
Trek* episode. I pass Autozam Revues and Toyota Starlets, Debonairs
and Charmants, Mazda Familias and Honda Todays (with Cat's Short
Story tissues in the back). Mickey Rourke grins down at me from a
bank of vending machines. The local dry cleaner hangs out a sign that
promises REFRESHING LIFE ASSISTANCE. At the intersection of

School-dori and Park-dori (as these science-fictive locales are called), dogs wait patiently for the lights to change, and everything in the whole firm-bordered area is so clear-cut that every single house is identified on maps at the number 12 bus stop.

Outside my window, toddlers cry "Mommy" and men in white shirts and black ties scale ladders to polish the sign outside the bank. Most mornings, a truck rumbles past, playing the unbearably mournful song of a traditional sweet potato salesman.

There are two small strips of stores in my "Western Convenience Neighborhood" (as the Japanese might call it), and both are laid out as efficiently, as artfully, as batteries inside some mini disc player. I can get fresh bread at the Deer's Kitchen bakery and éclairs (and Mozart) at Père de Noel. The Wellness building stands just across from a twenty-second-century health club, which offers *qigong* classes twice a week, its gray walls thick with autumn leaves, and the man at the Elle hair salon tells me (every time I visit) about his one trip abroad, to Hawaii. Right next to the Memphis Apartments, competing with the Elle, the Louvre Maison de Coiffure, and the Musée Hair and Make, is the Jollier Cut and Parm, and I had been in the neighborhood for three years before I realized that the name probably referred to Julia (as in Roberts). A ten-minute bus ride takes me to the Bienvenuto Californian trattoria down the street; the Hot Boy Club (with surfing shop next door); and a coffee shop, above an artificial lake, that used to be called Casablanca and contained the very piano that Dooley Wilson played for Humphrey Bogart.

At one level, of course, all these imported props could not be more synthetic or one-dimensional, and participate, as much as anything in Los Angeles or Hong Kong, in all the chill deracination of the age. The Japanese are probably less apologetic about embracing artifice and plastic replicas than anyone I know, and have few qualms about modeling their lives on the Spielberg sets they've seen on-screen. Those who worry that history is being turned into nostalgia, and community into theme park, could draw their illustrations from this suburb.

Yet the children in the neighborhood call every older woman "Auntie," and the Aunties feed whoever's child happens to be around. At dawn, old women take showers in freezing-cold water and shout ancestral prayers to the gods. The very cool clarity with which the neighborhood shuts me out, calling me a *gaijin,* or outsider person, is partially what enables it to dispense courtesy and hospitality with such dependability, and to import so much from everywhere without becoming any the less Japanese. Surface is surface here, and depth is depth.

The old ceremonies are scrupulously observed in Japan, even in a place where there are no temples and no shrines. Every year when the smell of daphne begins to fade from the little lanes, and the first edge of coldness chills the air, the baseball chat shows on TV transfer their interviews to sets melancholy with falling leaves, and Harvest Newsletters appear beside the Drink Bar at my KFC. And as soon as the five-pointed maples begin to blaze in the local park, it lights up with matrons, sitting at easels, transcribing the turning of the seasons on their canvases.

And sometimes, on these sharpened sunny days, when the cloudless autumn brightness makes me homesick for the High Himalayas, I fall through a crack somehow, and find myself in a Japan of some distant century. Not long ago, as I was looking out on a light so elegiac that it made me think of the magical transformations of the Oxford of my youth (where Alice found her rabbit hole and a wardrobe led to Narnia, and where the Hobbit sprang out of some dusty Old Norse texts), I went out for my daily morning walk along the shiny, flawless streets, held as ever in a tranquil northern stillness of tethered dogs and mapled parks and grandfathers leading toddlers (in Lovely Moment hats) by the hand.

Men were washing their white Oohiro Space Project vans in the street, and girls, or sometimes robots, were crying out "Welcome"

from the computer shop with the two kittens for sale (at five hundred
dollars a pop) in the window. Fred Flintstone in a White Sox cap
invited me to a local softball league, and a Mormon, by a park,
promised some form of enlightenment. A simple prelude of Bach's
floated down from the upstairs window of the stationery shop. And,
just behind the power plant, which I'd passed almost every day for
five years, I chanced, for the first time ever, upon a flight of stairs,
leading down into a valley.

I followed the steps down, and ended up in a thick, dark grove of
trees. I passed out of it and found myself inside another country:
green, green rice paddies shining in the blue-sky morning, and narrow, sloping streets leading up into the hills. Two-story wooden
houses, and a small community ringed by hills. Grandmothers were
working in traditional white scarves outside their two-story homes,
and as I passed one, she favored me with a gold-toothed smile. "It's
warm," she said, and so was she. "Look at me! I'm working in my
socks!"

I walked on farther through the silent village streets, past flower-
ing persimmon trees and a central oval pond. Then I turned back,
and greeted the old woman—my friend now—as I passed. I climbed
the fifty-four steps, and the hidden world fell behind me as a dream.

Four-year-old boys were playing catch in Harvard T-shirts; women
walked with parasols to shield their faces from the sun.

Japan will never be entirely my home, of course, and Japan would
never really want me to come any closer than I am right now. It
assigns me a role when I enter (a role that diminishes every foreigner
with glamour, and marvels at his stammerings as at a talking dog),
and asks me to go about my business, and let it go about its own. It
offers politeness and punctuality without fail, and requests in
exchange that I accept my fixed role in the bright, cheerful pageant
that is official life here. Coming from quicksand California, where
newcomers are warmly welcomed to a vacuum and no one really

knows where he stands in relation to anyone else, I find a comfort in the culture's lack of ambiguity.

Magic realism, the literary form native to our floating world, tells us that the simplest fact of our neighbors' lives may read like fairy tale to us. The forgotten, tonic appendix to that is that our lives, in their tiniest details, may seem marvelous to them, and one virtue of living in so strange a place is to be reminded daily of how strange I seem to it. Whenever I am tempted to laugh at the notebook on my dinner table that says "This is the hoppiest day of my life," or the message from the abbess of a famous local nunnery that prays (in the English translation) for "Peace on the earth and upon every parson," I recall that the real sense of local comedy, for the Japanese all around, is me: an unshaven, disheveled, seemingly unemployed Asian who speaks like a three-year-old and seizes the senior citizen "silver" seats on the bus. "The most peaceful place on earth," Canetti writes, "is among strangers."

This is a way of saying only that many of us are exiled amongst strangers now, and it makes most sense to embrace the odd fusions we cannot resist. For me, I can relish all the conveniences and courtesies of Japan (which come to a foreigner without the value-added tax of social responsibility), and savor, too, the fact that the most ordinary transactions are extraordinary (to me). Every time I call the local Federal Express office, I get put on hold to the sound of the *Moonlight* Sonata, and when I turn on the TV (bilingual, and with headphones attached), it is to find an exotically dubbed drama—from California, as it happens—called *The Wonder Years*. Even the places that have least romance to me—especially the rainy redbrick England that is the stuff of childhood—pass through a kind of magic looking glass and reemerge in dreamy dissolves of country houses and Beatrix Potter figures, pretty young boys on sunlit lawns and the "University of Oxford" shirt my girlfriend gives me from the Piccolo Sala store.

Japan treats its residents as coddled children, and so the props of infancy are all around, though found in the terms of my own distant past. Paddington Bear smiles down at me from street corners (not least because he's the mascot of one of Japan's leading banks), and those signs on the local train not advertising a Royal Riding School are announcing the arrival of Thomas the Tank Engine at the local theme park. Noddy books are scattered across the shelf of the desk where I work, and when I go to the Lawson Station around the corner, I find Smarties (here mysteriously rechristened Marble chocolate) and Mentos, Maltesers, and McVitie's chocolate digestives (in bite-sized haiku form). Japan's response to globalism, it sometimes seems, is a promiscuous consumption of all the cultures in the world, at the level of their surfaces—all of them converted into something so Japanese that I can feel as if I'm reading Proust in German.

Yet deeper than such toddlers' props, I recognize in the neighborhood the outlines and emotions of the safe, protected England I knew when young, with its orderly, changeless universe of corner shops and drizzly afternoons, tea served promptly at 5:00 p.m. I recognize, more than the words, the codes and silences, the emphases that politeness fights back or the force of all the things unsaid. I recognize the imperial shelteredness, the island suspiciousness of the personal pronoun, the Old World cultivation of private hopes and habits that leave the status quo alone.

On its surface, Japan is more alien than anywhere I know; but underneath the surface, it speaks the language I was trained to hear.

I am reminded of how little I belong here—how alien I am to Japan's image of itself—each time I return to the place I like to treat as home. At the Immigration desk, the authorities generally scrutinize my passport with a discernible sense of alarm: a foreigner who neither lives nor works here, yet seems to spend most of his time here; an alien who's clearly of Asian ancestry, yet brandishes a British passport; a postmodern riddle who seems to fit into none of the approved categories.

After I've been reluctantly waved on to the customs hall, I collect
my bag and park my cart in a line of obviously law-abiding Japanese
tourists returning from their holidays in California. When it's my
turn to be questioned, I am confronted with a customs officer who is,
for some reason, always very young and uncommonly fresh-faced.
He (or sometimes she) goes through the standard list of queries:
where have I come from? How long will I stay? What am I doing
here? Then, abruptly, he asks, "You have marijuana, heroin, LSD,
cocaine?" No, I say, I don't. "You have ever had marijuana, heroin,
LSD, cocaine?" he goes on, waving, now, a laminated picture of these
forbidden substances. No, I say, not always able to keep a straight
face. "Porno video?" No.

"Please open your bag."

At this, he pores carefully over all my belongings—the stacks of
faded notes in a hand even I can't read; the scattered bottles of hotel
shampoo, which have already begun to leak and deface everything in
their vicinity; the Olympic pins I'm bringing for my girlfriend's children, and the elaborate set of inhalers I need to protect myself from
Japan's allergy-producing cedar trees.

Then, almost inevitably, he comes upon a tiny red tablet of
Sudafed antiallergy medicine. Gravely, he mutters something to a
colleague. Whispers are exchanged. Then, nervously, they radio a
superior, and, with brusque politeness, I am led away, by at least two
officers, to a distant room. My guards look anxious and unhappy, as if
they recall that the only time Paul McCartney was separated from
Linda was as the result of a Japanese customs check.

In the back-room interrogation center, my home from home, I
know the drill by heart, having visited so often, and proceed to take
off my clothes, till I am down to my underpants. Meanwhile, as many
as seven uniformed officials gingerly go through my possessions, surveying every last bottle of leaked shampoo, every last sticky Mento in
my coat pocket, even the temple charm in my wallet. My shoes are
shaken out, my toothbrush holder is fearfully inspected, a stick of
incense is held up as if it contained cannabis.

Then I am subjected to a barrage of questions. Why do I carry over-the-counter allergy pills that contain a stimulant as proscribed as LSD or cocaine? What prompted me to bring antihistamines into a peace-loving island? Will I formally consent to hand over my drugs to the Japanese authorities, and authorize a confiscation of my tablets, while signing a confession?

I am more than happy to do all of that, sometimes saying so in such amiable gibberish that the officials, fingers sticky with shampoo, tell me, "Okay, okay. You'd better leave before you miss the last train." But my answers only compound their dissatisfaction. "Where were you born?" one asks me, while another tests my case for false bottoms. "England," I say, as they scrutinize a Hideo Nomo telephone card. "No, where were you really born?" "Oxford, England," I say, "as it says on my passport." "What are you doing here?" I show them my *Time* business card, my Time Inc. photo ID, even my name in a copy of *Time* magazine. I show them a whole book I wrote on Japan, interviews I've conducted in Japanese magazines, notes on Japanese topics I'm working up. Unhappy with this, they try a spot quiz. "Who is Masako-san? What is the importance of Kyoto? Where are you really from?"

Sometimes, sensibly enough, I have made sure that not a single antihistamine tablet could be found within a hundred-yard radius of my person. But, really, that's beside the point, since it's not my allergies that trouble them. Once, I was strip-searched for making a phone call from the customs hall, once for going to the men's room. Once, I was taken aside because my overcoat was *"abunomaru* (I was flying to the Himalayas), and once I was even stopped as I was going out of the country ("Why is your photo so creased?" "Because so many Japanese officials have pored over it"), and the British embassy was hastily faxed on a Sunday night to authorize my departure.

What concerns the Japanese, obviously, is just that I'm a Global Soul, a full-time citizen of nowhere, and, more specifically, one who looks like exactly the kind of person who threatens to destroy their civic harmony. During the Gulf War, I was routinely treated as if I were Saddam Hussein's favorite brother; at other times, I have been detained on the grounds of resembling an Iranian (41,000 of whom have stolen into Japan and live illegally, in tent cities in Tokyo parks, or nine to a shabby guest-house room, undermining the local economy with fake telephone cards). The rest of the time, I am suspected of being what I am—an ill-dressed, dark, and apparently shiftless Indian without a fixed address.

The newly mobile world and its porous borders are a particular challenge to a uniculture like Japan, which depends for its presumed survival upon its firm distinctions and clear boundaries, its maintenance of a civil uniformity in which everyone knows everyone else, and how to work with them. And it's not always easy for me to explain that it's precisely that ability to draw strict lines around itself—to sustain an unbending sense of within and without—that draws me to Japan. In the postmodern world, to invert Robert Frost, home is the place where, when you have to go there, they don't have to take you in.

My daily life in Nara is itself a curious artifact, belonging to a kind of existence that even I could not have imagined only a decade ago, before "home office" fax machines and Global Village modems, with international telephones on every other street corner, made centrifugal lives possible. In terms of the world I grew up in, almost none of it makes any sense, but in terms of the world we're entering, it forms the outlines of a complete sentence.

I go to sleep every day here by 9:00 p.m., in part so as to wake up at 5:00 a.m., when my employers (thirteen time-zones away) are at their desks (their office hours stretching from 11:00 p.m. to 7:00 a.m., Nara time). My research facility, if I need to check on something, is an English-language bookstore ninety minutes away by train, and my version of the Internet is a copy of the *World Almanac*.

The person I see most often, outside my immediate household, is the Federal Express boy who comes to collect and deliver packages from distant Osaka. In the newly shrunken world, I can complete articles or even books without having to exchange a word with editors, and can draw out money in a local department store from a bank account on the other side of the planet.

For breakfast, I generally enjoy some combination of asparagus cookies or chlorella biscuits, chaperoned by what is here known as "Royal Milk Tea," and for lunch I go to a convenience store round the corner, where all the goods of England and America are on sale, yet nothing is quite as I would expect. Little old women are photocopying Chopin scores to the sound of piped-in Clash songs, and teenagers with safety pins all over their faces are consulting magazines with names like *Classy* and *Waggle* and *Bang*. Though the whole place is only four aisles wide, it is crammed with wild plum chews and mangosteen candies, tubs of Grand Marnier pudding and vitamin jelly drinks. There are ice-cream sandwiches here made of Darjeeling tea, tandoori-flavored potato chips, and Kiss Mints that come in flavors of litchee and lime, kiwi, "Wake-up," and "Etiquette." There are "Moisture Desserts" and cups of "Mango Dream Snow," injunctions on packages to "Listen to the sweet murmurings of vegetables. You'll feel pleasure and find a smile." Once, while munching from a bag of potato puffs, I looked down, to see three characters prancing around the bag, and identified as Jean and Paul and Belmonte.

Usually, in the afternoons, I go to the post office next door, where all the clerks look up as I enter, as at the arrival of their daily soap opera. My principal means of communicating with the world at large is fraught with hazards: the envelope I'm using (from my company) is too large—measured against a transparent green ruler the workers wield—or I've neglected to attach a *Par Avion* sticker. Once I was rebuked for including too long a PS on the back of an envelope, and once, during the holiday season, I came in, only to be presented with a special invoice for thirty dollars when it was discovered that my New Year's greetings exceeded the regulation five words.

Afterwards, I walk around the local park, past the "bad boy" son of the electrician, polishing his Corvette till it's red as his waist-length hair, past the dogs that bark furiously at my alien scent and children who back away as if at the sight of the summer horror blockbuster from California. At one street corner in this placid country neighborhood, there is a set of vending machines where I can buy forty-nine kinds of cigarettes, thirty-six alcoholic drinks, ninety-two nonalcoholic drinks, and a bewildering array of brightly colored cans advertising Corn Potage soup and Melon Cream soda, Calorie Mate Block and Drafty Beer. In the supermarket, grannies handle radishes with black-fingered gloves and the shifty character beside me at the butcher shop sports a gold star on his breast that says ASSISTANT SHERIFF, LARIMIE.

Japan is notorious for treating all the world as a kind of giant souvenir store, from which it can mix and match at will, and many a newcomer, to Kyoto, for example, is taken aback to find the old imperial capital gaudy with "Think Potato" bars, "Amazement Spaces," and stores styling themselves "American Life Theater" (while the Eagles' "New Kid in Town" is piped into the geisha quarter). Yet the impersonality of Japan, to me, is that not of a country that hasn't matured into character so much as of one that keeps its passions to itself. The public world strives to be generic, to keep friction and confusion to a minimum; individuality flowers behind closed doors.

And though the reach of such daily oddities is only shallow, I often think of that moment in Christopher Isherwood's *A Single Man,* in which a woman from Sarah Lawrence reproaches California for offering "unreal places" instead of history and nuanced depth. Instead of Gothic cathedrals, she implies, it serves up Motel 6.

At this, Isherwood's stand-in narrator replies with passion, pointing out that it's precisely the unreality of the look-alike motel that prevents one from taking it too seriously; synthetic surfaces, he says, are a good deal less likely to keep one enthralled to them than that whole "old cult of cathedrals and first editions and Paris models and white wine." California encourages transcendence, he argues, precisely because its surfaces are so empty.

A position easier for an Old World exile to take, perhaps, than someone native to its state of permanent revolution; yet a salutary reminder that a place of hollow surfaces has some advantages over one of seductive ones. It's only the invisible things that make us feel at home.

My next-door neighbor in the four-apartment building where I pass my days is a Baptist minister who speaks perfect English, from his student days in Chicago, and dispenses his wisdom from a drab second-story apartment in the building across from ours, with a cross on the balcony outside and a sign reminding potential parishioners that attendance of a service brings with it a free English lesson. Whenever he passes me on the stairs, he looks away as if confronted by an agent of Beelzebub's. By contrast, the apartment upstairs from mine is occupied by a *yamama* (or "young mother" crossed with "Yankee mother," as the cunning Japanese term has it), who greets me with extravagant delight every time we meet, her long hennaed hair flying as she wrestles with two toddlers, a stroller, and the exigencies of her leopard-skin attire.

Occasionally, Jehovah's Witnesses appear at my door, with copies of *The Watchtower* in Japanese and, rallying at the sight of me, pass over a page on which their prayers are printed in fifty languages. Occasionally, telemarketers call up to plug some international phone service, but they are quickly scared off by my indecipherable answers. The world is here if one wants to follow it, even in this historically most closed of cultures: my local English-language paper carries even the scores of the Albanian and Luxembourg soccer leagues, and the monthly English-language magazine has notices for the Baha'i Communities of Osaka/Kobe, the Synagogue Ohel Shelo-moh, even the Norwegian Seamen's Church (close to its ads for "culture friendships" and "marriage-minded Canadians").

But what the people in my small apartment block enforce, every day, is that, increasingly nowadays, a sense of home or neighborhood can emerge only from within; I have never talked to the Baptist minister or to the rock 'n' roll mother, but for both of them, in opposite ways, I am a symbol of a world they cannot touch. And I, in reverse, can't begin to sustain the illusion that I know very much about them (as I might do "at home"). The Global Age reminds us of how little we really know about the people we pass on the stairs every day; identity will have to be deepened without much help from outside.

Every few weeks in Nara, in order to pay the bills, I take a bus down the street to a bank with stained-glass windows, where the cashier, as she changes my dollar traveler's checks into yen, hands me a Nara Bank toothbrush, to ease the silence, or, as often as not, two packages of Kleenex. One woman, on the Foreign Exchange floor, greets me every time I visit with a rapturous "Pico-san, long time no see!" and congratulates me on going back to California to see my mother, or on not doing so, and protecting my family here. When she is absent, her place is taken by a grimacing superior who glowers at me with obvious distaste, and pages through my passport in the hope of finding an irregularity.

Afterwards, I generally stop in at the library, my only real source of English-language news, and then at the Tsutaya Culture Convenience Club, where, when I rent, say, *Chungking Express* (in Cantonese, with Japanese subtitles), I am offered a choice between a small box of Kellogg's Genmai Flakes and a 289-page book listing all the store's animated videos. Though not enormous, the Culture Club has special sections for every actor you can think of (and many whom you can't), right down—or up—to Charlotte Gainsbourg, Vanessa

Paradis, and Moira Kelly, and brings home to me that even the things I know get translated into something other here (as *Jerry Maguire* becomes *The Agent*, and *Up Close and Personal, Anchor Woman*). When I watched Forrest Gump's rise to fame on video in Japan, I was surprised to see the hero, during the turmoil of the sixties, attending UCLA (as the Japanese translate Berkeley), though that is probably no stranger than the local baseball broadcasts, with their talk of "dead balls," "timely errors," and "sayonara home runs," and their habit, when the tying run's on third, with two outs in the ninth, of breaking for an ad for sanitary napkins, or switching to the next show because the time is up.

In short, the very notion of what is here and there—what is familiar, what is strange—has to be reconfigured in the modern world. In Japan, it is the apparently familiar things—the Western things (played out here, as it were, in katakana script)—that are most strange to me, as I have found it to be the tempura palaces or the Buddhas by the hot tub that are most curious, often, for Japanese visiting America. Speaking a foreign language one has scarcely learned is easier, perhaps, than trying to negotiate a tongue in which all the letters are the same, but ineffably scrambled, so that *home* appears as *oh me,* and *life* comes out as *file.*

And once a year, on the night of the harvest moon, I make a trip to the center of Nara, the imperial Buddhist capital of thirteen hundred years ago, and see costumed dancers in wooden boats ceremoniously floating around a pond into which a heartbroken empress once threw herself. A four-story pagoda is reflected in the water, and men in grass skirts brandish burning torches against the dark. Every now and then, the nighttime is pierced by the long, plangent wails of a bamboo flute.

The courtesans in their boats look out at us like wraiths, faces ghostly white and kimono the color of blood against their crow black braids. The wind sends red lanterns fleeting against the trees. Old women, hunched over, carry luminous globes up hills like shadows from a Hiroshige print, and schoolgirls at the stands nearby giggle over Marilyn Monroe telephone cards and hand puppets in the shape of Buddha.

Somehow, at this ceremony for tourists (many of them Japanese, who are tourists in their own history), I see something I recognize.

Perhaps the way in which my neighborhood most solidly uplifts and steadies me is by virtue of its tonic blend of cheerfulness and realism, measured (as I see it) with the wisdom of a culture that's been around long enough to know how to mete out its emotions. To many I know from the New World, the Japanese response to every setback, from terrorists to burning houses to long hours, crowded trains, and sudden deaths—*Shikataganai,* or "It can't be helped"—sounds fatalistic, and too ready to surrender power to the heavens. But to me, coming from a California where it sometimes seems as if everyone is restlessly in search of perfection in his life, his job, his partner, and himself, it feels bracing to hear of limits that imply a sense of past as well as of future. A republic founded on the "pursuit of happiness" seems a culture destined for disappointment, if only because it's pursuing something that, by definition, doesn't come from being sought; a culture founded, however inadvertently or subconsciously, on the First Noble Truth of Buddhism—the reality of suffering—seems better placed to deal with sorrow, and be pleasantly surprised by joy. In a world that's overheating with the drug of choice and seeming freedom, Japan, for all its consumerist madness, suggests, in its deeper self, a postglobal order that knows what things can really be perfected (streets, habits, surfaces) and what cannot.

In practical terms, this very serenity—some would say complacency—is perhaps what gives an air of pink-sweater innocence to protected neighborhoods such as mine. I do not believe the Japanese are more innocent than anyone else, but they are, perhaps, more concerned with keeping up appearances, especially of innocence, and whole communities are urged to play their part in this display of public sweetness (it is certainly the only culture I know where women, to look seductive, don't narrow their eyes, but widen them). Much of this can be converted in translation into what is regarded as hypocrisy, but it can also suggest a prudent drawing of boundaries in a world where they are in flux, and a sense of which illusions can be serviceably maintained, and which cannot (as the ad outside my building ambiguously promises: HONEST COSMETICS TO MAKE YOU FOREVER YOUTHFUL AND BEAUTIFUL).

The society urges its members to conceive of a purpose and an identity higher than themselves (people give you their business cards when you meet them here, but not their résumés or dogmas). And even punky nose-ring boys and scruffy Indians are implicitly urged to tend to responsibilities beyond their mortal bodies. I find myself picking up stray pieces of trash as I walk down the street (almost as reflexively as I find myself, now, bowing to a public telephone as I put it back in its cradle on my return to California); getting up from my seat in the bank, I stop to brush it clean as I would never do "at home."

The homes we choose, in short, deserve a tolerance we might not extend to the homes we inherit, and in a world where we have to work hard to gain a sense of home, we have to exert ourselves just as much to sustain a sense of Other. I choose, therefore, to live some distance from the eastern hills of Kyoto, which move me like memories of a life I didn't know I had. To visit the city of temples from here involves a ninety-minute pilgrimage by bus and train, and second train, and then another train, so that every trip has an air of ceremony and anticipation. Thus Kyoto is unclouded for me by the routines of paying bills and cleaning clothes. And coming to it from a suburb of white Ascots and Clever coffee shops, I still catch my breath when I see the lanterns in the autumn temples, leading up into the bamboo forests, as into another life, or hear the temple bells ringing along the Philosopher's Path at dusk.

Once every six months or so, I take my girlfriend back to her hometown (her Oxford, in a sense), and for six hours we rent a car and drive deep into the countryside. The very novelty of motion, in a space of our own, with a tape deck of our own, is itself a small enchantment, and Kyoto swings open, often, like a heavy gate admitting us to a deeper, ancestral quiet.

One cold winter night, we went there to celebrate a ninth anniversary of sorts and, awakening in the dark, saw the year's first snow coming down to cover the old spires and the few wooden buildings remaining in the center of town. Going out into the freshened chill, still hushed and smoky in the early morning, we rented a car and drove it up into the northeast, traditional area of demons and therefore monasteries, towards Mount Hiei.

As we left the town behind and began climbing the narrow, winding roads of the old mountain, we found ourselves in a festival of silver, the first car admitted up the mountain since the snowfall, and the only car in sight in a world of silence and whiteness for as far as we could see.

Everything was newly minted, virginal in the fresh snow, and the pines were still coated with a sugar lining against a sky now wide-awake and blue. We drove up and up, into a wonderland of sorts, with nothing around but green trees and white, chunks of snow falling from their branches, and everywhere a newborn hush.

The large parking lots with their vending machines stood empty; the occasional tall red torii gates were fringed with white.

We moved along the road in a suspended state of wonder, through a soundless trail that cut high into the dark mountain. Stopping at last, we got out in a silent landscape of huge trees and silver everywhere. The sky was blue and the day was windless. There was no sound anywhere, nothing but dark trees, white lacing, stone Buddhas fringed with snow. A steep slope led up to a temple, hidden away in a grove like a secret pendant against a heart. Huge clumps of white kept falling and there was nothing else to be heard.

Outside Shyaka-do, we sat on a wooden platform while a gong sounded within and a man prepared the day's austerities in front of a large Buddha. My stockinged feet were cold on the wooden steps, and as far as I could see, across the valley, there were just ranks of pines, in whitened rows, extending towards the cloudless sky. Then, briefly, four young monks in blue work clothes, tramping into the forest, headbands white against their shaven scalps. And the silence and the whiteness and the calm.

We sat for a while in the secret sanctuary, quiet on this quiet day. Then we drove back into the high rises and belching trucks and maddened pachinko parlors of the ancient capital.

A large part of the liberation of being here comes, I think, from the enforced simplicities that accompany a very foreign life. Living far from anywhere, without a bicycle or private car, I conduct my days, nearly always, within the boundaries of my feet; living without newspapers or magazines—and a television most of whose words are modern Greek to me—I can be free, a little, of the moment and get such news as I need from the falling of the leaves, or the Emerson essays on my shelf. Living in a small room, moreover, prompts me to be sparing, and to live only with the books and tapes that speak to me in ways I can respect. And not knowing much of the local tongue frees me from gossip and chatter and eavesdropping, leaving me in a more exacting silence.

This can, of course, be an evasion more than a transcendence, and in any case, I cannot hold very much to these austerities: I fly back to California every now and then to pay my bills, and sometimes I can't resist turning on the computer to see how the Lakers are doing. I cannot refuse technology too aggressively when it is technology that allows me to communicate with bosses half a world away, and to get on a plane when I need to see a dentist. Yet being in so alien an environment is the first step towards living more slowly, and trying to clear some space, away from a world ever more revved up. In our global urban context, it's an equivalent to living in the wilderness.

Once, after I'd been living here, on and off, for three years, I decided I needed a typewriter: the machine I was using, an ancient Japanese manual, was as arthritic, almost, as myself, and the only other implements I had for composing my articles were a box of $1.19 pens, a limited supply of paper, and an entirely illegible scrawl. I picked up a local magazine and started going through its classified section, finding at last the name of a company that offered simple, cheap electric typewriters similar to the one I'd had in college. I called them up, faxed them some forms, deposited a payment at the post office, and waited.

A few days later, as if by magic, a Black Cat messenger appeared at my door with my salvation in his hands. Eagerly, I began typing all the articles I'd previously handwritten, and before long, thanks to my expertise, the correction tape was all used up. Suddenly, I was helpless (having survived quite happily for years without a typewriter). Fretfully, I called up the company, got some more forms, faxed them back, deposited a further payment at the post office, and waited. Soon a whole box of correction tapes arrived. By then, however, the regular ribbon was worn out.

Again I was at a loss, stranded, with no apparent way to complete the article I'd started. I rang up the poor salesmen again, completed more forms, made more trips to the post office, and paced up and down like an expectant father. The problem, of course, lay not in the machine but in me, and I was reminded, firsthand, of how quickly we become the servants of our tools, habit-bound machines ourselves.

The story is as old as the camel and the tent—we're always possessed by our possessions—but it reminded me forcibly that the less one has, the less one has to worry about (a lesson that having one's house burn down, and all one's projects and hopes go up in smoke, ought to teach, but somehow does only on paper). And it brought me back to some of the defining principles of the society all around me, which more or less patented the notion that if you decorate a simple room with a single chrysanthemum, it will concentrate the mind and consecrate the flower. It pulled me back, too, to a simpler time, when small pleasures were big and old sensations new. If some of us feel nostalgic for childhood, for all its limitations, that is mostly because we long for a time when days could be eternities and the mind would be where the body is. In a small way, in Japan, with few belongings, no space, and not much savoir faire, I'm carried back to that state of quick enjoyment, where phone calls are so occasional that they're actually welcome and every movie, seen once a month perhaps, seems special.

I dwell, of course, in a kind of parallel universe here, and it takes my girlfriend (who's away at work most of the day) to explain to me that the frightened, kindly woman at the convenience store is, in fact, the cruel owner's wife and the lady who sells me croquettes has a daughter at the local junior high school.

One summer evening, after I'd been here for perhaps four years, she offered to take me on a tour of the neighborhood on her motorbike, and suddenly, five minutes from our flat, I was in a sleek, unanticipated world of Big Boy burger joints and Château d'Or bistros, with the Hotel Silk Road nearby. In parts, the area looked like Atlanta with subtitles, a random suburb made for those with wheels, and appointed with the look-alike global props of Book Bahn, Sushi Land, and Bottle World. Here was the standard jabberwocky of the convenience universe in the latest International Style—Mr. Pachinko, Taco Donald's, boys in baseball caps that said WHAT'S NEXT? SEX trooping into Neo-Geo Land.

In parts, though, it was something other, and as we drove, the shopping centers fell away, often, and gave onto open fields, and rice paddies, and farmers working outside straw-thatched houses, in villages still so linked that the news of the community was transmitted to every single house by speaker at seven o'clock each night.

And as the sky turned indigo, and a huge pulsing moon rose above the hills, suddenly we came upon something even stranger: huge transparent modern buildings, complex with tubes and workspaces, like the innards of a laptop, erected in the middle of nowhere. The signs said they were the Nara Institute of Science and Technology, here in the vastness of old green hills, and other tidy notice boards nearby explained, in English and Japanese, that they were the first signs of a whole Kansai Science City, which would one day extend for forty miles in every direction, linking all the areas of western Japan into a Silicon Valley East.

A road sign pointed us to Hi-Touch Research Park, and scale models showed the outlines of an urban corridor that would pulse in our midst like an answering machine blinking with some message from the future.

I had been staying in Nara for half the Heisei Emperor's reign, and yet had never known that I was in the middle of some cosmic city of the new millennium, and suddenly to come upon these spacecraft was vertiginous, like being lifted up so high that one could see one's home as a dot on some enormous canvas, fashioned by a meta–Thomas Pynchon. All the driving ranges, all the Family Marts and Tomato gas stations and billboards of Felix the Cat I'd taken to be the things of commuting doctors were, in fact, part of some Techno-City of tomorrow that would, among other things, help to displace the green hills that stirred me so deeply.

We got back on the bike, and drove past rice paddies and village streams and wooden houses huddled against the dusk, then turned a corner, and came upon a sign for PARK-DORI, the quiet street I walked down thrice a day.

· · ·

The person with whom I shared all these adventures was, of course, a little like the society itself to me, alluring both for the parts I could recognize and for the parts that were beyond my ken; daily, she recalled to me that the point of familiarity is to make one comfortable with mystery. All of us know too well that no place is more foreign than the face asleep by our side, under the distant moon; yet in our modern world, such old truths gain especial force, as more and more of us find ourselves sharing homes with our own private Japans, half strange and half strangely familiar.

Every couple has its private tongue—that could be said to be the distinguishing sign of being a couple; but, in my case, the setup is even stranger, since I share no public tongue with my partner. Because my Japanese has never been good enough to teach her English, nor her English good enough to teach me Japanese, we can communicate only in a kind of fluent pidgin, with English words thrown into Japanese constructions. It sounds a little like the way the neighborhood looks to me.

What this means, though, is that we're free, for the most part, from subtexts, and from the shadows and hidden stings that words can carry; I can't make puns with her, spin ambiguities, or engage in very much verbal subterfuge, and she can't pore over my words to see what they mean or what they don't mean, what covert weapons they hide or betray. Speaking across a language gap means speaking less to win than to communicate.

The global village has given more and more of us the chance to move among the foreign, and so to simplify and clarify ourselves in this way; even in the neighborhoods where we were born, often, we find ourselves speaking by gesticulation, or enunciating very slowly, like language tapes, to saleswomen and telephone operators. And living a little bit away from words means living a little bit away from the surfaces they carry: my partner of more than twelve years has little sense of who I am in terms of brand names and labels—what my job means, what my schools connote, who I am on my CV—and I, likewise, can't confine her to the answers on an application form. Neither of us can read a word the other has written, and so we have to apprehend one another, to a small degree, in some way deeper than the known.

For me, being surrounded by a language I can't follow means, at the lowest level, that I can sleep while the television's going full blast (so long as it's not in English), and am never disturbed by all the chatter outside my window about O.J. or Diana's death. The one steady companion I've had all my life (the English language) is done up here in a foreign garb, of "live house" music clubs and "Viking-style" breakfasts, "pocket bell" beepers and "hammer price" auctions. And living out of a linguistic suitcase, I'm reminded of what I find on every foreign trip, which is that, leaving home, I'm convinced I don't have all I need; and, within a few days, I feel I have three times more than I require. The extra words (the extra goods) get in the way.

Best of all, in Japan, bringing strange eyes to the things the Japanese take for granted, I can see the places that I might otherwise take for granted (England or India or California) through the marveling eyes of those who take them in from right to left: once I took my girlfriend's seventy-four-year-old father for the only foreign trip he'd taken since the war, to California. Suddenly, in this incomprehensible space, he was a child again, rolling up his trousers and dodging the Pacific surf, collecting shells to take back home. Everything was new to him—albeit translated into the terms he knew—and before he'd even boarded the plane, he'd emptied a roll of thirty-six exposures. For the duration of the eleven-hour flight, he sat with his hands pressed against the window, peering out into the dark.

Such minglings are more and more the fabric of our mongrel worlds, as more and more of us cross borders in our private lives, or choose to live with foreign cultures in our arms. In Toronto, in Hong Kong, even in the Olympic Village nowadays, I seem to see as many couples dissolving nationalities as other kinds of distinctions, and so bringing to light unimaginable new cultures in which the annihilation of traditional identity is turned to something higher.

. . .

In Kyoto once, on my way with my girlfriend to the Holiday Inn, I saw a foreigner, tall and sweet-faced, walking down the street with a Japanese woman in one hand and a Japanese-English dictionary in the other. The hotel itself, set along the Kamo River, on a narrow street with the northern hills behind it, is not unlike that couple—all the global properties of the Atlanta-based chain reproduced in a setting that could only be Japan. There is a hundred-lane bowling alley there, a driving range, tennis courts, and a room-service menu in English; but when you go to the hotel swimming pool, you are reminded, by written rules, that it is "restricted to guests with tattoo or under influence of alcohol."

One day, as we were sitting in the lobby of this hybrid place, an elderly woman looked over at my girlfriend, and then leaned over to talk to her. "Excuse me, can I ask you something?" She was Japanese, it turned out, and it was Sunday morning, and the Wedding Hall and Holiday Hall were filling up around us. "What is it like communicating with a foreigner? Do you have problems with religion, customs, other things? How do you get yourself across?" My partner, used to my propaganda, replied that we probably communicated better than if we had too many words, and were free from at least a few distractions; words tend to be most divisive in a common language.

Satisfied, the woman sat back and surveyed the men all around, patting her bouffant hairdo.

A few minutes later, a trim black American, with a gold stud in his ear, sauntered in with his tall Japanese wife (in knee-high boots and miniskirt) and a baby in a stroller. Seeing my girlfriend, the baby cried, "Mama!"

Perhaps the deepest obligation of any foreigner in a place he loves that's not his own is to remember, daily, that his paradise is a fallen one, if only because it is an everyday reality to those around him, and offers conveniences far outside the reach of most people on the planet. And whenever I read the books of Haruki Murakami, the highly contemporary Japanese novelist who has seen his country from the perspective of living in Europe and teaching at Princeton, while translating Raymond Carver and John Irving into Japanese, I recognize that Japan can appear as soulless, to a native, as sad with loneliness and loss, as London or LA can to me.

In the six hundred pages of his magnum opus, *The Wind-Up Bird Chronicle,* Murakami delivers a series of X rays on modern, affectless Japan that amount to a virtual autopsy on a culture that's lost dimension and depth, and dwindled into a reflexive creed of "I don't think, therefore I am." Almost all his characters have VACANT signs hanging up outside their souls, and float through life as through the pages of a glossy magazine, hardly more substantial than the images they devour. "I was like a walking corpse," says one character, and another says, "I was now a vacant house."

"I had turned into a bowl of cold porridge," a young woman explains, and the friendly unemployed narrator volunteers at one point, "I am a weed-choked garden, a flightless stone bird, a dry well." Life is a numbing haze of Percy Faith orchestra Muzak and Dunkin' Donuts mugs of coffee and cinder-block abortion clinics (so without weight or direction that it comes to seem like a waking dream).

Perhaps the most shocking thing in Murakami's synoptic novel is that he comes almost to express nostalgia for the atrocities of the war, and the campaign in Manchuria, when people at least had lives instead of lifestyles, and a sense of intensity and humanity that arose from a close acquaintance with suffering (by contrast, the contemporary narrator blandly reports, "My reality seemed to have left me and now was wandering around nearby"). The other, quieter shock of his book is that all its dislocated fashion victims and Sprite-drinking teenagers, sleepwalking through their planless days as if on Prozac, might be dropping in from an Ann Beattie story. The hero wears a "yellow promotional Van Halen T-shirt" and listens to FM radio while cooking up spaghetti; the women he runs into are called Nutmeg, Malta, and Creta. "I felt a strange emptiness inside, a helpless kind of feeling like that of a small child who has been left alone in an unfamiliar neighborhood," the narrator confesses, and it isn't hard to see that the foreign country where he is stranded is a suburb of a chill and soundproofed future. Japan to Murakami certainly looked no better than Hong Kong or Atlanta did to me.

And so I sit at a small blond-wood desk in a child's bedroom, with a stubby Hello Kitty pencil, a Japanese folder that says PERK UP YOUR SPIRITS (TRY TO TAKE THINGS JUST AS THEY COME), and a T-shirt (given to me in California) that says, I DISLIKE FEELING AT HOME WHEN I'M ABROAD—GEORGE BERNARD SHAW, and write the essays in this book. On the desk in front of me is a pencil-box that says WELCOME TO MY HEART, a ruler from the Norman Rockwell Museum in Stockbridge, Massachusetts (how it got here, I don't know), and a small James Dean mirror with my quasi-stepdaughter's name on it, a memento from a school trip to the Temple of Clear Water in Kyoto.

The items are the ones to be found in many a teenager's room anywhere, but here they make up a kind of anthology of foreign worlds brought into this unremarkable modern flat: a huge sombrero from the Yucatán; a mock-Californian license plate that says IAN; a large poster of Hideo Nomo pitching for the Los Angeles Dodgers; and, next to a Japanese fan advertising the local Hanshin Tigers, a button from the Istanbul 2004 Olympic Committee.

I sit against the midnight blue pillow and listen for the sound of a motorbike, a familiar footfall on the stair.

That this is my home, I realize now in incidental ways; I can tell when the trees in the park are going to change color, and when the vending machines will change their offerings from hot to iced. I know when my girlfriend will bring out the winter futons from the cupboard, and when her daughter will change her school uniform from white to blue. I read Thoreau on sunny Sunday mornings, as Baptist hymns float over from across the way, and think that in our mongrel, mixed-up planet, this may be as close to the calm and clarity of Walden as one can find.

One midsummer day two months ago, I took Hiroko to Kyoto on the final day of Obon, the traditional holiday in August when most faithful Japanese return to their hometowns to pay respects to their departed ancestors, and when the departed ones themselves are believed to return to earth for three days. It is a time of solemn obsequies and traffic jams on the expressways, and it is the time when, quite by chance, thirteen years before, I'd stumbled upon a Kyoto alive with ghosts and lanterns, and decided to return.

Heading now towards the eastern hills, the two of us walked along a broad avenue of trees, with the night before us, through a receiving line of lanterns, white, with the names of stores in black upon them. At the end of the gravel path, we passed through a huge wooden gate, into an area thick with the smell of incense and the sound of muttered prayers, men in priestly raiment hovering all about. Old, old men, from another age, walked past in kimonos, half-doubled over, to visit loved ones at their gravestones. Cicadas buzzed deafeningly, and lanterns began to glow as the sky darkened.

We followed the old men through a small entranceway to the south, and came out in a world of shining lanterns, for as far as we could see, all across the slope above us, zigzagging towards the heavens like fireflies trembling in the dark. Below us, at our feet, were the lights of the modern city, cacophonous, fluorescent, a distant hum; above us, stretching towards the sky, a shivering sea of golden lights, soundless somehow, and strangely disembodied, as if about to float off into the night.

We walked up the steep slope, with its worshipers at headstones, and followed the paper lanterns up and up, past rows of illuminated graves, till it felt as if we were bobbing on the sea of golden lights. There was nothing really to anchor us, and nothing to see but the tremulous lights, and the ghosts who were whispering farewells. To my amazement, I realized that the moment I'd seen before, on my brief first trip, a decade before, had been real, and not, as I'd half-imagined, some fabrication of jet lag and culture shock and wishful thinking. More searchingly, I realized, too, how miraculous it had been to come across the sight while here for only three days, on a stopover in Kyoto, and staying in a high-rise hotel on the wrong side of town: the gate was open only three nights a year, and in all the succeeding thirteen years, I'd never seen this field of ghostly lanterns.

I pointed out the magic to Hiroko (who, though born here, had never seen the scene before), and she, a part of it, confirmed that it was true.

Then we walked back into town and dined on a summer platform, along the Kamo River, while five great bonfires were lit up along the northern and eastern hills, spelling out a Chinese character. We moved, through girls in *yukata* and figures carrying lanterns, up to the northeast quarter, to stay in an acupuncturist's flat in an apartment block with Global in its title.

That night, I fell into a deep, deep sleep, and found myself in a country house in England. There were only a few other people there: some flop-haired schoolboys, a woman who'd been kind to me in youth—and Hiroko. It was a lazy Sunday morning, and we were doing nothing more special than reading the Sunday papers and making the occasional witticism. Everything had a languid, undirected air; once, we went for a walk, in green, green hills, encircled in mist; once, I asked something about Egypt before the war.

Somewhere, Lou Reed was playing "Heroin" and upstairs there were some fashion magazines, and a few half-familiar figures drifted in and out. All the unremarkable languor of a weekend in the country.

And something in this unexceptional scene felt absolutely right. I couldn't find the words, and I didn't need to find them, but as I slept, I heard myself saying, of the everyday English scene, "This is my home. This is where I belong. Usually, I'm not very sociable, but this is me. This"—I meant the large redbrick houses, the gray afternoons, the musty light and dullness, the sense of nothing special going on— "is who I am." Words I never thought to say in waking life, but here, suddenly, I could not just feel and see all the days of my childhood but taste them and be inside them, in this distant science-fiction land, on the night when departed spirits find their way back home.

Then I woke up, to the sounds of a bright Sunday morning in the northeast quarter of the ancient imperial capital of Japan, in the tenth year of the era known in English translation as "Achieving Peace."

Acknowledgments

I would like to thank the many people who helped me on and off the page during the writing of this book. In Toronto, Paul Tough was my cheerleader and guide, well beyond the call of duty, for many years (from New York to LAX, as well), and the incomparable Louise Dennys and Rick Young took me into their enchanted world and made me feel that their city was the civilized heart of the planet; David Rothberg and Alicia Peres were hospitable friends, over and over, and Guy Lawson and Tom Perlmutter were strikingly generous with their wisdom. Marge O'Regan graciously showed me the future of the city, and Noelle Zitzer gave me the archbishop of Toronto's new name.

During more than a decade of covering Olympiads, I am especially grateful to the cheery stalwarts of the *Time* team, who kept me afloat in all kinds of multicultural venues, especially Susanna Schrobsdorff, Larry Mondi, Joe Ferrer, Paul Witteman, and Maryanne Golon, not to mention my one man technology team, Laman Tsufura.

In Hong Kong, Richard and Sharon Rawlinson were wonderful and inimitable cronies to me, as they have been for decades, on several continents, always on hand with a spare room and good counsel; and I owe a debt, too, to Don and Ann Morrison, and their staffs, especially Isabelle Ng, for help with Vietnamese refugees.

My parents, before I knew it, were supporting the consequences of my global lifestyle, in ways I would not recognize till later, and bestowing on me all the blessings of their various homes in Oxford, Bombay, and California.

In Japan, my best reader and lifeline for many years has been Michael Hofmann, who gets to the heart of things with a wisdom that's rare; in this case, he characteristically went through every comma and last letter of my manuscript, noting where I repeated the word *orange* and seeing how a single line break could open up a universe. Often, writing sentences, I was spurred by the wish to pass his infallible radar for sifting the global surface from the soul.

In New York, the great caretakers of this project, for many years, were the unrivaled Lynn Nesbit and Sonny Mehta, and I owe a huge debt of thanks to my longtime editor, Charles Elliott, and to my new one, Dan Frank, who took me on as a writer and, with an intuition and insight that are increasingly legendary, suggested I read more of the writer I love most, and prompted me towards more thoughtfulness with his own.

Cullen Stanley and Tina Bennett, at Janklow & Nesbit, indefatigably passed my words around; Jennifer Weh and Carol Edwards helped transmit them; and around the West Coast, the inspired readings of Mark Muro and the global kindness of Mark Wexler were invaluable, too, on many fronts.

I do not have a research assistant I can thank, alas, or a secretary or typist; but my travel agent, Sue Crispin, has kept me happily in the air for years with imperturbable aplomb, while Pam Henstell, at Knopf, has organized my official movements seamlessly; and, like anyone who longs to keep abreast of our fast-moving future, I travel vicariously through the *New Perspectives Quarterly*, the only magazine I know that keeps globalism in steady but shifting perspective. Its editor, Nathan Gardels, had the inspired idea of bringing all the world's great minds and spirits together in one place, in his maga-zine—not trying to get them all into one room, but traveling himself from place to place to bring them into the same conversation. It is a happy coincidence that his global forum is the official voice of the same Center for the Study of Democratic Institutions that first brought my father (and so my mother and me) to the New World.

Finally, my great companions throughout the living and writing of this book were Hiroko Takeuchi and her children Sachi and Takashi; and, embarrassing though it is to mention, the ceremonious rhap-sodies of Handel, the craggy transports of Van Morrison, our modern Blake. In a world where the sense of "home" can prove so elusive, they root us firmly in the lasting.

CUBA AND THE NIGHT

This novel's central character is another place: the melancholy, ebullient, and inconsistent island that is Castro's Cuba. Richard, the jaded photojournalist who is our narrator, thinks he believes in nothing, yet almost against his will, he falls in love with a ravishing cubana named Lourdes who may just be using him for a ticket to America. At the same time, Lourdes fears that she may be nothing more than a Caribbean souvenir. What ensues is a voluptuously atmospheric story of passion and regret.

Fiction/0 679-76075-X

FALLING OFF THE MAP

Some Lonely Places of the World

What does the elegant nostalgia of Argentina have in common with the raffish nonchalance of Australia? And what do both of these countries have in common with North Korea? They are all some of the "lonely places" explored by Pico Iyer, cut off from the rest of the world by geography, ideology, or sheer weirdness. Whether he is documenting the cruising rites of Icelandic teenagers or being interrogated by tipsy Cuban police, Iyer is always uncannily observant and acerbically funny.

Travel/Adventure/0-679-74612-9

THE LADY AND THE MONK

Four Seasons in Kyoto

When Pico Iyer decided to go to Kyoto and live in a monastery, he did so to learn about Zen Buddhism from the inside. But then he meets Sachiko, a vivacious, attractive, highly educated wife of a Japanese "salaryman." With his characteristic lightness of touch, Iyer fashions a marvelously ironic yet heartfelt book that is at once a portrait of cross-cultural infatuation—and misunderstanding— and a delightfully fresh way of seeing both the old Japan and the very new.

Travel/Adventure/0-679-73834-7

TROPICAL CLASSICAL

Essays from Several Directions

Iyer continues his one-man reinvention of the essay in this eloquent book, which soars from the remotest places on the planet
to the frontiers of contemporary literature, culture, and manners.
He chats with the Dalai Lama and assesses books by Salman
Rushdie and Cormac McCarthy. Glittering with aphorisms, over-
flowing with insight, and often laugh-out-loud funny, this is Iyer
at his globe-sprinting best.

Travel/Essays/0-679-77610-9

VIDEO NIGHT IN KATHMANDU

And Other Reports from the Not-So-Far-East

Mohawk haircuts in Bali. Yuppies in Hong Kong. And in the new
People's Republic of China, a restaurant that serves dishes called
"Ike and Tuna Turner." These are some of the comical, poignant,
and unsettling images that Pico Iyer brings back from the Far East
in this brilliant book of travel reportage. Iyer approaches his subject with a camera-sharp eye and a willingness to go beyond the
obvious conclusions about the hybrid cultures of East and West.

Travel/Adventure/0-679-72216-5

VINTAGE BOOKS
Available at your local bookstore, or call toll-free to order:
1-800-793-2665 (credit cards only).